"Percolating with full how-tos for 23 window projects, plus dozens more inviting ideas in the "Sketchbook" chapter, this book will energize you to action, even if you've never sewn window treatments before. Easy-to-follow formulas built into the instructions invite you to document your project's yardage require-ments and dimensions as you go, breaking down seemingly daunting tasks into simple steps. Unfamiliar with a technique or term? The "Window Treatments 101" section and to-the-point glossary will fix that in a flash. And both pros and novices will appreciate the tips and tricks shared in "insight boxes" throughout the i_____ *den your creative hori*...

—...usan Voigt-Reising,
...kmark" Columnist

"Don...   ...*comes to home
deco*...   ...*y-step instructions
and*...   ...*e confidence to
crea*...   ...*corative trims is
unm*...   ...*kes Donna one of
our*...

Janet M. Pray,
...Sewing Expo, Inc.

"Save...   ...*treatments...the
instr*...   ...*ve great success!"*

Sandra Betzina,
...GTV's *Sew Perfect*

"Don...   ...*it comes to profes-
siona*...   ...*t part of this book
is th*...   ...*one will under-
stan*...   ...*ow just what
ma*...   ...*e size and type of
sev*...   ...*h treatments are
sui*...

"I lo...   ...*of us who own
hig*...   ...*one-of-a-kind
win*...   ...*es.

"If y...   ...*ents that will
con*...   ...*sonality all on a
bud*...

Sue Hausmann,
...*merica Sews* and
...*ng Machines, Inc.

More Splash Than Ca$h®
Window Treatments

Over 250 Ideas, Inspirations, and Techniques
for Beautiful Windows

Donna Babylon
Victoria Waller

Windsor Oak
PUBLISHING

Library of Congress Cataloging-in-Publication Data

Babylon, Donna
   More splash than cash window treatments : over 250
ideas, inspirations, and techniques for beautiful
windows / Donna Babylon, Victoria Waller. -- 1st ed.
   p. cm.
   Includes index.
   ISBN 0-9668227-1-4

   1. Draperies. 2. Window shades. 3. Valances
(Windows) 4. Cornices. 5. Windows in interior
decoration.   I. Waller, Victoria. II. Title.
III. Title: Window treatments

TT390.B265 2003   645'.3
                    QBI02-200645

Cover, Interior Design, and Illustrations: Norm Myers
Technical Illustrations: Ann Davis Nunemacher
Illustrations: Natalie Sorenson
Photography: T. R. Wailes
Editorial Services: PeopleSpeak
Indexing: Rachel Rice
Graphic Assistants: Brian Lange, Jordan Myers, and Katie Myers
Photo Stylist: Susan B. Hummel
Photo Assistants: Tom Fleming, Patrick Frate
Studio: Daddy's Garage
Caterer: Mom's Kitchen
10 9 8 7 6 5 4 3 2 1

Table of Contents

Table of Contents

Part II: Sketchbook.................. 169

Part III: Window Treatments 101: ... 179
A Crash Course in Sewing without Pulling Your Hair Out

Introduction

Why make your own window treatments? The cost savings alone can be reason enough! In addition, a world of endless colors, sizes, and styles awaits you. When you create your own window treatments, you are not limited to the basic colors and mass-produced ready-made versions that are available in catalogs and department stores. No longer do you have to make do with a treatment that is too big, too small, or the wrong color. You can have the perfect window treatment that reflects your own unique decorating style.

Packed with over 250 ideas, inspirations, and techniques, this book invites you to explore the many options available for window decorating. You'll be happy to know that many of these treatments are very easy to make (even if you have no previous experience) and present low-cost options when adding this very important decorating element to a room.

"I don't know how to sew!" is not an excuse if you really want to create your own window treatments. True, many projects include a sewing machine as a construction tool, but a large number require only a few quick seams. Rest assured, we created each project from start to finish in a way that ensures your success. We worked out all of the bugs and tailored our instructions to help you avoid any disappointments.

Our goal was to provide you with stylish designs that are easy to construct, along with ample instructions to help you make each project successfully. A professional approach to the construction process ensures that the end product is one you can be proud of for years to come.

Making your own window treatments may be a new and exciting challenge for you, so we hope that you find this book to be a friendly guide as you tackle your projects. Think of us as your personal coaches as we take you step by step through the entire process—suggesting tips along the way that will help you save money and avoid missteps. We take our role as creative advisors very seriously and have included only tried-and-true methods that create pleasing results.

How should you use this book? The layout is simple. The main projects are divided into six categories. Each project includes a list of tools and supplies you'll need, suggestions for fabrics, and recommendations on window shapes. We also list techniques you should be familiar with to complete the project. But don't worry if some terms are unfamiliar to you; we have included an entire section, called "Window Treatments 101: A Crash Course in Sewing without Pulling Your Hair Out," that explains all the techniques in detail. Part II is a "Sketchbook" that features over 50 treatments that are so simple to make, only a few descriptive sentences are needed to start you on your way to duplicate these designs. In addition, we've sprinkled More Splash Than Cash tips throughout the book to help you save money while decorating. Finally, a detailed glossary and index ensure that the information you're looking for is at your fingertips.

"More Splash Than Cash" doesn't mean cheap. It means that the cash you spend—whatever amount that may be—is well spent and that the resulting window treatments will be enjoyed and admired for many years.

Acknowledgments

Donna would like to thank her parents who continually allow her to disrupt their lives with her projects; all the employees at Babylon Vault Company, including Bo Darr, Steve Koontz, Randy Myers, Paul Albaugh, Gary Baker, Buddy Petry, Terry Petry, Bob Warehime, William Miller, Woody Yelton, and Ray Arrington, who worked very hard to get the "photography studio" in shape (and who graciously helped with last minute fixes); Kitty Stein of Workroom Concepts, who reviewed the text from a professional workroom point of view; Sandra Placide, CMT, who kept Donna balanced; Suzanne Singleton of 29 Angels Publishing, who offered many suggestions from the perspective of a nonsewer as well as a fellow publisher; Susan Hummel, Tom Fleming, and Patrick Frate, who were great troopers during a marathon photography shoot; Sandra Hughes of Sew Business, who loaned equipment; Rita Farrow for continuous encouragement; Sheila Zent, Donna's sewing soul mate, who supports her every design change and creative whim; Jean Fidler, for her fabulous sewing skills; Norm Myers, graphic designer, whose insight, vision, and talent is never-ending; Ann Nunnemacher, technical illustrator, who can take rudimentary sketches and make them beautiful; Sharon Goldinger of PeopleSpeak, a very tolerant editor who went with the flow in what seemed like a continuous roller coaster ride; Sharon Castlen of Integrated Book Marketing, who always sees a silver lining; "fur children" Ashley and Teakah, who provided comic relief and lots of head butts; and Stephanie Caprarola, who is missed, who always had time to paint a wall, move boxes, and provide encouragement.

Victoria would like to thank Jerry Fried, who always had faith in her and whose memory still inspires her to work harder than she thinks she can; Norah Hodgins, who has shared her sewing secrets and skills; Tom Hawkins, who has taught Vicki all she knows about her computer (and has endless patience); Ruth Carey and Dianne Giancola, for going above and beyond the call of duty to critique the manuscript; and Michele King for listening to Vicki whine about the whole process. Special thanks to Susan Fried for her support and friendship. Finally, Vicki thanks her cat, Ty, who—although he slept on every window treatment, fought with the neighbor cats and wanted in when he was out and out when he was in—kept Vicki's chair warm every time she got up and dusted her sewing machine with his tail.

Both of us would like to thank the manufacturers who generously provided us with product to produce the window treatments in this book:

Swavelle/Mill Creek Fabrics
Concord Fabrics
Dan River®
Spectrum Fabrics
Covington Fabrics
JB Martin Company, Inc.

Rockland Industries, Inc.
Prym-Dritz Corporation
Hollywood Trims® by Prym-Dritz Corporation
Velcro USA Inc.
Rubber Stampede

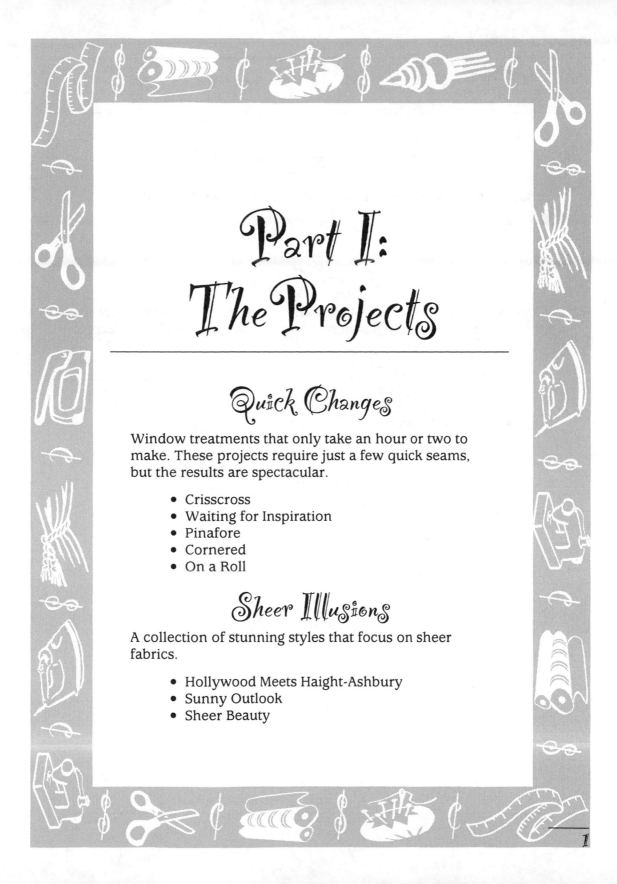

Part I: The Projects

Quick Changes

Window treatments that only take an hour or two to make. These projects require just a few quick seams, but the results are spectacular.

- Crisscross
- Waiting for Inspiration
- Pinafore
- Cornered
- On a Roll

Sheer Illusions

A collection of stunning styles that focus on sheer fabrics.

- Hollywood Meets Haight-Ashbury
- Sunny Outlook
- Sheer Beauty

Simply Sensational

Simple-to-make window treatments with fabulous design details.

- Tying the Knot
- Leaf Motif

Classic Choices

Window treatments that include special touches that turn the window into something to see, not just to see through. Classic styles for all decors.

- Knot Sew
- Skirting the Issue
- The Envelope, Please
- Beaucoup Scoops
- Friendly Borders
- Au Provence

Tradition with a Twist

Designs that transform a window from mundane to extraordinary.

- Double Your Pleasure
- Inside Outlook
- Walk on the Wild Side
- Regal Simplicity

Just Plain Fun

Window treatments that are sure to bring a smile to your face.

- Flutterby
- Pointed in the Right Direction
- Cancan

1 Crisscross Valance

This valance has design flair without the fuss. Add your own embroidery designs to the corners to make it a one-of-a-kind creation. Use it to cap a window requiring no other coverage, or place it over simple pull-down shades or blinds. Use solid-colored opaque or sheer fabric for embroidery opportunities, or leave the valance unadorned for a look that is clean and easy. Who could ask for more?

QUIETLY UNADORNED OR RICHLY EMBEL-LISHED WITH EMBROI-DERY, THIS STYLE IS SURE TO PLEASE. COLOR PHOTOGRAPH IS ON PAGE 117.

Suggested Window Shapes

This treatment is suitable for single windows, casement windows, or dormer windows. The recommended window width is limited only by the width of your fabric as seams are unsightly. Use multiple valances for wider windows.

Techniques to Know before You Begin

If you need to brush up on your skills in any of these areas, turn to part III.

- Accurate Measuring
- Usable Fabric Widths
- Turning and Cutting Corners and Points
- Cutting Fabric
- Covering Buttons
- Sewing on Buttons

·················· *Materials Needed* ··················

FROM THE FABRIC STORE
- decorator fabric
- matching thread
- removable fabric marker
- tension rod (also available at discount and department stores)*
- two tassels, 3 inches long
- embroidery thread as desired
- 3/4-inch-diameter (size 30) half-ball cover buttons

RECOMMENDED NOTIONS
Refer to the list of basic notions on page 180.

FROM THE HOME IMPROVEMENT CENTER
Refer to the list of basic tools and supplies on page 180.

Suggested Fabrics: Choose linen or a linen-like fabric, batiste, or a crisp cotton sheer. Prints are not recommended for the construction method provided.

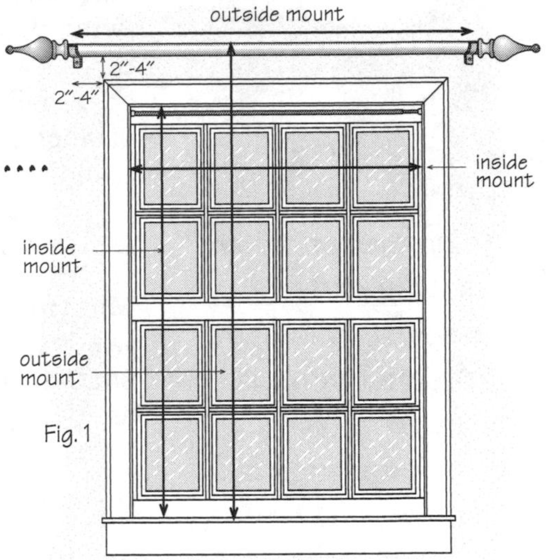

Fig. 1

Fabric Calculations

1. For an inside mount, install the tension rod inside the window frame as close as possible to the top edge. If using a decorative rod, mount the rod brackets 2 to 4 inches above the top edge of the window frame and 2 to 4 inches out from each side of the frame.

2. To determine the finished width of the valance, measure the width from one inside edge of the window to the opposite inside edge of the window or the distance between the two brackets if using a decorative rod (fig. 1). Write the number here: _____.

3. To determine the cut width of the valance, add 1 1/8 inches for seam allowances and ease to the finished width. Write the number here: _____.

* For windows that are too wide for a standard tension rod, consider using a shower curtain tension rod or a decorator rod for an outside mount.

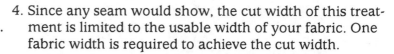

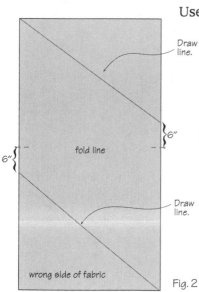

Tip

FOR VERY NARROW WINDOWS, YOU MAY BE ABLE TO CUT BOTH THE FRONT PANEL AND THE SELF-LINING FROM ONE WIDTH OF FABRIC. (GREAT FABRIC SAVINGS!) TO CHECK THIS, MULTIPLY THE CUT WIDTH OF THE VALANCE BY 2. IF THIS NUMBER IS SMALLER THAN THE USABLE WIDTH OF THE FABRIC, PURCHASE ONLY THE CUT LENGTH.

4. Since any seam would show, the cut width of this treatment is limited to the usable width of your fabric. One fabric width is required to achieve the cut width.

5. To determine the finished length, measure from the top of the rod to the top of the window sill. Divide this measurement by 2 for the finished length (fig. 1). Write the measurement here: _____. This valance is self-lined and simply folds over the rod to create the illusion of two panels. To determine the cut length of the folded valance, double the finished length and add 1 inch for seam allowances. Write the number here: _____.

6. To calculate the amount of decorator fabric needed, multiply the cut length by 2 for the self-lining. Write the number here: _____.

7. Divide this number by 36 and round up to the nearest $1/4$ yard. Write the number here: _____.

8. Plan for one covered button for every $3^1/2$ to $4^1/2$ inches of the finished valance width. Add two buttons to this total to determine the number of buttons required. Write the number here: _____.

Construction

Use a $1/2$-inch seam allowance unless otherwise instructed.

1. Lay the fabric on a flat work surface. Use a carpenter's square to mark and cut a straight edge at one end of the decorator fabric. Measure from this straight edge to cut two pieces of decorator fabric to the cut length and cut width measurements.

2. Fold one piece of fabric only, right sides together, matching the top and bottom edges. Use a straight pin to mark the fold line at each cut edge. Unfold the fabric so it is wrong side up. Starting at the pin-marked fold, measure along the right-hand long cut edge toward the top edge of the fabric. Place a mark 6 inches from the fold. Starting at the fold, measure along the left-hand long cut edge toward the bottom edge of the fabric, and place a second mark 6 inches from the fold. Draw a straight line from the upper left-

Draw line.

6"

Draw line.

fold line

6"

wrong side of fabric

Fig. 2

hand corner of the fabric to the first mark, and draw another straight line from the lower right-hand corner to the second mark, creating a parallelogram (fig. 2). Place the marked fabric on the remaining fabric right sides together, lining up all cut edges. Cut along the marked lines (fig. 3).

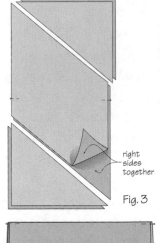

right sides together

Fig. 3

3. If you plan to embroider your fabric, do so now. If you are not going to add an embellishment, skip ahead to step 5. Choose an embroidery design that will fit into the long points. To choose the correct corners for embroidery, pin the two pieces of fabric wrong sides together, aligning all edges. Fold the fabric along the original pin-marked fold line so that the top panel has the long point on the right side. Use a straight pin to mark the two long corners facing up. Using a removable fabric marker, place a light arrow indicating the "up" direction in the seam allowance (fig. 4). Unpin the fabric pieces.

4. Stitch the embroidery design following the direction of the arrows in the marked corners. Center the design $1^1/2$ to $3^1/2$ inches from the cut edges of the fabric (fig. 5). See the sidebar for embroidery suggestions.

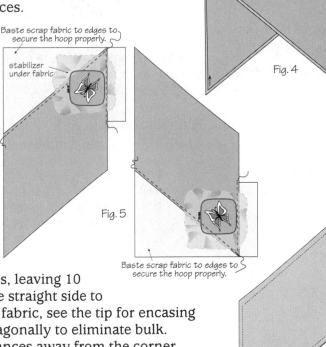

Baste scrap fabric to edges to secure the hoop properly.

stabilizer under fabric

Fig. 4

Fig. 5

Baste scrap fabric to edges to secure the hoop properly.

5. Pin the fabric pieces right sides together. Double-check the position of the embroidery before stitching. Stitch together along the sides and diagonal edges, leaving 10 inches unstitched along one straight side to turn. If you are using sheer fabric, see the tip for encasing seams. Trim the corners diagonally to eliminate bulk. Next, taper the seam allowances away from the corner (fig. 6). Turn the fabric right side out. For sharp corners, use a point turner to gently push the inside of the corners out. Press the seam edges so that neither fabric is visible from the opposite side. Handstitch the opening closed.

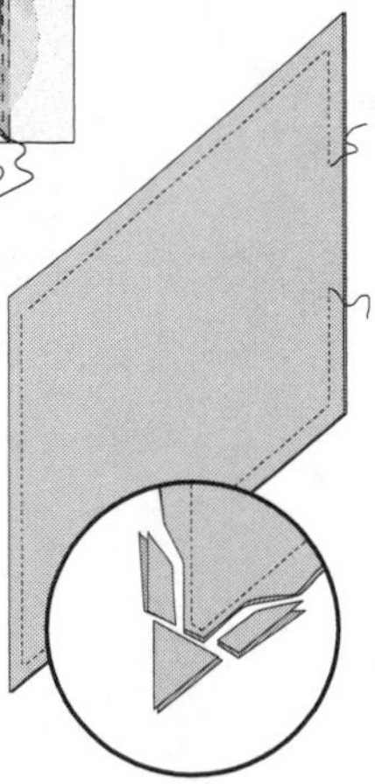

Fig. 6

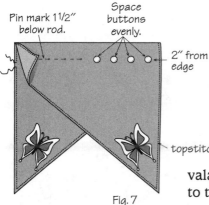

Pin mark 1 1/2″ below rod.

Space buttons evenly.

2″ from edge

topstitch

Fig. 7

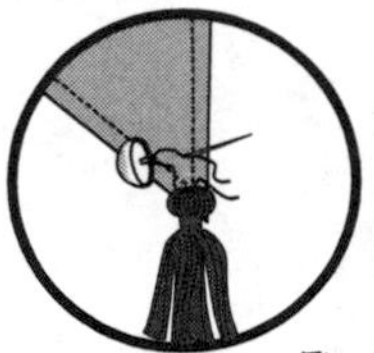

Handstitch button and tassel to point.

Fig. 8

Tip

EMBROIDER MINIA-
TURE DESIGNS THAT
COORDINATE WITH
THE LARGE EMBROI-
DERY MOTIF ONTO
FABRIC SCRAPS.
WHEN COVERING
BUTTONS, CENTER
THE MINIATURE MOTIF
ON THE COVER
BUTTON FORM FOR
TRULY ONE-OF-A-
KIND BUTTONS.

6. Pin the edges. Topstitch 1/2 inch from the pressed edge around all sides (fig. 7).

7. Fold the fabric so that the embroidered design faces forward and the points are equal in length. Mark the fold line with a pin. Drape the valance over the rod so the pin-marked fold line sits at the top of the rod.

8. To plan the button positions, place a pin 1 1/2 inches below the bottom of the rod. Remove the valance from the rod. Measure the distance from the fold to the pin mark. Write the distance here: _____.

9. Cover the buttons with matching fabric. Set two buttons aside for the tassels. Place the folded valance right side up on a large work surface. Space the buttons evenly across the top edge with the end buttons 2 inches from each side (fig. 7). The distance from the fold to the buttons should equal the measurement from step 8 above. Attach the buttons by stitching through all layers. The space above the buttons is the rod pocket.

10. Place the 1/2-inch loop of one tassel at the back of a covered button. Handstitch one button and a tassel to the topstitched line at each long corner of the valance so the tassel hangs away from the valance (fig. 8).

Installing and Dressing

Slide the rod through the opening above the covered buttons. Mount the tension rod flush to the top inside of the window, or place decorative rod in brackets.

Rooms with a View

We think this window treatment would look great in windows where total privacy is not required, such as a hallway or entry window, kitchen, bathroom, or office.

·················· *Easy Does It!* ··················

Binding Sheer Seams

Sheer fabric is often chosen for window treatments because it is translucent. This see-through quality may also reveal the raw edges of the fabric within, which are not so appealing.

To remedy this, encase the seam edges in a sheer meshlike binding. This binding is available in the notions department of fabric stores. Use a neutral color that blends with the dominant color of your fabric for the best coverage. First trim the seam allowance on your project to an even 1/4 inch. Gently pull the binding to determine its natural curl. Place the raw edge of your fabric inside the curl. Straight stitch along the seam allowance to catch the top and bottom edges of the meshlike binding, pulling it gently as you sew. Stop about 1/2 inch before any tapered or trimmed corner or point (fig. 9).

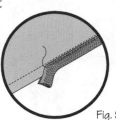

Fig. 9

To Embroider

Follow the instructions in your sewing machine manual to embroider your fabric. Test the embroidery design first on the same fabric as your window treatment. To position, trace the shape of the inside of the embroidery hoop onto the test fabric along with any centering marks. Place the finished sample right side up on the actual cut valance. Transfer all traced lines with thread marks; then use the thread marks to position the hoop.

The valance point must fit completely into the embroidery hoop. If necessary, enlarge the point of the valance by basting scrap fabric to the edges of the valance (fig. 5). With stabilizer against the wrong side of the fabric, place the fabric into the hoop. Test several water-soluble and tear-away stabilizers to choose the most appropriate kind for your project. We recommend that you use rayon thread for the shiniest stitch. Follow your individual machine instructions to create a mirror image of the embroidered design for the second valance point.

2 Waiting for Inspiration

THESE SIMPLE-TO-SEW PANELS ARE THE PERFECT PALETTE FOR YOUR CREATIVE TOUCH. COLOR PHOTOGRAPH IS ON PAGE 117.

These simple tied panels float to the floor in anticipation of the master-piece to come. The simple construction means no pleats to measure, no sections to stitch together, and no lining to attach—a perfect example of the "less is more" philosophy. Each panel starts with a finely stitched hem and finishes with ribbon ties. The beauty is in the details—your details. These plain hemmed panels can be anything you want them to be. Add a hand-painted mural, a rubber-stamped border design, or creative stitching to this empty canvas. Let the creative juices percolate and then decorate!

.... Suggested Window Shapes ....

This treatment is suitable for single or double windows.

...... Techniques to Know before You Begin ......

If you need to brush up on your skills in any of these areas, turn to part III.

- Accurate Measuring
- Usable Fabric Widths
- Cutting Fabric
- Hems
- Installing Rods, Brackets, and Holdbacks

.... *Materials Needed* ....

FROM THE FABRIC STORE

- decorator fabric
- matching thread
- brass- or nickel-colored eyelet kit, size extra large
- 1 1/2-inch wide satin or sheer ribbon

RECOMMENDED NOTIONS

Refer to the list of basic notions on page 180.

FROM THE HOME IMPROVEMENT CENTER

These are specific supplies needed for this project. Also refer to the basic list of tools and supplies on page 180.

- decorative wall hooks or curtain holdbacks (make sure the hooks clear the top edge of the window frame)
- hammer to attach eyelets

FROM THE CRAFT STORE

- optional: rubber stamps with large surface designs or stencils
- optional: fabric paint
- optional: cosmetic sponges, small foam brush, or stencil brush
- optional: kraft paper

Suggested Fabrics: Choose an evenly woven, solid-colored fabric with no right or wrong side, such as duck, twill, linen, handkerchief linen, voile, lawn, cotton organdy, or silk organza. If you plan to paint, stencil, or rubber-stamp the surface, we recommend cotton fabric in a natural or very light color.

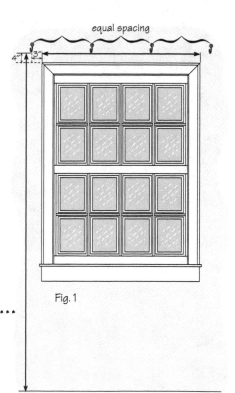

Fig. 1

Fabric Calculations

1. Measure the width of your window from outside edge to outside edge (fig. 1) and add 6 inches. Divide this number by an odd number (we used

three in our example) equal to the number of panels. This will determine the finished width of each panel. Write the number here: _____. The maximum recommended width per panel is 27 inches. If your division results in a wider measurement, plan additional panels to decrease the individual panel width.

2. The panels hang from wall-mounted hooks or curtain holdbacks. You will need a hook for each panel, plus one additional hook (e.g., four hooks for three panels or six hooks for five panels). Mount a hook at each corner of the window frame, 4 inches above the top edge and 3 inches out from each side of the window frame. Mount the remaining hooks in even increments equal to the finished width of each panel, 4 inches above the top edge of the window frame (fig. 1).

3. Add $8^1/_4$ inches to the finished width of each panel for the cut width. Write the number here: _____.

4. Measure from the bottom of the hooks to the desired finished length and subtract 3 inches to allow for the ribbon drop (fig. 1). Write the number here: _____.
Add $8^1/_2$ inches for the cut length. Write the number here: _____. (Note: For added grace on unpainted panels, plan for them to drape across the floor about 6 inches. If you would like this look, add 6 inches to your cut length.) To calculate how many finished panels can be cut from one width of fabric, divide the usable width of the fabric by the cut width of one panel. Round each number down to the nearest whole number. Write the number here: _____.

5. To determine the number of fabric widths required to make this treatment, divide the total number of panels by this number and round up to the nearest whole number. Write the number here: _____.

6. To calculate the yardage required, multiply the cut length by the number of fabric widths required. Divide by 36 and round up to the nearest $1/_4$ yard. Write the amount here: _____.

7. You will need about 2 yards of ribbon per panel for the ribbon ties.

Construction

1. Place one panel flat on a large work surface. Use a carpenter's square to mark and cut a straight edge at one end of the fabric. Be sure to cut off the selvages. Cut the panel to the width and length determined in Fabric Calculations. Repeat for the remaining panels.

2. Double 2-inch hems will be stitched on all sides of each panel. First, at the top and bottom edge of each panel, fold under and press 4 inches toward the wrong side. Tuck under the top edge of the hem 2 inches to meet the fold (fig. 2).

3. Repeat step 2 for the side edges of each panel. Do not stitch the hems yet.

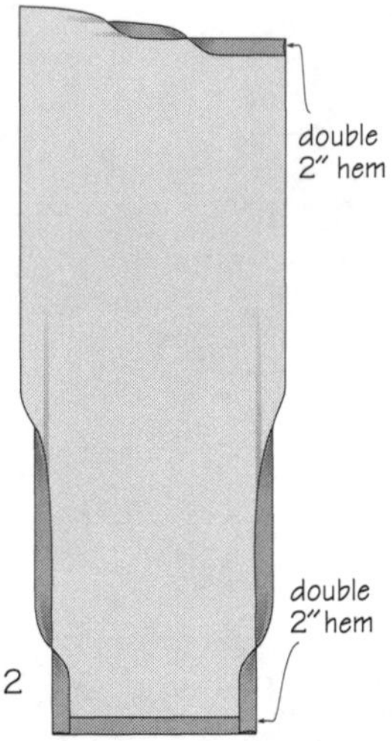

4. Place one panel on the work surface with the wrong side facing up. Open up the pressed-in hem at one corner (fig. 3a). To miter the corner, diagonally fold the point toward the wrong side across the innermost intersection of the fold lines and press (fig. 3b). Unfold. Create a new fold across the outermost intersection of the fold lines and press (fig. 3c). Cut off the fabric at this new diagonal line.

5. Refold the hems, keeping the corner fabric tucked inside. The hems will meet at a 45-degree angle to form a mitered corner. Press again (fig. 4a–4b). If the diagonal folds form a ridge on the right side of the panel, reopen the folded corner and trim away the inside diagonal fold to eliminate bulk (fig. 4c).

6. Repeat steps 4 and 5 for each corner at the top and bottom edges of each panel. Do not stitch the hems or mitered corners until the eyelets have been tested on scrap fabric. If necessary,

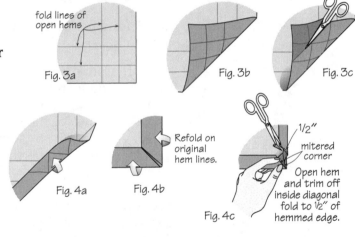

double 2" hem

double 2" hem

Fig. 2

fold lines of open hems

Fig. 3a

Fig. 3b

Fig. 3c

Fig. 4a

Fig. 4b

Refold on original hem lines.

1/2"

mitered corner

Open hem and trim off inside diagonal fold to 1/2" of hemmed edge.

Fig. 4c

Fabric scraps add thickness for eyelets.

Fig. 5

Testing Eyelets

Eyelets sometimes require added thickness to achieve a good fit. Make a test sample using scraps of your fabric and an extra eyelet to determine if you need extra thickness. If the eyelet does not fit snugly, add layers of fabric to help fill in the gap between eyelet sections and test again. You may also use a small square of cotton batting or felt to add thickness. Cut this square just slightly larger than the eyelets and insert it between the fabric layers. Center the hole of the eyelet over the insert and attach the eyelet.

If it is necessary to add thickness, insert this extra layer into each folded hem at the marked eyelet positions before stitching the hems (fig. 5). Eyelets may not be suitable for very thin or sheer fabric. Buttonholes can be substituted in this case. It may still be necessary to add strength to thin fabric to prevent possible tearing at the buttonhole. Cut a small piece of iron-on interfacing of a weight suitable for the sheerness of your fabric. Fuse it to the wrong side of the fabric in the marked eyelet or buttonhole locations before stitching the hem.

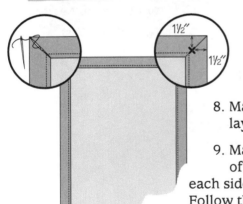

add extra layers of fabric at the top corners for the eyelets (fig. 5). (See the tip on page 15.)

7. Handstitch the diagonal folds of each mitered corner together (fig. 6).

8. Machine stitch the hems of each panel through all layers along the inside hem edge (fig. 6).

9. Mark the positions for the eyelets at the top corners of each panel. Place a mark 1 1/2 inches in from each side and 1 1/2 inches in from the top edge (fig. 6). Follow the package instructions to attach the eyelets.

Fig. 6

Options

PAINTING, STAMPING, OR STENCILING

1. Protect your work surface from paint seepage with brown kraft paper. To create a continuous image when painting your panels, place the panels wrong side up on a large work surface and line them up evenly. Use masking tape or duct tape to tape the panels together so the edges butt

but do not overlap. Turn the panels right side up. Tape the joined panels to the work surface. Creative souls can start to paint with fabric paint now.

2. The rest of us need a bit more guidance. Work with large rubber stamps designed for home décor. These stamps have well-defined areas with less detail. Apply fabric paint to the raised stamp surface with a cosmetic sponge or foam brush being careful not to allow paint into the crevices of the design area.

3. When stamping fabric, press firmly on the entire stamp surface to be sure the complete design has been transferred to the fabric. You may want to do several test images on fabric scraps before placing them on your finished panels. When stamping or stenciling over the taped joined edges, place the stamp or stencil over the joined line for a continuous image. If using stencils, adhere the stencil to the fabric with tape or stencil adhesive to hold it in place while you apply the fabric paint.

4. Heat setting the fabric paint may be required. Follow the manufacturer's instructions for heat setting.

Hemstitching

For a hem with more detail, use a wing needle and a decorative machine hemstitch. Cut each panel 4 inches narrower than instructed above. Press a single-layer hem 2 inches to the wrong side, mitering the corners. Follow your machine's instructions to hemstitch along the cut edge of the hemmed sides. Be sure to encase the raw edge of the fabric in your stitching. See page 32 for hemstitching tips.

Machine Embroidery

If simplicity isn't your cup of tea, these hemmed panels offer an irresistible empty palette for machine embroidery or appliqué.

Installing and Dressing

1. Cut the ribbon into 36-inch lengths—two for each panel.

2. Place the panels right side up on a large work surface. Slip one ribbon through each eyelet. Tie a bow with a

Tip

CARRY THE SAME STAMPED DESIGN FROM THE WINDOW PANELS TO THE WALL AND CREATE A CUSTOMIZED WALL BORDER. YOU CAN ALSO ADD THE SAME STAMPED DESIGN TO EXTRA FABRIC AND MAKE COORDINATING THROW PILLOWS.

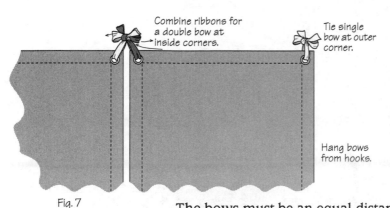

Combine ribbons for a double bow at inside corners.

Tie single bow at outer corner.

Hang bows from hooks.

Fig. 7

single ribbon at the outer corner of each of the two end panels. Tie the bows between panels with the two ribbons (one from each panel). Pin these ribbons together about 3 inches from the eyelet and treat the cut ends as one to form one bow.

The bows must be an equal distance from the top edge of the panels (fig. 7). You can test this by hanging the panels from the hooks.

3. Once you are certain the bows are to your liking, tighten the bows so they do not slip and remove any pins. For especially slippery ribbon, consider tacking the knot with several small hand stitches.

4. Hang the panels from the hooks.

Rooms with a View

We think these panels would work well in living or family rooms, dining rooms, screened porches, or bedrooms.

················· *Easy Does It!* ·····················

Eyelets

Hammering eyelet sections together on a high work surface can be ergonomically incorrect as well as hard on the eardrums. Work on a lower surface when hammering. Place a small block of wood under the eyelet to absorb the shock of the hammer and to protect the work surface. Cover the block of wood with a small piece of fabric to keep the back of your curtain panel clean.

3 On a Roll

Standard roll-up shades have been around for a while. They are certainly practical but just a little boring. By creating multiple minishades and varying the length of each, you triple the interest! You can make them all in different colors, with coordinating ribbon ties. Or make them all in the same color just to play it safe. Privacy can be accomplished by rolling down the shades, but you can let the sun shine in one roll at a time—or not. This treatment is easy, efficient, and just a little quirky.

.... Suggested Window Shapes ....

This treatment is suitable for single or double windows, casement windows, corner windows, dormer windows, angled windows, cathedral windows, oval windows, octagonal windows, or hexagonal windows.

...... Techniques to Know before You Begin ......

If you need to brush up on your skills in any of these areas, turn to part III.

- Accurate Measuring
- Fabric Repeats
- Cutting Fabric
- Cutting Multiple Fabric Widths

- Preparing a Mounting Board
- Installing a Mounting Board
- Hems

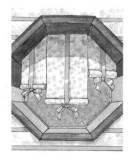

WITH A SLIGHT ALTERATION TO THE TOP EDGE, THIS WINDOW TREATMENT FITS NICELY IN ODD-SHAPED WINDOWS. COLOR PHOTOGRAPH IS ON PAGE 118.

······················ *Materials Needed* ······················

FROM THE FABRIC STORE

- decorator fabric
- thread to match decorator fabric
- coordinating ribbon (grosgrain or double-faced satin)

RECOMMENDED NOTIONS

Refer to the list of basic notions on page 180.

FROM THE HOME IMPROVEMENT CENTER

These are specific supplies needed for this project. Also refer to the basic list of tools and supplies on page 180.

- 1-by-2-inch board
- screws, 2 inches long (at least two, plus one for every 36 inches)
- heavy-duty staple gun with 1/2-inch long staples
- 3/8-inch-diameter wooden dowel rods

Suggested Fabrics: Choose a lightweight to medium-weight fabric, such as batiste, quilt-weight cotton, lace, voile, handkerchief linen, muslin, or gingham. Select a fabric that has no right or wrong side. Usually this is a woven fabric. Avoid a fabric where the design has only been printed on the surface. The back of this fabric is often unattractive. Woven plaids, checks, and solids are ideal for this project. Large prints that would need to be matched horizontally are not recommended.

··

Fabric Calculations

1. This window treatment is suitable for either an inside or outside mount. Select the mount that you would like at your window. Note: For an inside mount, the depth of the window frame must be at least 1 1/2 inches to accommodate the width of the mounting board.

2. Determine the length of the mounting board. For an outside mount, and if the window has a frame, measure the width of the window from outside frame edge to

---

MORE $PLASH THAN ¢ASH ·

·*Tip*· ✂
DON'T CUT INTO YOUR GOOD DECORATOR FABRIC AFTER 9PM. MOST MISTAKES HAPPEN WHEN YOU ARE TIRED.

outside frame edge (fig. 1). Add 1 to 2 inches on each side. Write the number here: _____. If the window does not have a frame, measure the opening and add 1 to 2 inches to each side as well. For an inside mount, measure the opening and subtract ¹/2 inch (fig. 1). Write the number here: _____. Regardless of the mount, the length of the board is the measurement to use when determining the individual size of the roll-ups.

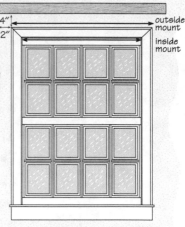
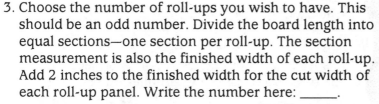

Fig. 1

3. Choose the number of roll-ups you wish to have. This should be an odd number. Divide the board length into equal sections—one section per roll-up. The section measurement is also the finished width of each roll-up. Add 2 inches to the finished width for the cut width of each roll-up panel. Write the number here: _____.

4. To determine the cut length of each roll-up, measure from the top edge of the window to the sill and add 12 inches. Write the number here: _____.

5. Add the cut widths of the roll-ups together to determine the total cut width. If this number is less than the usable width of the fabric, simply purchase enough yardage to equal the cut length measurement. If it is greater than the usable width, divide the total cut width of the roll-ups by the usable width of fabric and round up to the nearest whole number. If you need more than one width of fabric, multiply the number of widths needed by the cut length of the fabric. Write the number here: _____.

6. To determine the yardage, divide this number by 36 and round the number up to the nearest ¹/4 yard. Write the number here: _____. This is the amount of fabric you will need to make this window treatment. Note: You'll need extra fabric if you decide to cover the mounting board with the decorator fabric.

7. You will need two lengths of ribbon for each roll-up. The cut length of each ribbon is equal to the length of the window plus 7 inches.

8. Purchase enough dowels to cut individual lengths to fit within the individual finished width of each roll-up shade.

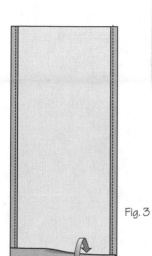

Fig. 2

1/2″

1″

Construction

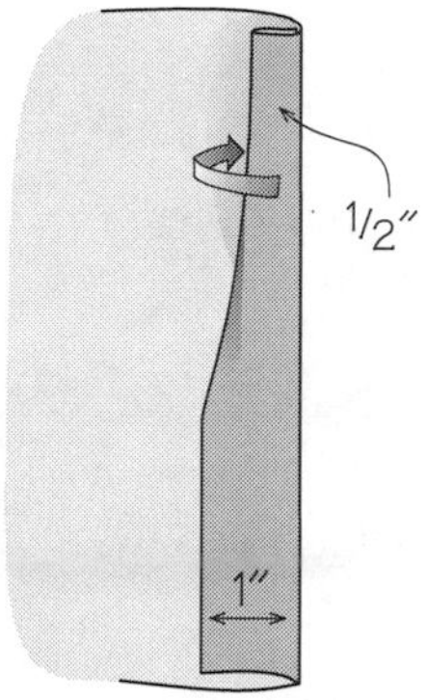

1. Lay the fabric flat on a large work surface. Use a carpenter's square to mark and cut a straight edge at one end of the fabric.

2. Refer to the cut width and length measurements determined in Fabric Calculations. Cut the appropriate number of roll-ups needed for your window.

3. To form the side hems, fold over and press 1 inch toward the wrong side of the fabric. Tuck in the raw edge of the fabric 1/2 inch to meet the fold. Stitch the hem (fig. 2). Repeat for each roll-up.

4. To form the bottom hem pocket for the dowel rod, fold over and press 1 1/4 inches toward the wrong side of the fabric. Tuck in the raw edge of the fabric 5/8 inch to meet the fold (fig. 3). Stitch the hem.

5. Cut two lengths of ribbon for each roll-up as determined in step 7 of Fabric Calculations.

6. Find and mark the exact center of the top edge of each roll-up. Place a ribbon on each side of the fabric, centered at this mark. Line up the cut edge of the ribbons with the top cut edge of the roll-up. Pin; baste through all layers. Repeat for each roll-up (fig. 4).

7. Serge or zigzag stitch along the top edge for a clean finish, catching both the ribbons and the fabric (fig. 5).

8. Cut the dowel rods 1/4 inch shorter than the finished width of each roll-up. Insert rods into pockets.

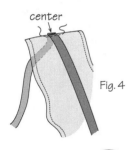

Fig. 3

double 5/8″ hem for dowel rod

center

Fig. 4

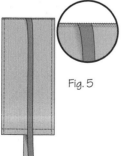

Fig. 5

Installing and Dressing

INSIDE MOUNT

1. Prepare the mounting board by either painting it to match the wall color or by covering it with the decorator fabric.

2. Place the mounting board flat on the work surface with the wider side of the board facing up. Arrange each roll-up right side up and side by side on the board with the

serged or zigzag edge against the back edge of the board (fig. 6). Staple in place.

3. Install the board against the inside of the window frame so the flat side of the board with the staples is flush against the top inside of the frame. The roll-ups should "waterfall" over the top narrow edge of the board (fig. 6).

4. Refer to the photograph and roll up each strip toward you (do not include ribbons) until you reach the desired height. Tie the ribbons in a bow around the rolled end to secure it. Trim the ribbons if desired.

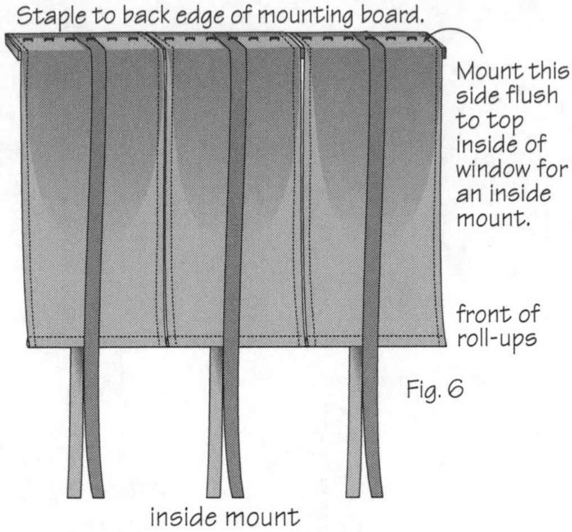

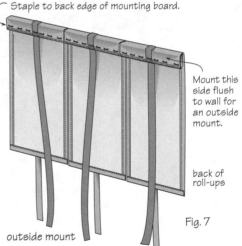

Staple to back edge of mounting board.

Mount this side flush to top inside of window for an inside mount.

front of roll-ups

Fig. 6

inside mount

OUTSIDE MOUNT

1. Prepare the mounting board by either painting it to match the wall color or by covering it with the decorator fabric.

2. Place the mounting board flat on the work surface with the wider side of the board facing up. Arrange each roll-up right side up and side by side on the board with the serged or zigzag edge against the back edge of the board. Staple in place.

Staple to back edge of mounting board.

Mount this side flush to wall for an outside mount.

back of roll-ups

Fig. 7

outside mount

3. Install the board above the window frame so the flat side of the board with the staples is flush against the wall. The roll-ups should "waterfall" over the top narrow edge of the board (fig. 7). Use a level when positioning the board.

4. Refer to the photograph and roll up each strip toward you (do not include ribbons) until you reach the desired height. Tie the ribbons in a bow around the rolled end to secure it. Trim the ribbons if desired.

Rooms with a View

We think this window treatment would look great in a bedroom, bathroom, entryway, child's room, kitchen, or informal dining nook.

4 Pinafore

SUN-FILLED ROOMS ARE EVEN MORE CHEERY WITH THIS WINDOW TREATMENT. COLOR PHOTOGRAPH IS ON PAGE 118.

The word pinafore conjures up visions of girls in ruffled dresses topped with gingham aprons happily playing in a meadow full of flowers. Is it possible to transfer such a halcyon vision to a window treatment? Certainly! This breezy curtain dressed in two cheerful fabrics is the happy result. Construction is easy. The main body of the curtain attaches to the upper section with buttons (hence the resemblance to a pinafore). We chose coordinating flower-shaped buttons to complete the vision. Hang these curtains at your window. And, just for a moment, let your mind drift back in time to carefree days and flower-filled meadows.

Suggested Window Shapes

This treatment is suitable for single or double windows, dormer windows, or casement windows.

Techniques to Know before You Begin

If you need to brush up on your skills in any of these areas, turn to part III.

- Accurate Measuring
- Installing Rods, Brackets, and Holdbacks
- Usable Fabric Widths
- Cutting Multiple Fabric Widths

- Fabric Repeats
- Matching Repeat Designs
- Sewing on Buttons
- Cutting Fabric
- Hems
- Sewing French Seams

.... *Materials Needed* ....

FROM THE FABRIC STORE

- fabric for the top section
- fabric for the bottom section
- thread to match fabrics
- buttons (at least ³/₄ inch in diameter)
- paper-backed fusible tape (³/₄ inch wide)
- decorative rod, finials, and mounting brackets (also available at department stores)

RECOMMENDED NOTIONS
Refer to the list of basic notions on page 180.

FROM THE HOME IMPROVEMENT CENTER
Refer to the list of basic tools and supplies on page 180.

Suggested Fabrics: Choose lightweight to medium-weight fabrics such as batiste, eyelet, quilt-weight cotton, lace, voile, muslin, or gingham. Select a woven fabric that is the same on the front as the back and has no right or wrong side. Avoid a fabric where the design has only been printed on the surface. The back of this fabric is often unattractive. Woven plaids, checks, and solids are ideal for this project.

Fig. 1

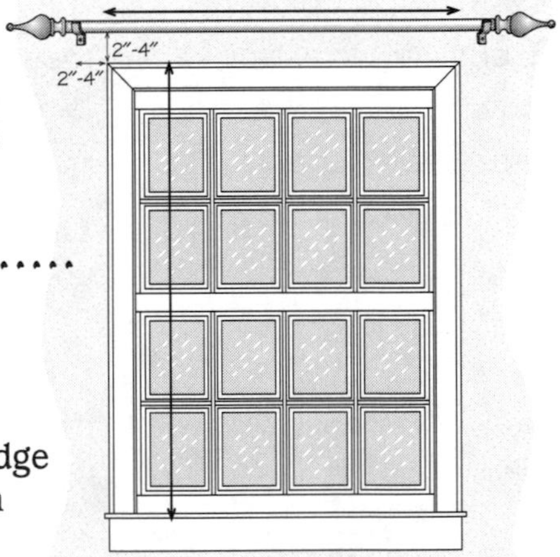

2"-4"

2"-4"

....

Fabric Calculations

OVERALL CURTAIN MEASUREMENTS

1. Mount the rod brackets 2 to 4 inches above the top edge of the window frame and 2 to 4 inches out from each side of the frame (fig. 1).

2. Measure the distance between the brackets (fig. 1). Write the measurement here: _____. To determine the finished

width of each panel, divide this measurement by 2 for two panels. Add 15 inches for the cut width of both the top and bottom sections for each panel. Write the number here: _____.

3. To determine the number of fabric widths required for both the top and bottom sections, compare the width of fabric you are using to the cut width of each panel. Depending on the size of your window, you may be able to cut two panels from one width of fabric. If this is the case, you only need to purchase the cut length to make this window treatment. Otherwise, to determine the number of fabric widths required, divide the usable width of the fabric by the cut width. Round up to the next whole number. Write the number here: _____.

4. Determine the finished length of the overall curtain by measuring from the top edge of the window frame to the desired finished length. We suggest sill length (fig. 1). Write the measurement here: _____.

5. The number of buttons required is entirely up to you. As a general rule, the larger the button, the fewer you need. For buttons as small as 3/4 inch, plan for at least one button per tie.

TOP SECTION

1. For the visible length of the top section, divide the overall finished length by 5 1/2 and round to nearest whole number. Write the number here: _____.

2. To determine the cut length of the top section, add 6 inches for the hems and the overlap to the above number. Write the number here: _____.

3. The cut width of the top section was determined in step 2, Overall Curtain Measurements.

4. To calculate the yardage, multiply the cut length by the number of widths needed. Write the number here: _____. If the fabric has a repeat design, multiply the repeat distance by the number of widths and add this figure to the total. The extra fabric will allow you to match the designs.

Tip

MORE $PLASH THAN ¢ASH ·

IF YOU DON'T WANT TO MAKE NAIL HOLES IN A FRESHLY PAINTED WALL, HANG A LIGHTWEIGHT ROD FROM LARGE RIBBON LOOPS THAT HAVE BEEN THUMBTACKED TO THE TOP EDGE OF THE WINDOW FRAME. THIS IDEA IS PERFECT FOR APARTMENT DWELLERS WHO HAVE TO LEAVE THEIR LODGINGS IN PRISTINE SHAPE WHEN THEY MOVE OUT.

5. Divide this number by 36 and round up to the nearest $1/4$ yard. Write the number here: _____. This is the amount of fabric you need for the top section.

BOTTOM SECTION

1. For the finished length of the bottom section, subtract the visible length of the top section from the overall finished length. Write the number here: _____.

2. To determine the cut length of the bottom section, add 9 inches for the hems and the overlap to the above number. Write the number here: _____.

3. The cut width of the bottom section was determined in step 2, Overall Curtain Measurements.

4. To calculate the yardage, multiply the cut length by the number of widths needed. Write the number here: _____. If the fabric has a repeat design, multiply the repeat distance by the number of widths and add this figure to the total. The extra fabric will allow you to match the designs.

5. Divide this number by 36 and round up to the nearest $1/4$ yard. Add 1 yard for the ties. Write the total here: _____. This is the amount of fabric you need for the bottom section.

Cutting Instructions

1. Lay the fabric flat on a large work surface. Use a carpenter's square mark and cut a straight edge at one end of each fabric.

2. Cut each fabric to the individual cut width and length measurements determined in Fabric Calculations. If you need more than one width to achieve the cut width of your curtain, cut additional fabric to the same length, matching motifs. Sew the fabric widths together, making sure the design motifs match at the seam. Use a French seam to join the fabric widths.

3. Trim equal amounts from both side edges to obtain the cut width measurement.

Tip ✂

SAVE YOUR FABRIC SCRAPS! USE THEM TO MAKE COORDINATING PILLOWS, LAMPSHADE COVERS, TABLE RUNNERS, OR TABLE TOPPERS FOR TRUE MORE SPLASH THAN CASH DECORATING!

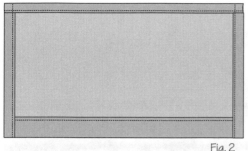

Fig. 2

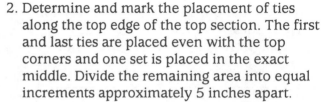
Fig. 3

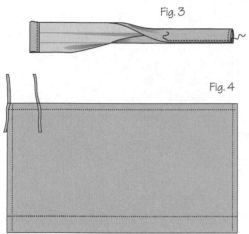
Fig. 4

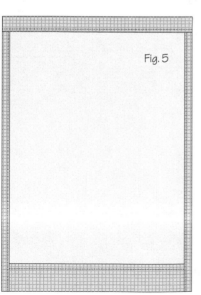
Fig. 5

Construction

TOP SECTION

1. Hem the bottom edge first with a double 1 1/2-inch hem. Then hem the side edges with a double 3/4-inch hem. Finally, hem the top edge with a double 3/4-inch hem. Topstitch the hems in place (fig. 2). Repeat with the second top section.

2. Determine and mark the placement of ties along the top edge of the top section. The first and last ties are placed even with the top corners and one set is placed in the exact middle. Divide the remaining area into equal increments approximately 5 inches apart.

3. Add up the number of ties determined by the spacing in step 2. For each tie, cut a strip of the bottom-section fabric that measures 1 3/4 inches by 36 inches. Fold both short ends of each strip under 1/2 inch toward the wrong side. Fold both long sides 1/4 inch toward the center of the wrong side. Then fold the entire tie in half lengthwise toward the wrong side; match all folded edges and pin. Stitch across each short end and along the folded edges to finish (fig. 3).

4. Find the center of each tie. Pin this center point to the marked points along the top edge of the top section. Secure by stitching across the tie at each point several times (fig. 4).

5. Repeat steps 1 through 4 for the second panel.

BOTTOM SECTION

1. Hem the bottom edge first with a double 3-inch hem. Then hem the side edges with a double 3/4-inch hem. Finally, hem the top edge with a double 1 1/2-inch hem. Topstitch the hems in place (fig. 5). Repeat with the second bottom section.

2. Place the finished top and bottom sections on a large work surface so the top edge of the bottom

section overlaps the bottom edge of the top section 1 1/2 inches (fig. 6). The top edge of the bottom section should be even with the stitched hem of the top section.

3. Place the 3/4-inch fusible tape with the adhesive side facing the wrong side of the top edge of the bottom section (fig. 6). Follow the manufacturer's instructions to fuse the bottom section to the top section. This adhesive will help prevent the curtain from gapping between the buttons.

4. Repeat steps 1 through 3 for the second panel.

5. Refer to the photograph and arrange the buttons evenly across the width of the panel. Handstitch the buttons in place through all layers.

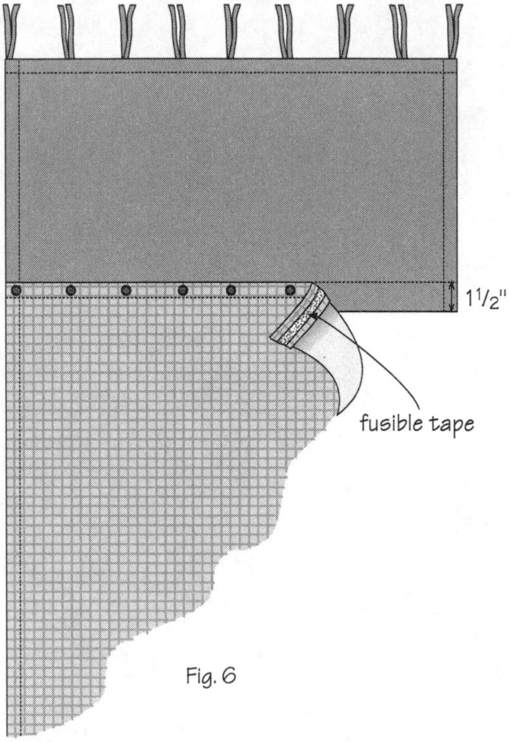

1 1/2"

fusible tape

Fig. 6

Installing and Dressing

Tie the ties evenly into bows. Slide the rod through the ties, under each bow. Use the photograph as a guide to arrange the folds in each panel.

Rooms with a View

We think this window treatment would look great in a bedroom, sunroom, bathroom, child's room, nursery, kitchen, or informal dining nook.

5 *Cornered*

BEING CREATIVE WITH YOUR ROD PLACEMENT DOUBLES THE VERSA-TILITY OF THIS SIMPLE TREATMENT. COLOR PHOTOGRAPH IS ON PAGE 118.

Grandma used to painstakingly pull threads in fine linens and then wrap them with hand stitches in intricate patterns known as hemstitching. Many of these beautiful stitches are now available on home sewing machines at the touch of a button. If you would like to give hemstitching a whirl, this oh-so-easy valance is a perfect place to show off your skill. Napkins make the perfect accompaniment—like a valance for a valance! With such beautifully finished edges, it seems a shame to waste them on an occasional dinner party. Grandma would be so proud!

Suggested Window Shapes

This treatment is suitable for single or double windows, casement windows, or ranch windows. The recommended window width is 48 to 55 inches for the treatment as pictured. Hemstitched panels can be made for windows of any width, but the amount of overlap and position of the napkins may vary.

Techniques to Know before You Begin

If you need to brush up on your skills in any of these areas, turn to part III.

- Accurate Measuring
- Usable Fabric Widths

Part I – The Projects

- Cutting Fabric
- Sewing on Buttons
- Installing Rods, Brackets, and Holdbacks
- Hems
- Covering Buttons

······················ *Materials Needed* ······················

FROM THE FABRIC STORE

- solid-color linen or linen-like fabric for underpanels
- fine cotton or poly-cotton thread to match the fabric for decorative stitching
- matching thread to sew buttons on the napkins
- $3/4$-inch (size 30) half-ball cover buttons, one for each napkin
- paper for patternmaking
- zigzag embroidery presser foot
- $5/8$- to 1-inch-diameter decorative drapery rod with finials and brackets (also available at department stores)
- optional: wing needle

RECOMMENDED NOTIONS
Refer to the list of basic notions on page 180.

FROM THE DEPARTMENT OR LINEN STORE
- 18- to 20-inch square napkins (we used three)

FROM THE HOME IMPROVEMENT CENTER
Refer to the list of basic tools and supplies on page 180.

Suggested Fabrics: Choose a lightweight, evenly woven fabric, such as handkerchief linen, linen, or linen-like fabric in a solid color.

Tip

BEFORE DIVING INTO A PROJECT, THINK THROUGH THE ENTIRE PROCESS FIRST. BY TAKING THIS STEP, YOU'LL BE ABLE TO ANTICIPATE POTENTIAL PROBLEMS AND HAVE SOLUTIONS READY. BRUSH UP ON YOUR TECHNIQUES OR LEARN A NEW TRICK OR TWO BY REVIEWING PART III, "WINDOW TREATMENTS 101: A CRASH COURSE IN SEWING WITHOUT PULLING YOUR HAIR OUT."

Fabric Calculations

These instructions will result in two unlined valance panels with three napkin toppers. For windows that are less than 30 inches wide, plan for one panel and one to two toppers only. For windows wider than 55 inches, use additional panels and napkins.

1. Mount the rod brackets 2 to 4 inches above the top edge of the window frame and 2 to 4 inches out from each side of the window frame. Place the rod in the brackets.

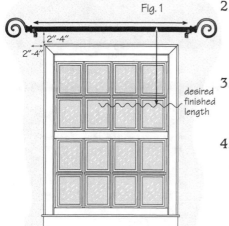

Fig. 1

2"-4"

2"-4"

desired finished length

2. Measure the distance between the rod brackets (fig. 1). Divide this measurement by two for two valance panels. This number will be the finished width of each panel. Write the number here: _____.

3. Add 4 1/2 inches to this number for hems. This is the cut width of each valance panel. Write the number here: _____.

4. Measure from the top of the rod to the desired finished length (fig. 1). (This should be 22 to 27 inches to balance with the size of the napkins.) Write the number here: _____. To determine the cut length, add 5 inches to this number for the rod pocket and hem. Write the number here: _____.

Making the Pattern

1. Cut the pattern paper to the cut width and cut length of one valance. All corners should be 90 degree angles. Divide the cut width measurement in half. Measure up from the bottom corners of the paper a distance equal to this amount and place a mark along each side edge. Mark the center point of the bottom edge of the paper. Draw a diagonal line from each side mark to the center of the bottom edge (fig. 2). Cut on the marked lines.

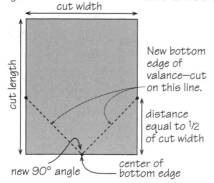

Fig. 2

cut width

cut length

New bottom edge of valance—cut on this line.

distance equal to 1/2 of cut width

new 90° angle

center of bottom edge

2. One of the angled bottom edges will be placed even with the grain of the fabric (fig. 3). Take this pattern with you to the fabric store when purchasing fabric. The pattern should be placed on the fabric in the same direction for each valance.

Construction

VALANCES

1. Lay the fabric flat on a large work surface. Use a carpenter's square to mark and cut a straight edge along one end of the fabric.

Part I - The Projects

2. Place the pattern on your fabric as in figure 3. It is very important for hemstitching to have the grain as accurate as possible. Cut two panels.

3. Create double 1¹⁄₈-inch hems on the diagonal edges. To start, fold each angled bottom edge under 2¹⁄₄ inches toward the wrong side. Press. Then tuck under the top edge of the hem 1¹⁄₈ inches to meet the fold and press again (fig. 4). Do not stitch.

4. Repeat step 3 for the two vertical edges of each panel (fig. 5). Do not stitch.

5. Place one panel on the work surface, with the wrong side facing up. Open up all of the pressed-in hems (fig. 6a). To miter the center bottom point, fold the point toward the wrong side across the innermost intersection of the fold lines and press (fig. 6b). Unfold. Create a new fold across the outermost intersection of the fold lines and press. Cut the fabric at this new diagonal line (fig. 6c).

6. Refold the diagonal double hems to create the mitered corner. Press the mitered corner. Pin to hold it (fig. 6d).

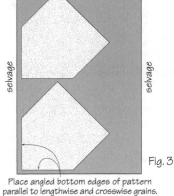

Fig. 3

Place angled bottom edges of pattern parallel to lengthwise and crosswise grains.

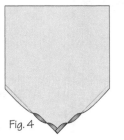

Fig. 4

Fig. 5

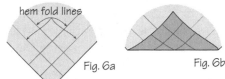

hem fold lines

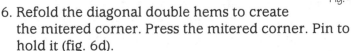

Fig. 6a   Fig. 6b 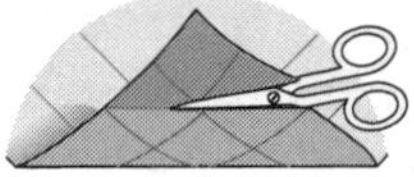   Fig. 6c

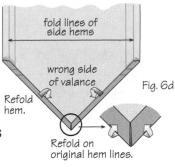

fold lines of side hems

wrong side of valance

Fig. 6d

Refold hem.

Refold on original hem lines.

7. Notice that the 1¹⁄₈-inch fold line for the side hem does not line up with the diagonal hem (fig. 7a). At the side corners, open the hem and roll the fabric out from under the folded corner until the fold lines for the

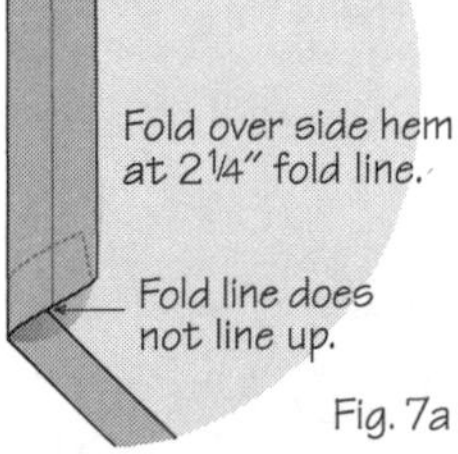

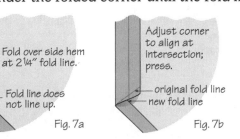

Fold over side hem at 2¹⁄₄" fold line.

Fold line does not line up.

Fig. 7a

Adjust corner to align at intersection; press.

original fold line
new fold line

Fig. 7b

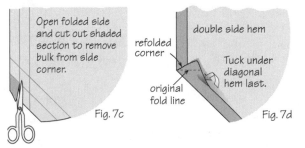

Open folded side and cut out shaded section to remove bulk from side corner.

Fig. 7c

double side hem

refolded corner

Tuck under diagonal hem last.

original fold line

Fig. 7d

hems intersect (fig. 7b). Press the corner. Refold the side hems on the vertical fold lines. To eliminate bulk in the side corner, open up the corner fold and cut a notch in the fabric to the first intersection of the hem fold lines (fig. 7c). Then, tuck in the mitered side corners (fig. 7d). Pin to hold.

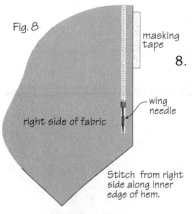
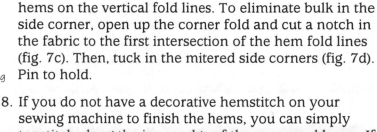

Fig. 8

masking tape

wing needle

right side of fabric

Stitch from right side along inner edge of hem.

8. If you do not have a decorative hemstitch on your sewing machine to finish the hems, you can simply topstitch along the inner edge of these pressed hems. If you choose to use a decorative stitch, always test the stitch on a scrap of fabric folded as thick as the double hem (including mitered corners). Stitch along the test fold and make any tension or stitch width adjustments before you stitch on your valance. Note: If you have trouble stitching over the thicker mitered corners, you may need to trim additional fabric from the inside of the corners. Do so carefully so that no raw edges become exposed. If you still find that your fabric is too thick to hemstitch neatly, cut the hems at the $1^{1}/8$-inch pressed edge and stitch the hemstitch so that it just covers this raw edge to prevent raveling.

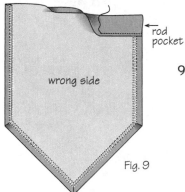
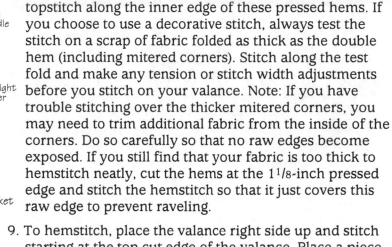

rod pocket

wrong side

Fig. 9

9. To hemstitch, place the valance right side up and stitch starting at the top cut edge of the valance. Place a piece of masking tape on the bed of your sewing machine to assist in guiding a straight stitch line. Stitch $1^{1}/8$ inch from the edge of the valance on the hem so that when the needle swings to its farthest left position, the thread wraps the inner pressed hem edge (fig. 8). See the following sidebar for more information on hemstitching.

10. For the rod pocket, press the top edge under $2^{1}/2$ inches toward the wrong side. Then press the cut edge under $1/2$ inch. Use a straight stitch to topstitch the rod pocket from side to side along the inner pressed edge (fig. 9).

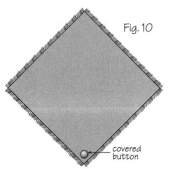
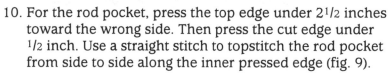

Fig. 10

covered button

NAPKINS

1. Use scraps of fabric from the valance to cover the buttons.

2. Fold a napkin diagonally from corner to corner.

3. Handstitch a button centered at the lower front point $1^{1}/8$ inches in from each side edge (fig. 10).

Hemstitching

The term hemstitching refers to a handstitched decorative hem consisting of pulled threads and elaborate thread-wrapped stitches. Sewing machines often have built-in or add-on stitches designed for machine hemstitching. Consult your machine manual to help you choose the best decorative stitch. Use a wing needle to accent the design. It punches large holes in the fabric as it stitches. Since this type of needle is wider than normal, be careful not to let the needle swing too wide or it may strike the throat plate and break. Test the stitch on scrap fabric before stitching the actual project.

For best results, use fine cotton or polyester-cotton thread so that multiple stitches can be made in one spot without the machine jamming. Buy extra thread and fill extra bobbins; hemstitching uses more thread than normal. Prewound bobbins designed specifically for machine embroidery are also available at most sewing machine stores. While not required, this thread may offer the most consistent stitch quality. A presser foot with a shallow raised area on the underside will allow space for the additional thread, as well as keep the fabric flat while sewing. Lower the top tension slightly to prevent puckering. Operate the sewing machine at a low speed to help control the stitch placement. The stitch should follow the hem edge exactly.

Examine the stitch pattern as you sew. At corners, stop the stitch with the needle in the fabric—usually the far right position at a point just before it moves forward, not backward. Stitch slowly or turn the hand wheel by hand for accurate positioning.

Installing and Dressing

1. Slide the valances onto the rod side by side.

2. Refer to the photograph to position the napkins. Place one napkin centered over each valance, aligning the points. Tuck under the points of the napkins closest to the brackets so that the napkin and valance edges are even. Place the third napkin centered between the first two. The point of the third napkin should be at the center of the window.

Rooms with a View

We think this window treatment would look great in a breakfast nook, kitchen, child's room, or bathroom.

6 *Sheer Beauty*

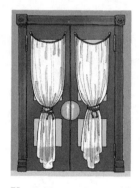

YOU HAVE TO AGREE THAT THIS TREATMENT LOOKS FABULOUS ON FRENCH DOORS, BUT IT IS JUST AS STUNNING ON OTHER WINDOWS. COLOR PHOTOGRAPH IS ON PAGE 119.

*I*nformal or "dressed to the nines"? While contradictory, both descriptions work well for this diaphanous window treatment. A sheer print and sheer solid are layered and gathered at the top with a cord and gracefully tumble from sheer heights to the floor. Tie the soft, seductive folds at the center or release them to the wind.

Suggested Window Shapes

This treatment is suitable for single windows, double windows, French doors, casement windows, picture windows, or bay windows.

Techniques to Know before You Begin

If you need to brush up on your skills in any of these areas, turn to part III.

- Accurate Measuring
- Installing Rods, Brackets, and Holdbacks
- Usable Fabric Widths
- Working with Sheer Fabrics
- Sewing French Seams

- Hems
- Cutting Multiple Fabric Widths
- Cutting Fabric
- Fabric Repeats
- Matching Repeat Designs

- Stitching Fabric Widths Together
- Working with Decorative Trims

···················· *Materials Needed* ·····················

FROM THE FABRIC STORE
- printed sheer decorator fabric
- solid-color sheer decorator fabric for lining
- 3/8-inch cord-edge (cord with an attached lip edge)
- 1 1/2 yards coordinating 3/8-inch cord*
- thread to match both fabrics
- 1 pair medallion-style holdbacks (also available at department stores)

RECOMMENDED NOTIONS
These are specific notions needed for this project. Also refer to the list of basic notions on page 180.

- size 70/10 universal sewing machine needle (for sewing sheer fabrics)
- size 80/12 universal sewing machine needle (for sewing cord-edge)
- fine handsewing needle to sew the hem
- zipper foot

FROM THE HOME IMPROVEMENT CENTER
Refer to the list of basic tools and supplies on page 180.

Suggested Fabrics: Choose voile, crinkled voile, or sheer matelassé.

Fabric Calculations
These instructions will make one curtain panel.

1. Mount the holdbacks 2 to 4 inches above the top edge of the window frame and 2 to 4 inches out from each side of the window frame. Note: If your molding measures 4 inches or wider, the holdback can be placed in the upper corner of the frame itself (assuming you are willing to drill into your woodwork).

* If coordinating cord is not available, purchase this additional amount of cord-edge and remove the lip. See Working with Decorative Trims.

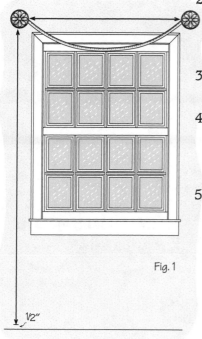

Fig. 1

½"

2. Measure the distance between the holdback medallions (fig. 1). Multiply this measurement by $2^1/2$. This is the finished width of the panel before it is gathered. Write the measurement here: _____.

3. To determine the cut width of the curtain, add 1 inch for seam allowances. Write the number here: _____.

4. To determine the number of fabric widths required, divide the cut width by the usable width of the fabric. Round up to the nearest whole number. Write the number here: _____.

5. Because of the swagged shape at the top of the curtain, the hem on this design will not be parallel to the floor. A slightly uneven hem is an inherent part of this design. To determine the finished length of this treatment, measure the distance from the bottom of the holdback medallion to a point $1/2$ inch above the floor (fig. 1). Write the number here: _____. Add 15 inches to this number for hems and seam allowance. This is the cut length. Write the number here: _____.

6. To calculate the total yardage of sheer decorator fabric and lining, multiply the cut length by the number of fabric widths needed. Write the number here: _____. If your fabric has a repeat design, multiply the repeat distance by the number of widths and add this figure to the total. The extra fabric will allow you to match the designs. Divide this number by 36 and round up to the nearest $1/4$ yard. This is the amount of decorator fabric needed to complete this window treatment. Write the number here: _____. This is also the amount of sheer fabric needed for the lining less any amount added for a repeat. If different, write the number here: _____.

7. Tape one end of a tape measure to the bracket of one holdback. Drape the tape measure, with some slack, across the window to the opposite holdback (fig. 1). The drape should simulate the desired curve of the top edge of the curtain. Note the measurement at the opposite bracket. Write the measurement here: _____.

8. To determine the finished width of the top gathered edge

of the curtain, subtract 2 inches from the draped tape measurement. Write the number here: _____.

9. To determine the amount of cord-edge to purchase, add ³/4 yard to the above measurement for loops and seam allowance. Write the number here: _____.

10. Save scraps of the printed sheer fabric to use later as belt loops for the cord.

Construction

Use a ¹/2-inch seam allowance unless otherwise instructed.

PREPARING THE CURTAIN PANELS

1. Lay the fabric flat on a large work surface. Use a carpenter's square to mark and cut a straight edge at one end of the decorator and lining fabrics. Trim the selvages evenly from both sides of the fabric. The easiest way to do this is to snip the cut edge and pull a lengthwise thread. Use the pulled thread as the cutting line. Measure from the straight edge and cut the fabric to the cut width and length as determined in Fabric Calculations.

2. If you need more than one fabric width to achieve the cut width, cut additional fabric to the same length, matching design repeats. Sew the fabric widths together using a French seam; make sure the design motifs match at the joined seam. Repeat for the lining fabric.

3. Hem the decorator and lining fabrics separately. Each layer has a double 6-inch hem. Stitch the hem (fig. 2). We strongly recommend handstitched hems for sheers.

4. Gather the top edge of the front panel. The gathered measurement between the side seam lines should equal the measurement determined in step 8 of Fabric Calculations. To gather, stitch two parallel rows of long stitches with the bobbin tension reduced. Pull both bobbin threads simultaneously to gather the fabric (fig. 2). Adjust the gathers evenly.

5. Repeat step 4 to gather the top edge of the lining.

ATTACHING CORD-EDGE AND CORD LOOPS

1. If you are using cord-edge for the belt, cut off and set

· ·*Tip*· · · ✂ ·

IF YOU CAN'T FIND HOLDBACKS TO MATCH YOUR FABRIC, SIMPLY PAINT THE METAL HOLDBACKS A COLOR TO COORDINATE WITH YOUR FABRIC.

MORE $PLASH THAN ¢ASH

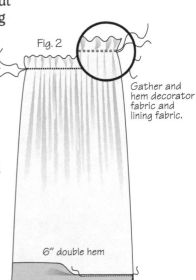

Fig. 2

Gather and hem decorator fabric and lining fabric.

6″ double hem

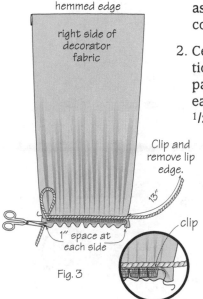

hemmed edge

right side of decorator fabric

Clip and remove lip edge.

13"

clip

1" space at each side

Fig. 3

aside the 1 1/2 yards required. Always wrap tape around the cord before cutting; then cut through the taped section.

2. Center the cord-edge (calculated in step 9 of Fabric Calculations) along the gathered edge of the right side of the front panel. About 13 inches of cord-edge should extend from each end. The cord itself should be placed just beyond the 1/2-inch seam line so your stitching is right against the cord. Begin and end the stitching 1 inch in from each side edge of the fabric. Use a zipper foot to stitch as close to the cord as possible, reinforcing each end with extra stitching. Clip the lip edge to the stitching line every inch in the gathered section (fig. 3).

3. Clip the lip edge to the cord 1 inch in from the cut side edge of the fabric. Be careful not to clip the cord. At the same point, clip the chain stitch connecting the lip edge to the cord. Pull the chain stitch and remove the lip edge from the cord extension at each end. (See page 218.) Be sure to tape the end of the cord to prevent it from untwisting.

4. Flush to the end of the stitching, form a loop with each cord end large enough to pass over the holdback medallion. The loops should be even in size. Lay the end of the looped cord in the 1-inch section at each end of the stitched cord-edge so the loop points toward the center of the curtain (fig. 3). Pin in place so 1/2 inch of fabric seam allowance remains at the side of each loop. Test the loop size before stitching by hanging the curtain over the holdback medallions. Then stitch over the cord on the gathering seam line. Reinforce with extra stitching to ensure stability. Trim the cord ends to 1/2 inch.

CREATING BELT LOOPS

1. Cut two pieces of scrap decorator fabric 1 inch wide by 4 inches long to make belt loops for the center belt. Fold the long edges of the fabric toward the wrong side so they meet at the center. Press. Fold the strip in half lengthwise, lining up the pressed edges. Sew the halves together, stitching close to the pressed edge (fig. 4). Fold the strip in half crosswise to form a loop.

2. Mark the center point along each vertical edge of the front

Fig. 4

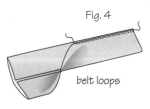

belt loops

curtain. Pin one fabric loop to the right side of each side edge, 5 inches below the center point. Stitch (fig. 5).

CONNECTING THE LINING TO THE CURTAIN

1. Pin the decorator fabric and lining right sides together along the gathered edges and sides. Make sure the top edges and the bottom hems of both layers are even. Stitch along the top and side edges in one continuous stitch line (fig. 6). Use a zipper foot to stitch along the gathered edge as close as possible to the cord-edge.

2. Trim the corners (fig. 6). Turn the curtain right side out. To create sharp corners, use a point turner to gently push out the corners from the inside. Press all edges so neither fabric is visible from the opposite side.

3. Fold the belt loops toward the back of the curtain and pin. Handstitch each loop to the lining about 1 1/2 inches from the side seam.

4. To make sure the lining at the top edge does not roll over the cord, stitch in the ditch along the top edge. Working from the front side, use a zipper foot to stitch in the narrow gap between the cord and the gathered edge of the fabric (fig. 7). The stitching should barely catch the top of the lining gathers on the opposite side.

Installing And Dressing

1. To hang the curtain, slip one cord loop over each hold-back at the top of the window.

2. Use cord (without a lip edge) to create the belt tie. (Remove the lip edge from the cord if you can't find matching cord.) Knot the cord tightly at each end. Trim the taped end or any excess cord flush to the knot. Thread the cord through the loops at the back of the curtain. Wrap the cord around the curtain once or twice to control fullness. Tie a knot at the front and allow the ends to hang loose. Blouse the fabric over the belt tie until the hem edge looks straight.

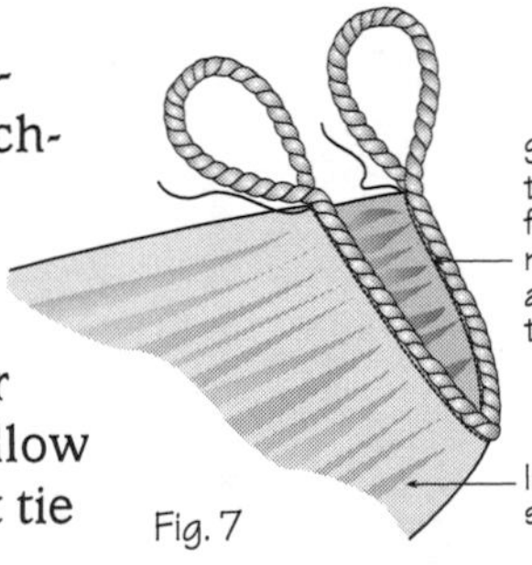

Rooms with a View

We think this window treatment would look great in a bedroom, sitting room, dining room, or sunroom.

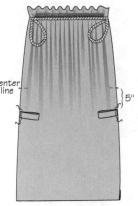

center line

5"

Fig. 5

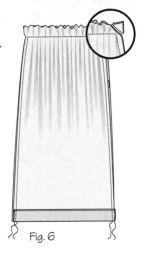

Fig. 6

Stitch in the ditch from the right side against the cord.

lining side

Fig. 7

7 Hollywood Meets Haight-Ashbury

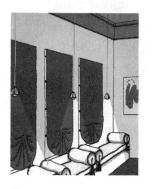

FABRIC SELECTION MAKES ALL THE DIFFER-ENCE. THIS WINDOW IS A CHAMELEON—IT CAN BE CLASSICAL OR A LITTLE ROCK AND ROLL. COLOR PHOTOGRAPH IS ON PAGE 119.

*T*wo layers of sheer fabric create liquid-like folds to form this fanned shade. Tie-dyed fabric and fun novelty fringe create an over-the-top combi-nation of Hollywood glamour and hippie chic. However, this luscious look will be just as effective with a more traditional choice of fabric. Very little construction is required to create this lively window treatment. Simple hand stitches perma-nently form deep folds to maintain the curved fan shape.

Suggested Window Shapes

This treatment is suitable for single windows, casement windows, or French doors. The maximum recommended shade width is 45 inches. Use multiple shades for wider windows.

Techniques to Know before You Begin

If you need to brush up on your skills in any of these areas, turn to part III.

- Accurate Measuring
- Preparing a Mounting Board
- Installing a Mounting Board
- Cutting Fabric
- Turning and Cutting Corners and Points

Part I – The Projects

- Working with Sheer Fabrics
- Working with Decorative Trims

················· *Materials Needed* ·················

FROM THE FABRIC STORE
- sheer decorator fabric
- sheer decorator fabric for the lining
- novelty fringe, such as ostrich fringe or ball fringe
- thread to match the decorator fabric
- heavy thread (such as carpet thread)
- 5/8-inch-wide grosgrain ribbon to match decorator fabric

RECOMMENDED NOTIONS
These are specific notions needed for this project. Also refer to the list of basic notions on page 180.

- point turner
- zipper foot
- size 70/10 universal machine needle

FROM THE HOME IMPROVEMENT CENTER
These are specific supplies needed for this project. Also refer to the basic list of tools and supplies on page 180.

- 1-by-2-inch board
- screws, 2 inches long (at least two, plus one for every 36 inches of board)
- heavy-duty staple gun with 1/2-inch long staples

Suggested Fabrics: Choose voile, crinkled voile, Georgette, chiffon, organza, or batiste.

Suggested Trims: Choose lightweight novelty trims such as ostrich fringe, confetti fringe, or ball fringe.

> **Tip**
>
> SEARCH FLEA MARKETS FOR UNUSUAL VINTAGE TRIMS AT BARGAIN PRICES. MANY GREAT FINDS ARE STILL ATTACHED TO ITEMS SUCH AS BEDSPREADS, APPAREL, AND DISCARDED WINDOW TREATMENTS.

·························

Fabric Calculations

1. Determine the measurement of your mounting board. If the window has a frame, measure the width of the window from outside frame edge to outside frame edge (fig. 1). If the window does not have a frame, measure the

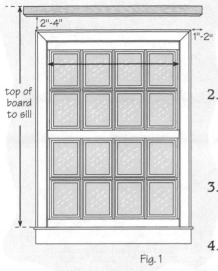

2"-4"

1"-2"

top of
board
to sill

Fig. 1

opening. The board should extend 1 to 2 inches beyond each side of the window. This is the length of your mounting board. Write the measurement here: _____. Cut the mounting board to this measurement.

2. Place the mounting board 2 to 4 inches above the window so one flat side is against the wall (fig. 1). Make a light pencil mark on the wall at the top edge of the board. Do not permanently attach the board to the wall at this time.

3. To determine the finished width of the shade, add $1/2$ inch for ease to the measured width of the mounting board (step 1). Write the number here: _____.

4. To determine the cut width of the shade, add $1 1/2$ inches to the finished width for ease and seam allowances. Write the number here: _____.

5. To calculate the cut length of this shade, first measure the window from the top of the mounting board to the top of the window sill (fig. 1). Write the measurement here: _____.

6. Divide the length of the mounting board (from step 1) by 4 and round up to the nearest $1/2$ inch. Add 1 inch for ease. Write the number here: _____. Add this number to the measured length of the window. This is the finished length of the window shade. Write the number here: _____.

7. To determine the cut length of the window shade, add 2 inches for seam allowances. Write the number here: _____. Example: If the length of the mounting board is 36 inches and the measurement determined in step 6 is 60 inches long, divide 36 by 4 to get 9 inches. Add 1 inch to get 10 inches. Add the 10 inches to the 60-inch measured length for a finished length of 70 inches. Then add 2 inches for a cut length of 72 inches.

8. To calculate the total yardage, divide the cut length of the shade by 36 and round up to the nearest $1/4$ yard. Write the number here: _____. This is the amount of decorator fabric and lining fabric needed to construct this window shade. Add $1/2$ yard of fabric to cover the mounting board. Write the total here: _____.

9. To determine the amount of fringe and gros-grain ribbon to purchase, add 3 inches for ease to the cut width determined in step 4. Write the number here: _____.

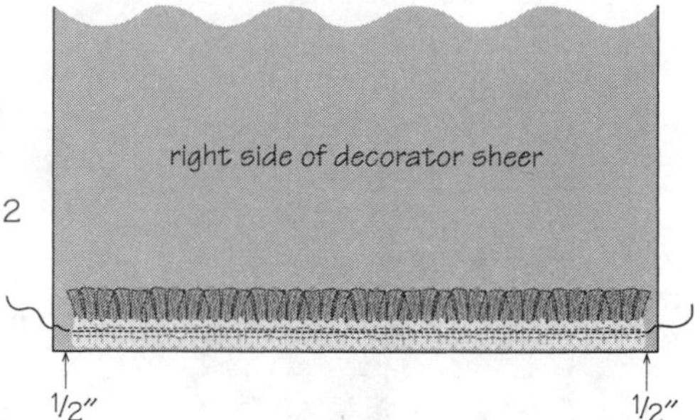

Construction

Use a $1/2$-inch seam allowance unless otherwise instructed.

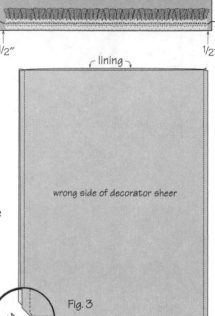

Fig. 2

right side of decorator sheer

1/2"   1/2"

lining

wrong side of decorator sheer

Fig. 3

Cut corners diagonally;
do not cut edge of fringe.

1. Lay the fabric flat on a large work surface. Use a carpenter's square to mark and cut a straight edge at one end of the sheer fabric.

2. Cut the fabric and the lining to the cut width and cut length determined in steps 4 and 7 above.

3. Pin the fringe to the right side of the bottom edge of the decorator fabric between the $1/2$-inch side seam allowances. Ease to fit. Line up the header edge of the fringe with the cut edge of fabric so the cut fringe ends point to the center of the fabric. The innermost row of trim stitching should be just beyond the $1/2$ inch seam line. Use a zipper foot to attach, stitching along the innermost row of fringe stitching, easing the trim to fit 3 to 4 inches at a time (fig. 2).

4. Place the fabric and lining right sides together and pin along the sides and bottom edge. Stitch on

Working with Novelty Trims

Most fringe styles have a protective row of chain stitching along the decorative edge to control the cut ends while handling. Leave it intact until the project is complete. However, some novelty trims, such as beads or the ostrich trim we used in our sample, do not have this protective stitching. To control the flyaway ends while sewing, flatten the cut ends with your hand to locate the header edge. Easing to fit, pin the header edge of the fringe to the fabric. (To ease, pin the fringe so it buckles slightly. Then flatten the buckle as you stitch.) To sew, guide the fabric with one hand, while the other holds the fringe ends away from the needle. Stitch slowly, a few inches at a time for maximum control. This is not as difficult as it sounds. It takes a bit of patience, but it's worth it!

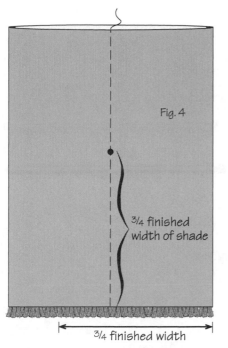

Fig. 4

³/₄ finished
width of shade

|← ³/₄ finished width →|

the same stitching line used to attach the trim. Cut the fabric corners diagonally to eliminate bulk (fig. 3). Do not cut the header edge of the fringe when you cut the corners. Turn the shade right side out. To create sharp corners, use a point turner to gently push the inside of each corner out. Press the edges so neither fabric is visible from the opposite side.

5. Place the lined shade flat on your work surface, lining side up. Pin a vertical line through the center of the shade. Use long hand stitches to baste the entire length of the shade along the pinned line (fig. 4).

6. Measure along the basted center line from the bottom of the shade, and mark a point equal to ³/₄ of the finished width of the shade (fig. 4).

7. Knot the end of the heavy thread and handstitch two identical rows of 1¹/₄-inch-long stitches from the bottom of the shade to the marked point. Stitch each row ¹/₈ inch away from the center row of basting (fig. 5). The last stitch at the marked point should come out on the lining side of the shade. Pull the thread up until the fabric is tightly pleated. Note: Since this shade is stationary, you may prefer a shorter length. Take additional stitches to shorten the shade if desired.

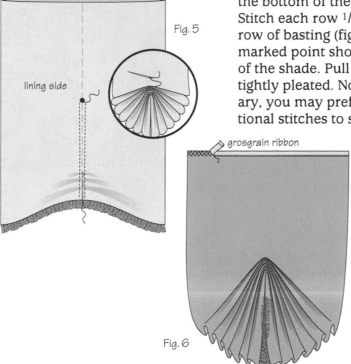

Fig. 5

lining side

grosgrain ribbon

Fig. 6

Make several small stitches through the top few pleats to secure the threads so the pleats stay in place.

8. For a clean top edge finish, serge or zigzag along the top edge of the shade. Pin the grosgrain ribbon along the right side of the top edge of the shade so that the ribbon extends ¹/₄ inch beyond the serged fabric edge. Fold the cut ends under ¹/₂ inch at each top

corner edge of the shade. Stitch (fig. 6). The ribbon will reinforce the sheer fabric in the area to be stapled.

9. Remove the basting stitches from step 5.

Installation and Dressing

1. Prepare the mounting board by covering it with decorator fabric. If using a sheer fabric, you may need several layers of fabric to hide the surface of the board.

2. Place the mounting board flat on the work surface with the wider side of the board facing up. Arrange the shade with the right side up and the free edge of the grosgrain ribbon against the back edge of the board (fig. 7). Staple in place.

3. Position the board at the mark you made in step 3 of Fabric Calculations with the staple side flush against the wall. The shade should "waterfall" over the top narrow edge of the board (fig. 7).

4. Arrange gathers evenly.

Rooms with a View

We think this window treatment would look great in a bedroom, bathroom, or living room.

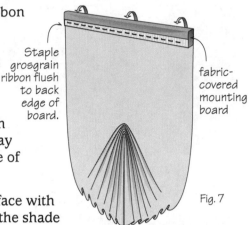

Staple grosgrain ribbon flush to back edge of board.

fabric-covered mounting board

Fig. 7

·························· *Easy Does It!* ··························

Ironing Sheers

Sheers can be woven in many fibers. Check the fiber content when you purchase your fabric, and set your iron accordingly. Cottons require medium to high heat, while polyesters need only medium to low. Nylon can stand the least heat, so set your iron to the lowest setting. Before ironing your window treatment, always test the iron on a scrap of fabric to choose the temperature and decide whether to use a steam or dry iron.

Tip

USE LEFTOVER FABRIC FROM YOUR WINDOW TREATMENT TO UNIFY YOUR DESIGN THEME. WHY NOT DECOUPAGE A TABLETOP OR DRAWER FRONTS FOR AN ARTFUL MORE SPLASH THAN CASH TOUCH?

MORE $PLASH THAN ¢ASH

8 *Sunny Outlook*

THIS SURE-TO-DELIGHT WINDOW TREATMENT CAN BE TWISTED OVER MANY WINDOW SHAPES. COLOR PHOTOGRAPH IS ON PAGE 119.

"Simplicity at its best" is the only way to describe this window treatment. A wisp of fabric is twisted ever so slightly to allow the sun to peek through while adding some softness and color to your window. A printed sheer fabric was teamed with a textured sheer to create this luscious look. The construction is very simple to do and the resulting window treatment is fantastic.

Suggested Window Shapes

This treatment is suitable for single or double windows, bay windows, French doors, casement windows, corner windows, dormer windows, or Palladian windows.

Techniques to Know before You Begin

If you need to brush up on your skills in any of these areas, turn to part III.

- Accurate Measuring
- Turning and Cutting Corners and Points
- Cutting Fabric
- Working with Sheer Fabrics

Materials Needed

FROM THE FABRIC STORE
- sheer decorator fabric

- sheer decorator fabric for lining
- one pair 4-inch-wide wall-mounted medallion-style holdbacks (also available in department stores)
- 7/8 yard of cording or ribbon to match the fabric
- thread to match the fabric

RECOMMENDED NOTIONS

This is a specific notion needed for this project. Also refer to the list of basic notions on page 180.

- size 70/10 universal sewing machine needle

FROM THE HOME IMPROVEMENT CENTER

Refer to the list of basic tools and supplies on page 180.

Suggested Fabrics: Choose lace, sheer fabric (printed or solid), voile, batiste, or crinkled voile. If using a print fabric, make sure the fabric design can be railroaded. This window treatment requires that the design look as good sideways as it does up and down. Not all fabrics are appropriate for this technique. Study the fabric closely to determine if the design does not have a specific direction (that is, you don't want stemmed flowers to appear to be lying on their sides).

Tip ✂

WHEN YOU'RE MAK-
ING WINDOW TREAT-
MENTS, IT IS IMPOR-
TANT NOT TO SKIMP
ON FABRIC. IF YOU
FALL IN LOVE WITH
A FABRIC THAT IS
OUTSIDE YOUR
BUDGET, DON'T
COMPROMISE BY
TRYING TO BUY LESS
FABRIC THAN SPECI-
FIED AND "MAKE
DO." INSTEAD, FIND
A LESS EXPENSIVE
FABRIC AND PUR-
CHASE ENOUGH.
YOU'LL BE PLEASED
WITH THIS DECISION.

MORE $PLASH THAN ¢ASH

Fabric Calculations

1. Mount the medallions 2 to 4 inches above the top edge of the window frame and 2 to 4 inches out from each side of the frame (fig. 1).

2. Along one side, measure down from the medallion to the desired finished length (fig. 1); mark this point with masking tape on the window frame. Place a corresponding tape mark at the opposite side of the window. For the cut length, add 1 inch for seam allowances to this measurement. Write the measurement here: _____.

3. To determine the cut width of your rectangle, start again at the medallion and measure down to the tape mark. Continue diagonally to the medallion in the opposite corner, then down the side of the window to

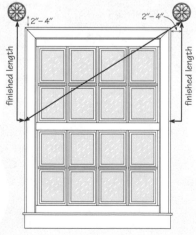

2"–4"   2"–4"

finished length

finished length

Fig. 1

the marked corresponding finished length point (fig. 1). Add 5 inches to this measurement for seam allowances and ease. This total measurement will be the cut width of your rectangle. Write the total here: _____.

4. To determine the yardage needed, divide the cut width by 36 and round up to the nearest 1/4 yard. Write the total here: _____. This is the amount of decorator and lining fabrics needed to construct this window treatment.

Cutting Instructions

1. Lay the fabric flat on a large work surface. Use a carpenter's square to mark and cut a straight edge at one end of the decorator and lining fabrics.

2. Beginning from this straight cut edge, draw a line 1/2 inch from and parallel to the selvage edge along the full length of the fabric. Cut on this line to remove the selvage.

3. To create the fabric rectangle, start at the corner of the two cut perpendicular edges to measure and draw a rectangle equal to the cut width and cut length measurement (fig. 2). Note: The cut width measurement will run along the lengthwise fabric edge. This is called railroading. Repeat this process with the lining fabric.

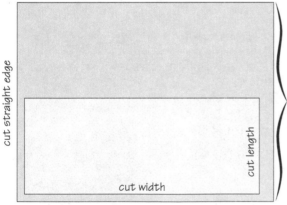

Fig. 2

cut straight edge

width of fabric

cut length

cut width

lengthwise grain of fabric (remove selvage)

Construction

Use a 1/2-inch seam allowance unless otherwise instructed.

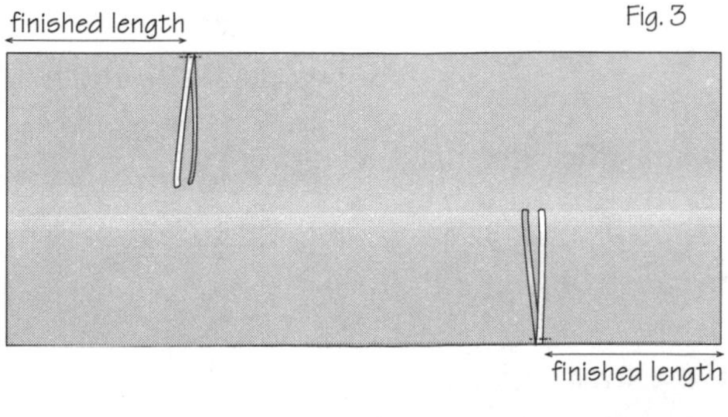

1. Measure in from the upper left corner along the long edge a distance equal to the finished length measurement. Mark this point with a pin. Measure the same distance in from the bottom right corner along the opposite long edge and pin-mark (fig 3).

finished length

Fig. 3

finished length

2. Cut the cording or ribbon into two equal pieces to produce the ties. Fold each tie in half. Pin the folded edge of one tie to each pin mark on the right side of the decorator fabric so the loose ends point toward the center of the valance (fig. 3). Machine baste the ties in place.

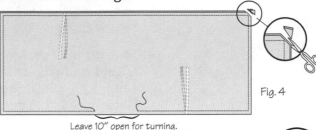

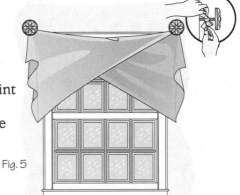

Fig. 4

Leave 10" open for turning.

3. Pin the lining and decorator fabrics right sides together. Stitch around all four sides of the rectangle, leaving a 10-inch opening for turning (fig. 4).

4. To eliminate bulk, trim the corners diagonally.

5. Turn right side out. For sharp corners, use a point turner to gently push the fabric out from the inside. Press the seam so neither fabric is visible from the opposite side.

6. Handstitch the opening closed.

Fig. 5

Installing and Dressing

Tie the cording or ribbon on the upper left side of the panel to the bracket on the left medallion. Then tie the opposite ties to the opposite medallion (fig. 5). The fabric will twist into shape automatically. Arrange the folds along each side in a pleasing design.

Rooms with a View

We think this window treatment would look great in a bedroom, bath, child's room, kitchen, or informal dining nook.

Easy Does It!

Stitching Sheers

When stitching sheer fabrics, always use a needle size that was designed for this weight of fabric (70/10). Always start with a brand new needle when stitching sheers. This will prevent unsightly pulled threads that are caused by an old, blunt needle.

Tip

YOU CAN USE INEXPENSIVE KITCHEN CABINET KNOBS OR DRAWER PULLS (AVAILABLE IN HOME CENTERS) INSTEAD OF MEDALLION-TYPE BRACKETS.

9 *Leaf Motif*

DRESSING UP READY-MADE CURTAINS WITH FREE-FORM VELVET LEAVES HAS NEVER BEEN SO EASY! COLOR PHOTOGRAPH IS ON PAGE 120.

epartment store curtains come alive with the addition of luscious three-dimensional embossed velvet leaves. The rich velvet texture and vibrant fall colors will transform plain-Jane ready-mades into a veritable whirlwind of color. Sophistication and appeal have rarely been so easy to achieve!

·············· *Suggested Window Shapes* ··············

This treatment is suitable for single or double windows, picture windows, corner windows, or casement windows.

······ *Techniques to Know before You Begin* ······

If you need to brush up on your skills in any of these areas, turn to part III.

- Accurate Measuring
- Installing Rods, Brackets, and Holdbacks

··················· *Materials Needed* ···················

FROM THE FABRIC STORE

- assorted colors (six to eight) of velvet with rayon and acetate fiber content (1/4 yard each) to coordinate with the ready-made curtain you are embellishing*

---

* For best results, use velvet that is made from both rayon and acetate fibers. You may use velvet scraps if they're large enough to accommodate a 6-inch square.

Part I – The Projects

- assorted 100 percent cotton fabrics to match each color of the velvet selected
- double-stick paper-backed fusible webbing
- assorted rubber stamps with a bold leaf design—four to six of various sizes and designs (also available at craft stores); do not use foam stamps for this process
- thread to match the ready-made curtain
- press cloth

FROM THE DEPARTMENT OR LINEN STORE

- ready-made tabbed curtains in a color of your choice with optional tiebacks
- decorative rod, bracket, and finials (also available at fabric and hardware stores)

RECOMMENDED NOTIONS

These are specific notions needed for this project. Also refer to the list of basic notions on page 180.

- squirt bottle
- embroidery scissors

FROM THE HARDWARE STORE

Refer to the list of basic tools and supplies on page 180.

Tip — INSTEAD OF PURCHASING A NEW SET OF CURTAINS, ADD EMBOSSED VELVET EMBELLISHMENTS TO AN EXISTING WINDOW TREATMENT TO GIVE IT A COMPLETELY NEW LOOK.

MORE $PLASH THAN ¢ASH

Construction

INSTALLING THE HARDWARE

1. Mount the rod brackets 2 to 4 inches above the top edge of the window frame and 2 to 4 inches out from each side of the frame (fig. 1).

2. Ready-made curtains come in predetermined length and width measurements. Select a size that is best for your window. To do this, measure from the top of the rod to the floor to determine the finished length of the curtain.

EMBOSSING VELVET

Embossed velvet is achieved by transferring a rubber stamp design to velvet with heat and pressure.

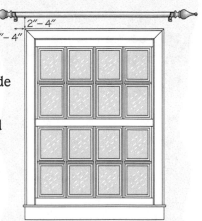

2"– 4"

2"– 4"

Fig. 1

1. Cut the velvet, cotton fabric, and fusible webbing into 6-inch squares. This size accommodates most size stamps and is very easy to handle. You will use one 6-inch square of fabric, lining and fusible webbing for each leaf. However, with careful planning, several different imprints of the same leaf may be produced from one 6-inch square.

Fig. 2

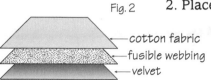

— cotton fabric
— fusible webbing
— velvet

2. Place the velvet with the right side, or nap side, down on the work surface. Remove one side of the paper from the double-stick fusible webbing. Place the webbing so the paper side is up with the sticky side against the back of the velvet square (fig. 2).

3. With a hot, dry iron (wool or cotton setting), glide the iron just above the layers without touching the iron to the paper. Pass the iron as close as possible to the paper so the heat will activate the adhesive. Note: Velvet nap is easily crushed. Any pressure placed on the fabric may destroy the nap. If the nap is destroyed, this technique will not work.

4. Remove the remaining paper from the webbing that is now fuse-basted to the velvet. Place the square of cotton fabric against this adhesive layer. The adhesive should be slightly sticky to the touch so the lining fabric will stay in place.

Fig. 3

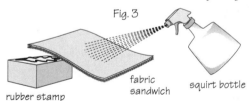

rubber stamp

fabric
sandwich

squirt bottle

5. Place the stamp, rubber surface up, on the ironing surface. Then place the entire fabric "sandwich" velvet side down on one of the stamps (fig. 3). Lightly mist the cotton fabric with water. Cover it with a press cloth.

6. Press the iron securely against the surface of the press cloth; do not move it around. Hold it in place for approximately 30 seconds. Use the part of the iron that does not have steam holes or the hole marks will be transferred to the velvet surface and ruin the design (fig. 4).

Fig. 4

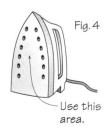

Use this
area.

7. Lift the iron up and carefully remove the velvet sandwich from the stamp surface. The stamp design will have been transferred to the velvet. Allow the fabric to cool before handling.

8. Repeat this process until all the leaves have been embossed.

9. With embroidery scissors, carefully cut around each leaf image just outside the flattened design (fig. 5). The three layers are now sealed together and the leaf will not fray.

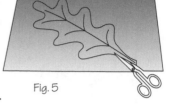

Fig. 5

10. Refer to the photograph and arrange the leaves as desired across the width of the top edge of the curtain panel. It is more interesting to have leaves appear to be windblown across the curtain, rather than in a rigid line.

11. Handstitch the leaves in place in an inconspicuous part of the leaf. If you want the leaves to remain flat and not flutter, tack each leaf in several positions.

12. Repeat this entire process with the tiebacks (if they were included with the curtains).

Installing and Dressing

1. Insert the rod through the tabs. Arrange the curtain evenly at each side of the window.

2. Attach the tiebacks where desired.

3. Refer to the photograph and arrange the folds as desired.

Rooms with a View

We think this window treatment would look great in a bedroom, living room, family room, dining room, or kitchen.

Suggested Placements for Tiebacks

Sill Length
Floor-length curtains or drapes fall into graceful curves if the tiebacks are placed at the height of the sill.

Placed Low
By placing tiebacks low (about two-thirds of the way down from the top of the curtains), an illusion of a tall, narrow window is created. This effect will obscure light because the curtains cover more of the window.

Placed High
To create an illusion of height, place the tiebacks about one-third of the way down from the top. This effect will also let in the most light.

10 Tying the Knot

You have heard about tying the knot at the altar. Why not tie the knot at the window? This soft valance becomes gracefully linear when suspended from knotted ties. The texture created by simple knots is enhanced by the use of a contrasting fabric texture. This rich combination helps to transform a basic valance into a creative solution perfect for windows of many sizes and shapes.

WINDOWS OF ANY WIDTH ARE PERFECT FOR THIS VALANCE. COLOR PHOTOGRAPH IS ON PAGE 120.

·············· Suggested Window Shapes ··············

This treatment is suitable for single or double windows, sliding glass doors, window walls, ranch (strip) windows, or French doors.

······ Techniques to Know before You Begin ······

If you need to brush up on your skills in any of these areas, turn to part III.

- Accurate Measuring
- Usable Fabric Widths
- Cutting Fabric
- Fabric Repeats
- Installing Rods, Brackets, and Holdbacks
- Cutting Multiple Fabric Widths
- Matching Repeat Designs
- Better Buttonholes

Part I - The Projects

- Stitching Fabric Widths Together
- Advantages of Lining Your Window Treatments
- Turning and Cutting Corners and Points
- Working with Sheer Fabrics
- Working with Decorative Trims

.... *Materials Needed* ....

FROM THE FABRIC STORE

- decorator fabric
- sheer fabric for ties
- blackout lining fabric*
- 3/16- to 1/4-inch cord-edge (cord with an attached lip edge)
- decorative rod, brackets, and finials**
- standard flat rod with a rounded return the same measurement as the decorative rod brackets**
- thread to match decorator fabric
- hook-and-loop tape (one side sew-in and one side adhesive-back)
- hook-and-loop tape adhesive (available in a tube)

RECOMMENDED NOTIONS

These are specific notions needed for this project. Also refer to the list of basic notions on page 180.

- point turner
- size 90/14 universal machine needle
- zipper foot or special piping foot

FROM THE HOME IMPROVEMENT CENTER

Refer to the list of basic tools and supplies on page 180.

Suggested Fabrics: For the valance, choose a medium-weight fabric such as duck, jacquard, sateen, linen or linen-like fabric, denim, broadcloth, or chintz. For the tabs, choose sheer voile or sheer crinkled voile.

* This treatment needs to have more structure than regular lining fabric can provide. Blackout lining adds the weight and body needed for the structure.

**This valance actually hangs from the standard curtain rod but gives the illusion that it is suspended from the decorative rod.

Fabric Calculations

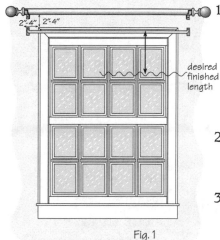

2"-4" 2"-4"

desired
finished
length

Fig. 1

1. Mount the brackets for the decorative rod 2 to 4 inches above the top edge of the window frame and 2 to 4 inches out from each side of the frame. Mount the standard flat rod so the returns are directly below the brackets for the decorative rod. The top edge of the flat rod should be even with the top edge of the window frame (fig. 1).

2. Measure the flat rod from end to end including the returns. This is the finished width of the valance. Write the number here: _____.

3. To determine the cut width of the valance, add 1 1/2 inches for seam allowances and ease. Write the number here: _____.

4. To determine the number of fabric widths required to achieve the cut width, divide the cut width of the valance by the usable width of the fabric. Round up to the next whole number. Write the number here: _____.

5. To determine the finished length, measure from the top edge of the flat rod to the desired finished length (fig. 1). Write the measurement here: _____. Add 1 inch for the seam allowances to determine the cut length. Write the measurement here: _____.

6. To calculate the total yardage of the decorator and lining fabrics, multiply the cut length measurement by the number of widths calculated in step 4. Write the number here: _____. If your fabric has a repeat design, multiply the repeat distance by the number of widths and add this figure to the total. The extra fabric will allow you to match the designs.

7. To determine the yardage needed, divide this number by 36 and round up to the nearest 1/4 yard. Write the number here: _____.

8. You need one tie for every two buttonholes. For each tie, you will need a rectangle of fabric that is 5 inches by 24 inches. Figure fabric amounts according to the width of your window and the number of ties you need. (Note: You can make ten ties from 3/4 yard of 54-inch-wide fabric,

MORE $PLASH THAN ¢ASH ·

Tip

BAMBOO POLES (AVAILABLE AT GARDEN CENTERS) OR EVEN TREE BRANCHES BRING A LITTLE OF THE OUTDOORS INDOORS AND ARE PERFECT TO USE AS CURTAIN RODS.

twelve ties from 3/4 yard of 60-inch-wide fabric, or eighteen ties from 3/4 yard of 90-inch-wide fabric.)

9. You will need a length of cord-edge equal to the perimeter of the entire valance, plus 1/4 yard for ease. Write the amount here: _____.

10. You will need a length of hook-and-loop tape equal to the finished width of the valance.

Construction

Use a 1/2-inch seam allowance unless otherwise instructed.

1. Lay the fabric flat on a large work surface. Use a carpenter's square to mark and cut a straight edge at one end of the decorator and lining fabrics.

2. Cut the fabric to the cut length measurement. If you need more than one width to achieve the cut width of your valance, cut additional fabric to the same length, matching motifs. Sew the fabric widths together, making sure the design motifs match at the joined seam. Do the same with the lining fabric.

3. Trim equal amounts from both side edges of the joined fabrics to obtain the cut width measurement.

4. Pin the cord-edge to the right side of the decorator fabric. Start at the center of an edge in an inconspicuous spot (e.g., along the side), not at a corner. Pin the cut cord end perpendicular to the cut side edge. Then, bend the cord so the lip edge aligns with the fabric edge (fig. 2). The cord itself should be placed just beyond the 1/2-inch seam line so your stitching is right against the cord. Use a zipper foot to stitch on the seam line over the folded cord end, then continue stitching as close to the cord as possible. Ease the cord to fit the fabric, working with 2 to 3 inches at a time around the entire perimeter of the valance.

5. At each corner, stitch to within 1 inch of the corner and stop with the needle in the down position. This allows you to pivot the cord-edge around the corner to create a sharp point. Clip the lip edge to, but not through, the innermost row of trim stitching exactly at the corner.

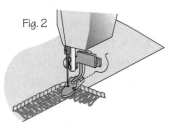

Fig. 2

Tip

IF YOUR EXISTING WINDOW TREATMENT MATCHES YOUR CURRENT COLOR SCHEME AND THE FABRIC IS STILL IN GOOD SHAPE, CONSIDER RESTYLING IT INSTEAD OF REPLACING IT. YOU MAY HAVE PLENTY OF FABRIC FOR A SIMPLE AND STYLISH WINDOW TREATMENT.

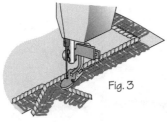

Fig. 3

Continue stitching to the corner, then stop again with the needle in the down position, raise the presser foot, pivot the fabric, lower the presser foot and continue stitching. End by overlapping the beginning cord and running the cut end of the cord-edge into the seam allowance as you did at the beginning (fig. 3). Stitch over the overlapped cords to finish. Trim any excess cord-edge even with the seam allowance.

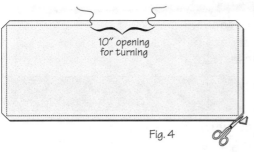

10" opening for turning

Fig. 4

6. Pin the decorator and lining fabrics right sides together. Stitch around all four sides, leaving a 10-inch opening along the top edge for turning (fig. 4). Continue to use a zipper foot so that you can stitch on the same stitching line used to attach the cord-edge, as close as possible to the cord.

7. Trim the corners diagonally to eliminate bulk (fig. 4).

8. Turn the valance right side out. To create sharp corners, use a point turner to gently push the fabric out from the inside. Press the seam so that neither fabric is visible on the opposite side.

9. Handstitch the opening closed.

10. Two buttonholes will be stitched along the top edge of the valance for each knotted tie. To determine the placement of the buttonholes, temporarily attach the valance to the lower rod with tape. Mark where you would like the outermost buttonholes to be placed.

11. To determine the number of buttonholes and the distance in between, measure the distance between the two marks. Divide this measurement by an odd number. Try different odd numbers until the result is a number between 6 and 8 inches (fig. 5). The odd number represents the number of spaces between the buttonholes and the result will be the distance between the buttonholes (e.g., a measured distance of $47^1/2" \div 7$ [the number of spaces] = 7.07, or about $7^1/16"$ [the size of the space]. You should have

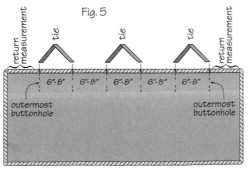

Fig. 5

return measurement — tie — tie — tie — return measurement

6"-8" 6"-8" 6"-8" 6"-8" 6"-8"

outermost buttonhole   outermost buttonhole

an even number of marks for the buttonholes and an odd number of spaces.

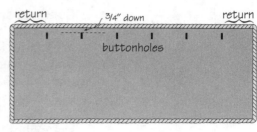

Fig. 6

12. Stitch a 1-inch-long vertical buttonhole at
each of these marks. The top edge of the
buttonhole should be 3/4-inch down from
the top edge (do not include the cord-edge
in this measurement) (fig. 6). Use scissors
or a seam ripper to cut open the buttonholes.

13. Cut the sheer fabric into the number of ties needed (one
tie per pair of buttonholes). Each tie is cut 5 inches by
24 inches. Fold the tie fabric in half lengthwise, right
sides together, so that the tie measures 2 1/2
inches by 24 inches. Begin at one folded
edge and stitch across one short end. Leave
the needle in the down position to turn the corner.
Continue stitching along the long edge, leaving a
10-inch opening for turning, and continue across the
other short end (fig. 7). Trim the corners diagonally to
eliminate bulk. Turn the tie right side out, press smooth,
and handstitch the opening closed.

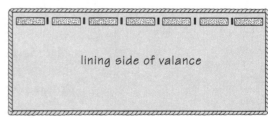

Fig. 7

14. Separate the hook-and-loop tape. Set aside the sticky-
backed hook (rough) portion for now. Cut the loop (soft)
side of the hook-and-loop tape into
sections that are 3/4-inch shorter than
the measurement between the buttonholes (step 11 above). Follow the package directions to apply the adhesive to
the wrong side of the loop pieces.

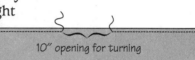

Fig. 8

15. Position the loop pieces on the lining
side of the valance between buttonholes (fig. 8).

Installing and Dressing

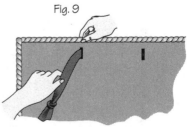

Fig. 9

1. Attach the adhesive-back portion of the hook-and-
loop tape to the front of the entire length of the
standard flat rod (including the returns). If the tape is
too wide, trim it to the width of the flat rod.

2. At one end of each tie, make a large single knot
approximately 1 inch from the end. Begin at one
outermost buttonhole and insert the tie through the

buttonhole from the front to the back (fig. 9). Pull the tie so the knot is against the buttonhole. Repeat this process with every other buttonhole. Be careful not to tie the knots too tight. They must be large enough so that they don't pull through the buttonholes.

3. Attach the valance to the flat rod by pressing the hook-and-loop tape together along the top edge of the valance. Take care so the top edge is even.

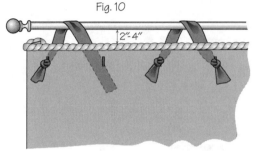

Fig. 10

4. Now place the decorator rod in its respective brackets. Refer to the photograph and bring the tie up and behind the decorator rod, down over the front of the decorator rod, and into the next buttonhole from the back of the valance to the front (fig. 10).

5. Tie another knot approximately 1 inch from the end. Then pull the tie so the knot is against the buttonhole.

6. Repeat this process for the remaining buttonholes.

7. Refer to the photograph and adjust the ties so they are even in length. It should appear as if the valance is hanging from the ties; the flat rod should not be visible.

Rooms with a View

We think this window treatment would look great in a living room, dining room, kitchen, bathroom, child's room, or bedroom.

11 *Knot Sew*

Sharp angles on a window give way to a graceful arch created by folds of fabric artfully held in place with knotted cording. The cording creates both structural dimension and intrigue on this simple-to-sew cornice-style window treatment. This unique arched design is a great choice for those who have existing Palladian, or arched, windows. Or for those who don't have these window shapes, the illusion can easily be created.

.... *Suggested Window Shape* ....

This treatment is suitable for single or double windows, corner windows (if they don't butt together in the corner), dormer windows, Palladian windows, arched windows, or casement windows.

...... *Techniques to Know before You Begin* ......

If you need to brush up on your skills in any of these areas, turn to part III.

- Accurate Measuring
- Installing a Mounting Board
- Usable Fabric Widths
- Cutting Multiple Fabric Widths
- Fabric Repeats
- Cutting Fabric
- Hems
- Matching Repeat Designs

EASILY ADD SHAPE AND DESIGN TO YOUR WINDOW WITH THIS VALANCE. COLOR PHOTOGRAPH IS ON PAGE 120.

- Stitching Fabric Widths Together
- Advantages of Lining Your Window Treatments
- Fabric-Covered Cording

.... *Materials Needed* ....

FROM THE FABRIC STORE
- decorator fabric   • thread to match fabric
- lining for the valance and inside the cornice
- 1-inch-diameter filler cord (enough for three knotted ties and for around the top of the cornice box)
- 1/2-inch plastic rings (12)
- 1 1/2 yards of nylon Roman shade cord

RECOMMENDED NOTIONS
These are specific notions needed for this project. Also refer to the list of basic notions on page 180.

- point turner   • zipper foot
- size 90/14 universal machine needle   • fabric glue

FROM THE HOME IMPROVEMENT CENTER
These are specific supplies needed for this project. Also refer to the basic list of tools and supplies on page 180.

- 1-by-4-, 1-by-6-, or 1-by-8-inch board   • wood glue
- 1/4-inch interior-grade plywood   • pushpins
- finishing nails
- angle brackets shorter than the projection of the board (at least two, plus one for every 36 inches of board length)
- screws, 2 inches long (two to four for each bracket)
- Heavy-duty staple gun with 1/2-inch long staples

Suggested Fabrics: Choose a medium-weight fabric, such as duck, jacquard, sateen, linen or linen-like fabric, denim, or broadcloth.

Making the Cornice Box
Directions for constructing the cornice box are the same for

Tip ✂

SOMETIMES, THE BEST WINDOW TREATMENT IS NONE AT ALL. OF COURSE, YOU HAVE TO CONSIDER HOW MUCH PRIVACY IS NEEDED BEFORE YOU "UNDRESS" YOUR WINDOWS. IF YOUR WINDOWS HAVE SPECIAL ARCHITECTURAL DETAILS, CONSIDER LETTING THESE FEATURES SPEAK FOR THEMSELVES.

all window sizes. The overall finished length of the window treatment is determined by the fabric panel.

1. Determine the width of the cornice box. If the window has a frame, measure the width of the window from outside frame edge to outside frame edge. If the window does not have a frame, measure the opening. The cornice box should extend 2 to 4 inches beyond each side of the measured window frame or opening. Write the measurement here: _____.

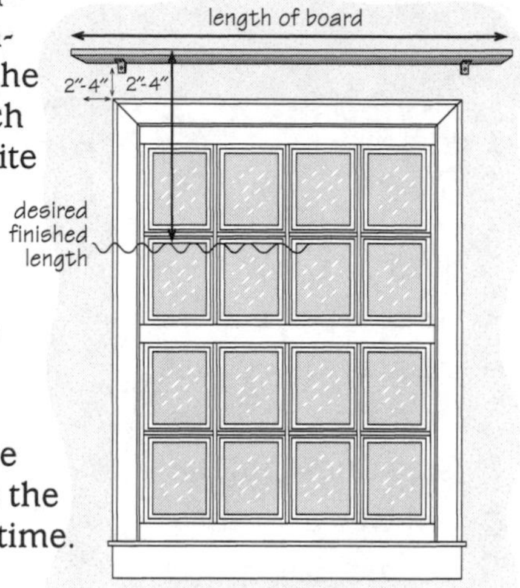

2. Cut one piece of the board to this measurement.

3. The cornice box is mounted 2 to 4 inches above the window. Place the board in position above the window like a shelf; mark the position of the angle brackets (fig. 1). Use a level to make sure the board is straight before screwing the brackets to the wall. Do not attach the board to the brackets at this time.

length of board

2"-4" 2"-4"

desired finished length

Fig. 1

4. For the side legs, cut two additional pieces from the remaining board, each 8 inches long.

5. Cut the face board from the plywood. The width is the same measurement as determined in step 1. The height is 8 inches plus the thickness of the top board (fig. 2).

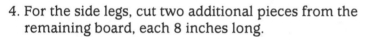

Fig. 2

8"

8" plus thickness of top board

6. Remove the top board from the brackets. Attach the legs to the underside of the top board, one leg flush to each cut end. Apply a bead of wood glue to the top edge of one leg and position it as indicated against the top of the board. Secure it with finishing nails (fig. 3). Repeat on the other side.

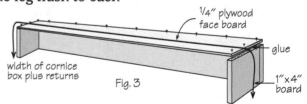

¼" plywood face board

glue

width of cornice box plus returns

Fig. 3

1"x4" board

7. Apply a bead of glue to the front edges of the two legs and the top board. Place the face board against the glued edges. Secure it with finishing nails (fig. 3).

8. Refer to Fabric Calculations for yardage for lining. Place the cornice on the work surface with the inside facing up. Cut strips of fabric to neatly cover the inside surface of the cornice box, allowing extra fabric all around to turn under.

Fold the edges under and glue the lining to the inside of the cornice box. No raw edges should be visible (fig. 4).

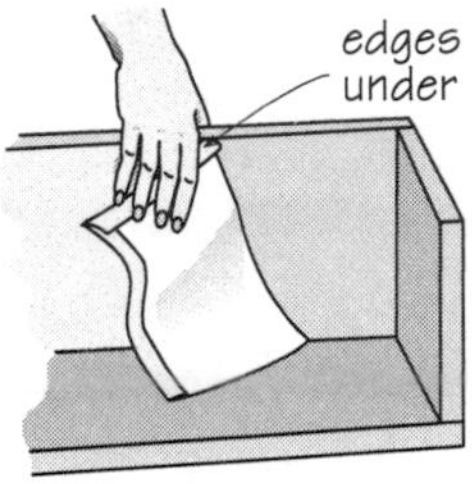

edges folded under

Fig. 4

9. Cut another piece of lining 1 inch larger than the inside dimension of the face board. Fold under all edges 1/2 inch to the wrong side. Glue the lining to the inside of the face board flush to the outer edge of the wood and covering the raw edges of the first lining strip.

Fabric Calculations

1. Measure the width of the cornice box plus the returns (fig. 3). Write the measurement here: _____. This is the finished width of the window treatment. Add 5 inches to this measurement for side hems and ease. This is the cut width measurement for the decorator fabric. Write the measurement here: _____. Subtract 6 inches from the cut width for the lining fabric. Write the number here: _____.

2. If the cut width of the panel is less than the usable width of the decorator fabric, then you only need to purchase enough fabric to accommodate the cut length measurement. If the number is larger than the usable fabric width, you will need to join additional widths together. To determine the number of widths required to achieve the cut width, divide the cut width by the usable width of the fabric. Round up to the next whole number. Write the number here: _____.

3. The cut length of the decorator fabric is 46 inches. The cut length of the lining fabric is 40 inches.

4. To calculate the yardage required of the decorator and lining fabrics, multiply the cut length measurement by the number of widths needed (determined in step 2). Write the number here: _____. If you need more than one fabric width and the fabric you have selected has a repeat design, multiply the repeat distance by the number of widths and add this figure to the total. Write the number here: _____. The extra fabric will allow you to match the designs.

5. Divide this number by 36 and round up to the nearest 1/4 yard. This is the amount of decorator and lining fabrics needed to construct this window treatment. Add

Tip

DON'T GET RID OF YOUR HORIZONTAL OR VERTICAL BLINDS WHEN UPDATING YOUR WINDOW TREATMENTS. JUST PAINT THEM A FRESH COLOR TO MATCH YOUR NEW FABRIC.

MORE $PLASH THAN ¢ASH

1 yard to the total yardage of the decorator fabric for covering the filler cord.

6. For a professional finish, measure the inside dimensions of the cornice box and purchase enough addtional lining fabric to cover the area.

Construction

Use a ¹/₂-inch seam allowance unless otherwise instructed.

1. Lay the fabric flat on a large work surface. Use a carpenter's square to mark and cut a straight edge at one end of the decorator and lining fabrics.

2. Cut each fabric to the individual cut length and width measurements determined in Fabric Calculations. If you need more than one width to achieve the cut width of your valance, cut additional fabric widths to the same length, matching motifs. Sew the fabric widths together; make sure the design motifs match at the joined seam. Trim equal amounts of fabric from both side edges to obtain the exact cut width.

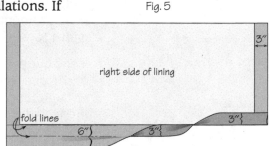

Fig. 5

right side of lining

fold lines

6" 3" 3"

3"

3. Place the lining and the decorator fabrics wrong sides together. The decorator fabric will extend approximately 3 inches from each side edge of the lining and 6 inches from the bottom (fig. 5). The top edges should be even.

4. To form the bottom hem, fold over and press 6 inches toward the lining. Tuck in the top of the hem 3 inches to meet the fold (fig. 5). Stitch the hem.

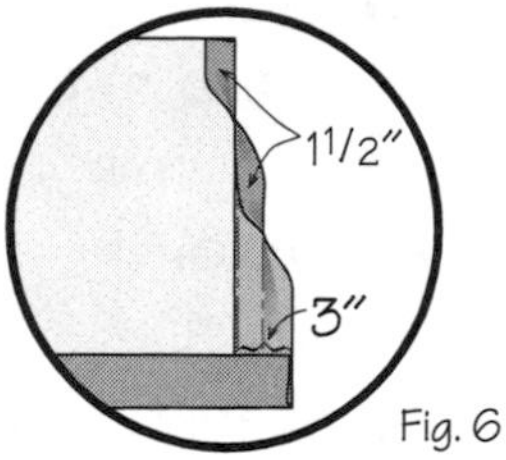

1¹/₂"

3"

Fig. 6

5. To form the side hems, fold over and press 3 inches toward the lining. Tuck in the raw edge of the fabric 1¹/₂ inches to meet the fold (fig. 6). Stitch the hem.

6. Serge or zigzag along the top edge for a clean finish.

7. Working on the back side, find the exact center of the valance. Pin to mark along the top edge of the hem (fig. 7).

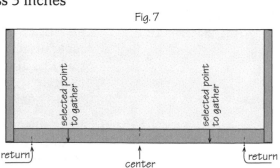

Fig. 7

selected point to gather

selected point to gather

return   center   return

Measure in from both finished side edges a distance equal to the return measurement. Pin to mark. Refer to the photograph and then select a point between the return marks and the center mark where the sides will be gathered into the arch shape. Pin to mark (fig. 7). Remove the pins at the returns. Test the shape by hand gathering the fabric at these new marks to create an arch shape. Adjust gather positions if desired.

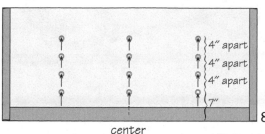

Fig. 8

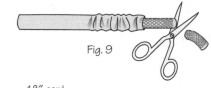

4" apart
4" apart
4" apart
7"

center

8. At each remaining pin mark, measure up 4 inches from the top of the hem in a straight vertical line and make four marks, 4 inches apart for the rings. The marks for the rings must match up horizontally as well as vertically (fig. 8).

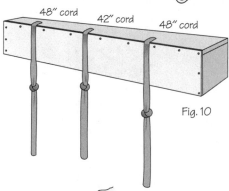

Fig. 9

9. Handstitch a plastic ring (through all layers) at each of these marks.

10. From the decorator fabric, make enough fabric-covered cord to go around the top edge at the sides and front of the cornice box plus 4 yards. Instructions for this technique are found on page 224.

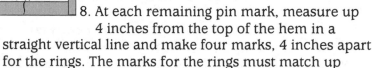

48" cord   42" cord   48" cord

Fig. 10

Installing and Dressing

1. Cut two pieces of fabric-covered cord, each 48 inches long. Cut another piece 42 inches long. Make a single overhand knot in the exact center of each piece.

2. At one end of each covered cord, open the casing and cut off 1 inch of filler cord from the inside (fig. 9). At the other end, open the casing and cut off 10 inches of filler cord. Flatten the 10-inch sections of fabric and staple the end to the top board in the center and at each side in positions corresponding to the rings on the back of the fabric panel (fig. 10).

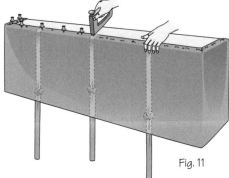

Fig. 11

3. Center the fabric panel on the cornice (over the covered cords) with the upper edge overlapping the top edge of the cornice by 1 inch and the sides flush to the back of the side legs

(fig. 11). Hold in place with pushpins. Staple in the center of the board and work toward each side, placing the staples about 1 1/2 inches apart. Miter the fabric at the corners where the fabric overlaps (fig. 12).

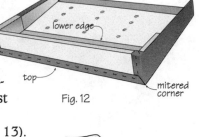

Fig. 12

5. Cut the Roman shade cord into three equal pieces. Use this cord to tie the four rings together in each vertical row. Tie the shade cord in a knot on the lowermost ring. Thread the cord up through each vertical row of rings. Pull the cord to gather the fabric into pleats (fig. 13). Gather the center row of pleats higher than the two side rows. When pleased with the arrangement, knot the ends of the cord tightly. Trim the ends of the cord close to the knot. Apply a dab of fabric glue to the knot and the ends of the cord to prevent the knot from slipping.

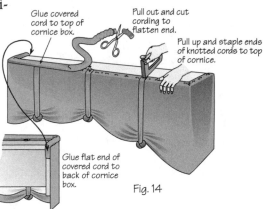

Fig. 13

6. Bring the loose ends of the fabric-covered cords up from the back of the panel and over the front fabric panel so they match the opposite ends that were previously stapled to the board. Staple them in place (fig. 14). The knot should be snug against the bottom of each pleated section.

7. Glue the remaining fabric covered cord along the top edge of the cornice box. Extend a 1-inch tail of covered cord beyond the back edge of the cornice box; then glue the cord along the top back edge of the return. Continue across the front and end at the top edge of the opposite return. Finish with a 1 inch tail of cord. At each end, open the casing of the cord tail, cut off 1 inch of the filler cord and flatten this 1 inch section. Glue it to the back of the board so it is concealed (fig. 14).

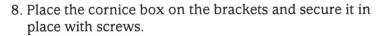

Fig. 14

8. Place the cornice box on the brackets and secure it in place with screws.

9. Refer to the photograph and adjust the folds.

Rooms with a View

We think this window treatment would look great in a bedroom, study, den, living room, dining room, entranceway, or home office.

12 The Envelope, Please

M ention "the enve-
lope" and it sounds
like a Hollywood awards
ceremony, doesn't it? You
will be nominated for an award of your own from your
family and friends when you create this envelope-inspired
window treatment. This winning combination stars two
complementary fabrics, with decorative trim and a covered
button as the supporting cast. The director in this produc-
tion is you. Get ready for rave reviews!

A PADDED CORNICE IS
A POPULAR CHOICE
FOR WINDOWS. WITH
THE ADDITION OF A
FEW DECORATIVE
TOUCHES, THIS STYLE
IS VERY ADAPTABLE.
COLOR PHOTOGRAPH
IS ON PAGE 121.

.... Suggested Window Shapes ....

This treatment is suitable for single or double windows,
dormer windows, sliding glass doors, ranch windows, and
casement windows.

...... Techniques to Know before You Begin ......

If you need to brush up on your skills in any of these areas,
turn to part III.

- Accurate Measuring
- Usable Fabric Widths
- Installing a Mounting Board
- Cutting Multiple Fabric Widths
- Turning and Cutting Corners and Points
- Cutting Fabric
- Matching Repeat Designs

Part I – The Projects

- Fabric Repeats
- Working with Decorative Trims
- Covering Buttons
- Sewing on Buttons

.... *Materials Needed* ....

FROM THE FABRIC STORE

- decorator fabrics for the cornice and flap
- drapery lining for the flap and inside the cornice
- thread to match the decorator fabrics
- 3/16- to 1/4-inch cord-edge (cord with attached lip edge)
- One 1 1/8-inch-diameter half-ball cover button
- ultraloft batting
- paper for patternmaking

RECOMMENDED NOTIONS

These are specific notions needed for this project. Also refer to the list of basic notions on page 180.

- size 90/14 universal machine needle
- point turner

FROM THE HOME IMPROVEMENT CENTER

These are specific supplies needed for this project. Also refer to the basic list of tools and supplies on page 180.

- 1-by-4-inch board
- finishing nails
- 1/4-inch interior-grade plywood
- wood glue
- angle brackets shorter than the projection of the board (at least two, plus one for every 36 inches of board length)
- screws, 2 inches long (two to four for each bracket)
- heavy-duty staple gun with 1/2-inch long staples
- spray adhesive

Suggested Fabrics: Choose a medium-weight fabric, such as duck, jacquard, sateen, linen or linen-like fabric, denim, or broadcloth.

••

Making the Cornice Box

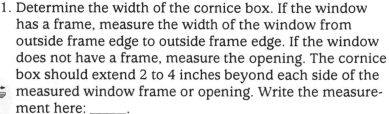

Fig. 1

length of board

2"-4" 2"-4"

desired
finished
length

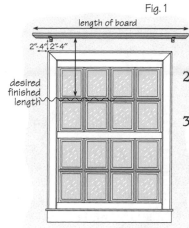

1. Determine the width of the cornice box. If the window has a frame, measure the width of the window from outside frame edge to outside frame edge. If the window does not have a frame, measure the opening. The cornice box should extend 2 to 4 inches beyond each side of the measured window frame or opening. Write the measurement here: _____.

2. Cut one piece of the 1-by-4 inch board to this measurement.

3. The cornice box is mounted 2 to 4 inches above the window frame or opening. At this time, place the board in position above the window like a shelf; mark the position of the angle brackets (fig. 1). Use a level to make sure the board is straight before screwing the angle brackets to the wall. Place the board on top of the brackets to finish taking measurements, but do not attach it yet.

4. Measure from the bottom edge of the board to the desired finished length (fig. 1). Write the measurement here: _____. Cut two additional pieces from the remaining 1-by-4-inch board to this measurement for the side legs.

5. Cut the face board from the plywood. The width is the same measurement as determined in step 1. The height is the length of the side legs plus the thickness of the top board.

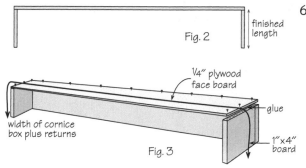

Fig. 2

finished
length

1/4" plywood
face board

glue

width of cornice
box plus returns

Fig. 3

1"x4"
board

6. Remove he board from the brackets. Place it on the work surface with the widest side of the board facing up. Attach the legs to the underside of the top board, one leg flush to each cut end (fig. 2). Apply a bead of wood glue to the top edge of one leg and position it as indicated against the top board. Secure it with finishing nails. Repeat on the other side.

7. Apply a bead of glue to the front edges of the two legs and the top board. Place the face board against the glued edges. Secure it with nails (fig. 3).

Fabric Calculations

If you are making this window treatment for a single window, only one flap needs to be constructed. However, if you are covering a wide window, construct one wide cornice and attach several smaller flaps. An uneven number of flaps is recommended. Plan the window treatment on paper to determine the number and size of flaps for your window.

CORNICE

1. Measure the width of the cornice box plus the returns (fig. 3). Write the measurement here: _____. This is the finished width of the window treatment. Add 6 inches to this measurement for the finishing allowance. This is the cut width measurement. Write the measurement here: ___.

2. If the cut width is less than the usable width of the fabric, then you only need to purchase enough fabric to accommodate the cut length measurement. If the cut width is larger than the usable fabric width, you will need to join additional widths together. To determine the number of widths you need to achieve the cut width, divide the cut width by the usable width of the fabric. Round up to the next whole number. Write the number here: _____.

3. To determine the cut length, add 5 inches to the height of the face board (determined in step 5 above) for the finishing allowance. Write the total here: _____.

4. To calculate the total yardage of the decorator fabric, multiply the cut length measurement by the number of widths needed (determined in step 2). Write the number here: _____. If you need more than one fabric width and the fabric you have selected has a repeat design, multiply the repeat distance by the number of widths and add this figure to the total. The extra fabric will allow you to match the designs.

5. Divide this number by 36 and round up to the nearest 1/4 yard. This is the amount of decorator fabric needed to cover the cornice box.

6. For a professional finish, measure the inside dimensions of the cornice box and purchase enough lining fabric to cover the area.

Tip

DO YOU HAVE AN EXISTING WINDOW TREATMENT THAT NEEDS SOME FRESHENING UP? INSTEAD OF REPLACING IT ENTIRELY, CONSIDER ADDING A NEW VALANCE OVER IT.

MORE $PLASH THAN ¢ASH

FLAP

1. Measure the width of the cornice box (do not include the returns). Add 5 inches to determine the cut width measurement of the decorator and lining fabrics. If making multiple flaps, divide the width of the cornice box by an uneven number and add 3 inches to determine the cut width of fabric needed for each flap. Write the number here: _____.

2. Measure the height of the face board. Add 4 inches for the cut length measurement. Write the number here: _____.

3. Follow steps 4 and 5 above to figure the required yardage for the flap. Repeat for the lining fabric.

4. To determine the yardage needed of cord-edge, measure the diagonal edges of the flap after it is cut.

Construction

COVERING THE CORNICE BOX

1. Cut a rectangle of batting 1 inch longer than the height of the face board and 1 inch narrower than its width including the returns (step 1 in Fabric Calculations, Cornice).

2. Cut the decorator fabric to the determined cut width and length measurements. Press under $1/2$ inch toward the wrong side along all raw edges of the fabric.

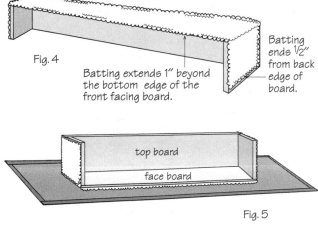

Fig. 4

Batting extends 1″ beyond the bottom edge of the front facing board.

Batting ends $1/2$″ from back edge of board.

top board

face board

Fig. 5

3. Apply the batting so it is flush with the top front edge, extending 1 inch beyond the bottom edge of the face board. It should stop $1/2$ inch in from the back edge of each board (fig. 4). Adhere the batting to the front of the cornice box with spray adhesive. Make sure the batting is applied smoothly.

4. Place the decorator fabric wrong side up on a work surface. Center the cornice box face down on the fabric (fig. 5).

5. Beginning with one side leg, wrap the fabric to the inside. Staple the fabric in the direct center of the inside of the leg (fig. 6). Repeat on opposite side, pulling the fabric taut before stapling.

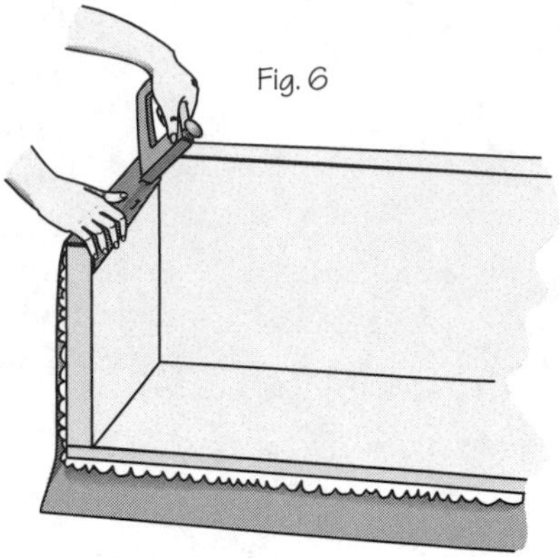

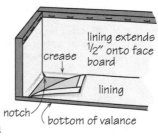

Fig. 6

6. Along the top edge, pull the fabric to the top of the board and staple once. Repeat along the bottom edge, pulling the fabric taut before stapling.

7. Turn the cornice box over and check to be sure the fabric is smooth and taut. Readjust if necessary. Then turn the cornice box over again and continue pulling and stapling the fabric to the inside of the box. Miter the fabric at the corners where the fabric overlaps (fig. 7).

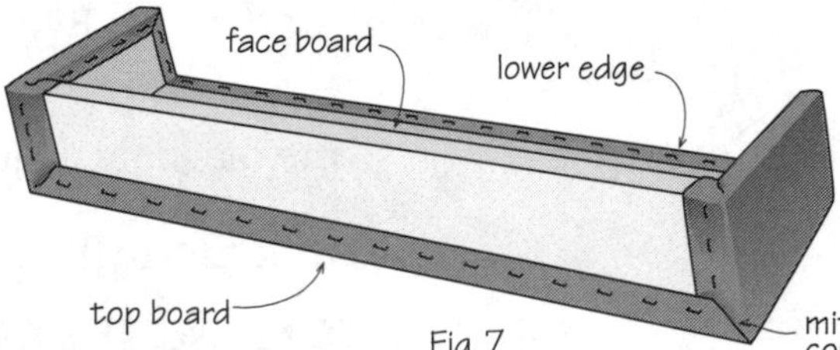

face board

lower edge

top board

Fig. 7

mitered corners

8. Place the cornice on the work surface with the inside facing up. Cut strips of lining fabric to neatly cover the inside surface of the cornice box, allowing extra fabric all around to turn under. Fold the edges under and glue the lining to the inside of the cornice box (fig. 8).

9. Cut another piece of lining 1 inch larger than the inside dimension of the face board. Fold under all edges 1/2 inch to the wrong side. Glue the lining to the inside of the face board flush to the outer edge of the wood and covering the raw edges of the first lining strip (fig. 9).

edges folded under

Fig. 8

FLAP

1. Make a paper pattern of the triangle flap shape. Use a rectangular piece of paper that is exactly 1 inch larger than the width of the padded cornice box and 2 1/2 inches longer than the height of the padded cornice box.

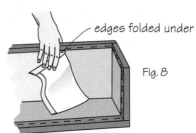

lining extends 1/2" onto face board

crease

lining

notch

bottom of valance

Fig. 9

2. Draw a line 1/2 inch in from both side edges and 1/2 inch from the bottom edge. These lines are the seam allowances.

3. To determine the exact center of the paper, fold the paper in half crosswise and align the short ends. Measure from

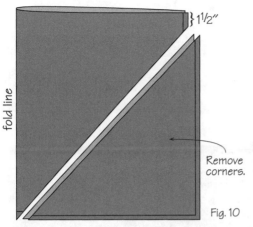

1 1/2"

fold line

Remove corners.

Fig. 10

the top of each side edge down 1 1/2 inches and mark directly on the seam allowance. Use a straight edge to draw a line diagonally from this point to the seam allowance line in the middle of the bottom edge (fig. 10).

4. Cut on the outermost lines to create the flap pattern.

5. Use a carpenter's square to mark and cut a straight edge at one end of the lining and decorator fabric for the flap.

6. Center the pattern on the flap and lining fabrics. Pin in place and cut out.

7. Serge or zigzag stitch along the top edge of both the decorator and lining fabrics for a clean finish.

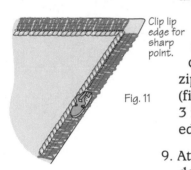

Clip lip edge for sharp point.

Fig. 11

8. Pin the cord-edge to the right side of the decorator fabric along one vertical edge, continuing to the adjoining diagonal edge. The cord itself should be placed just beyond the 1/2-inch stitch line so your stitching is right against the cord. To start, pin the end of the cord-edge flush to the top edge of the flap. Use a zipper foot to stitch as close to the cord as possible (fig. 11). Ease the cord to fit the fabric, working with 2 to 3 inches at a time. Be careful not to stretch the diagonal edges of the flap when sewing.

9. At the corners and at the point, leave the needle in the down position and raise the presser foot. Clip the lip edge to, but not through, the innermost row of trim stitching (fig. 11). This will allow you to pivot the cord-edge to create a sharp point. Turn the fabric, lower the presser foot, and continue stitching. End the cord-edge at the top edge of the flap.

10. Pin the decorator and lining fabrics right sides together. Use a zipper foot to stitch the two diagonal sides directly over the previous stitch lines.

11. To eliminate bulk, clip the corners diagonally.

12. Turn the flap right side out. To create a sharp corner, use a point turner to gently push the fabric out from the

inside. Press the seam so neither the lining nor the decorator fabric shows on the opposite side.

13. Cover the button with contrasting fabric or cording (see Regal Simplicity for specifics). Refer to the photograph and handstitch the button near the point on the flap.

Installing and Dressing

1. Center the flap on the front of the cornice. The upper edge of the flap should overlap the top of the board by 2 inches. Miter the corner for a neat finish.

2. Staple the flap to the board, starting in the center and working toward each side (fig. 12).

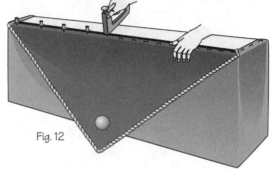

Fig. 12

3. Place the cornice on the brackets and secure the brackets to the top of the cornice.

Rooms with a View

We think this window treatment would look great in a living room, den, study, dining room, kitchen, bathroom, child's room, or bedroom.

-------------------------- *Easy Does It!* --------------------------

Spray Adhesive

When using spray adhesive, work in a well-ventilated area. Use all recommended safety equipment (goggles, mask, and so on) and respect all cautions on the label. Protect the work area from overspray by placing the item being sprayed inside a large open box that is sitting on its side. Cover overspray area with newspaper.

13 *Beaucoup Scoops*

MANY, MANY SCOOPS. MANY, MANY COMPLI-MENTS! COLOR PHOTO-GRAPH IS ON PAGE 121.

Casual and comfort-able are the words that come to mind when viewing this simple scooped treatment. Two complementary fabrics are sepa-rated with a row of narrow cord. Cheerful colors offer punch and personality to this family-oriented décor. Attached wooden rings allow the curtains to be easily pulled closed for privacy.

.... *Suggested Window Shapes* ....

This treatment is suitable for single or double windows, casement windows, bay windows, picture windows, a wall of windows, or sliding glass doors.

...... *Techniques to Know before You Begin* ......

If you need to brush up on your skills in any of these areas, turn to part III.

- Accurate Measuring
- Installing Rods, Brackets, and Holdbacks
- Usable Fabric Widths
- Fabric Repeats
- Stitching Fabric Widths Together
- Addressing Take-Up
- Cutting Multiple Fabric Widths
- Matching Repeat Designs
- Cutting Fabric

Part I – The Projects

- Advantages of Lining Your Window Treatments
- Making Smooth Curves
- Turning and Cutting Corners and Points
- Hems
- Using Drapery Weights
- Working with Decorative Trims

.... *Materials Needed* ....

FROM THE FABRIC STORE
- fabric for bottom section of curtains
- fabric for top section
- lining fabric
- matching thread
- four covered drapery weights plus one for each joined seam
- 3 yards of $3/16$- to $1/4$-inch cord-edge (cord with an attached lip)
- $1^1/2$-inch decorative drapery rod with finials and brackets (also available at department and hardware stores)
- 2-inch sew-on decorative rings to match rod (12)

RECOMMENDED NOTIONS
These are specific notions needed for this project. Also refer to the list of basic notions on page 180.

- point turner
- zipper foot
- optional: compass

FROM THE HOME IMPROVEMENT CENTER
Refer to the list of basic tools and supplies on page 180.

Suggested Fabrics: Choose linen or linen-like fabric, duck, jacquard, sateen, ticking, or denim. We suggest combining fabrics with different size prints and designs, including plaids, for the top and bottom sections.

Tip

PAINT YOUR EXISTING RODS, BRACKETS, FINIALS, OR HOLD-BACKS TO MATCH YOUR NEW TREAT-MENT. IT WILL SAVE YOU FROM INVESTING IN TOTALLY NEW HARDWARE AND WILL CREATE A STUNNING FINISHING TOUCH!

MORE $PLASH THAN ¢ASH

Fabric Calculations

These instructions will result in two identical curtain panels that are each 46 inches wide. This size is suitable for windows up to 60 inches wide at a fullness of 1 1/2 times the width of the window. (For narrower windows, the panels will be at 2 times fullness.) See the sidebar on page 82 for windows wider than 60 inches.

OVERALL CURTAIN MEASUREMENTS

1. Mount the rod brackets 3 to 4 inches above the top edge of the window frame and 2 to 4 inches out from each side of the window frame. (Mount the rod high enough to accommodate the amount of the ring drop. The top of the window frame should not show above the points of the scooped border.) Place the rod in the brackets. Hang a ring on the rod.

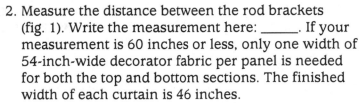

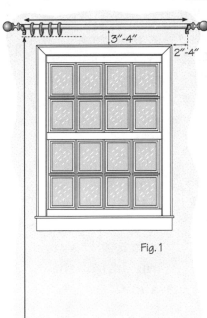

Fig. 1

2. Measure the distance between the rod brackets (fig. 1). Write the measurement here: _____. If your measurement is 60 inches or less, only one width of 54-inch-wide decorator fabric per panel is needed for both the top and bottom sections. The finished width of each curtain is 46 inches.

3. To determine the number of fabric widths needed for fabrics less than 54 inches wide, divide the cut width by the usable width of the decorator fabric. Round up to the next whole number. Write the number here: _____.

4. To determine the overall finished length of the curtain, measure from the bottom of the drapery ring to the desired finished length (fig. 1). Write that measurement here: _____. This measurement includes the top and bottom sections.

BOTTOM SECTION

1. The cut width of the bottom section is 52 inches.

2. To determine the cut length of the bottom section, subtract 1 1/2 inches from the overall finished length to allow for the top section and the attached rings. Write the number here: _____.

3. To calculate the amount of decorator fabric and lining needed for the bottom section, multiply the cut length measurement by the number of widths needed. Write the number here: _____. If your fabric has a repeat design, multiply the repeat distance by the number of widths and add this figure to the total. Write the total here: _____. Multiply by 2 for two curtain panels. Divide by 36 and round up to the nearest 1/4 yard. Write the amount here: _____.

TOP SECTION

The top section is self-lined.

1. The cut width of the top section is 47 inches.

2. The finished length of the top section is 10 inches. The cut length is 11 inches.

3. To determine the number of widths needed for the top section, divide the cut width by the usable width of the fabric. Round up to the next whole number. Write the number here: _____.

4. To calculate the yardage needed for the top section, multiply the number of widths needed by 11 inches (cut length). If the fabric has a repeat design, multiply the repeat distance by the number of widths and add this to your total. This extra fabric will allow you to match the designs. Multiply this amount by 4 for both curtains (two for the front of the curtain and two for the self-lining). Divide by 36 and round up to the nearest 1/4 yard. Write the amount here: _____.

Construction

If your window is wider than 60 inches, read the sidebar on page 82 before cutting.

BOTTOM SECTION

Use a 1/2-inch seam allowance unless otherwise instructed.

1. Place the fabric flat on a large work surface. Use a carpenter's square to mark and cut a straight edge at one end of the decorator fabric. Repeat for the lining fabric.

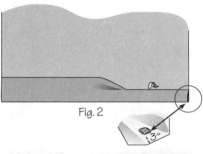

Fig. 2

Fig. 3

2. Cut two identical lengths of decorator fabric to the cut width and length determined in Fabric Calculations.

3. Cut two lining panels for the bottom section. The cut width of each lining panel is equal to the finished width measurement. The cut length is 3 inches shorter than the decorator fabric.

4. Hem the lining and curtain panel separately. First hem the curtain panel with a double 4-inch hem. Handstitch a drapery weight in each corner at least 3 inches from the side cut edge (fig. 2). Stitch the hem.

5. Hem the lining with a double 3-inch hem. Set aside.

6. Place the decorator and lining fabrics wrong sides together. The decorator fabric should extend 3 inches from each side of the lining. Pin. Make sure the top edges of the decorator and lining fabrics are even and that the bottom edge of the lining is 1 inch shorter than the decorator fabric. Baste the fabrics together along the top edge (fig 3).

7. Place the curtain on a large work surface. Hem the side edges with a double 1 1/2-inch hem (fig. 3). To avoid stitching the drapery weight, you may want to handstitch the side hems where they overlap the bottom hem.

8. Diagonally fold the bottom edge of the side hem to form a mitered corner. Press. Handstitch in place (fig. 3).

Fig. 4

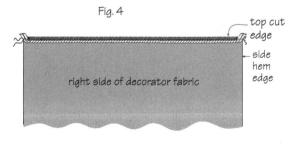

top cut edge

side hem edge

right side of decorator fabric

ATTACHING THE CORD-EDGE

Pin the cord-edge along the top edge of the right side of each lined bottom section. To start, pin the cut cord end perpendicular to the top edge, flush to the folded outside hem edge. Then, folding the cord-edge so the lip edge aligns with the top edge, stitch across the panel. Fold the cord toward the top edge again at the opposite side. Use a zipper foot, stitching over the folded cord to start and to finish (fig. 4). Repeat for the second panel. Set aside.

TOP SECTION

1. Place the fabric flat on a large work surface. Use a carpenter's square to mark and cut a straight edge at one end of the decorator fabric.

2. Cut four top sections to the measurements determined in Fabric Calculations.

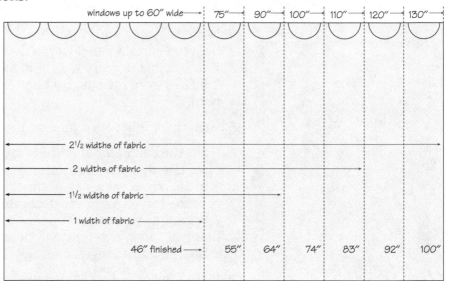

Fig. 5

windows up to 60" wide → | 75" | 90" | 100" | 110" | 120" | 130"

← 2½ widths of fabric →
← 2 widths of fabric →
← 1½ widths of fabric →
← 1 width of fabric →

46" finished → | 55" | 64" | 74" | 83" | 92" | 100"

3. The scoops are 8 inches wide by 5 inches deep, finished, with 1-inch points at each end and in between. Each panel has five scoops. (Wider panels have additional scoops, as shown in figure 5).

4. To make a pattern for each scoop, draw a rectangle 8 inches wide by 5½ inches high on a piece of paper. Fold the paper in half, aligning the 5½-inch ends of the rectangle. Place a mark on the top edge ½ inch in from the cut corner and a second mark on the fold ½ inch above the bottom edge (fig. 6). Use a compass or a round plate to draw a curved line joining the marks (fig. 7). Cut on this line. Open up the folded pattern. Smooth the bottom of the curve, if necessary. Make one pattern for each of the scoops on one panel.

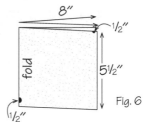

8"

½"

fold

5½"

Fig. 6

½"

5. Two top sections will be used for the front side of the curtains, and two will be used for facings. Place the patterns on the wrong side of one top section flush to the top cut edge, so the outer edge of the paper rectangle is 1½ inches from the cut side edge of the fabric. Space the patterns 1 inch apart, repeating across the top section, with the last rectangle ending 1½ inches from the

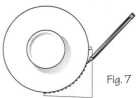

Fig. 7

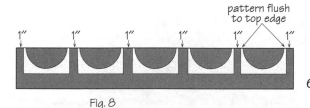

pattern flush
to top edge

1"   1"   1"   1"   1"   1"

Fig. 8

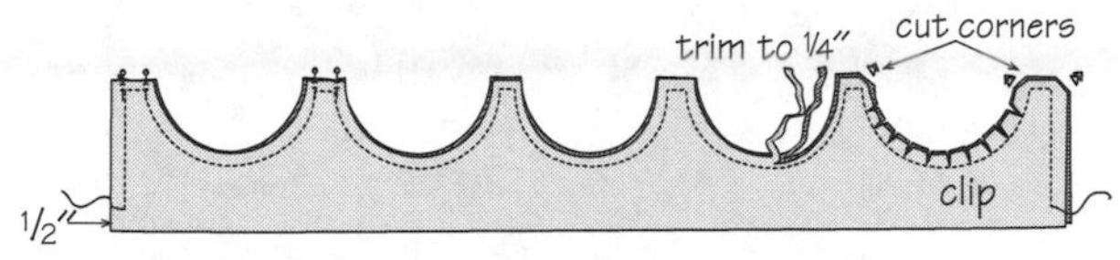

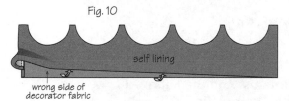

trim to ¼"   cut corners

clip

½"

Fig. 9

opposite edge (fig. 8). Cut along the curved line for each scoop. Use this section as the complete pattern to cut the remaining three top sections.

6. Pin one front top section to one self-lining, right sides together, along the short ends and scooped top edge. Stitch, beginning and ending ¹/2 inch from the long cut edge. Trim the seam allowance to ¹/4 inch. Clip the curves every ¹/2 inch. Cut the corners diagonally to remove bulk (fig. 9). Turn the top section right side out.

For sharp points, use a point turner to gently push out the corners from the inside. Press. Repeat for the second top section.

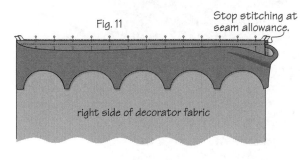

Fig. 10

self lining

wrong side of
decorator fabric

7. Fold and press under the long un-stitched edge of the self-lining ¹/2 inch toward the wrong side (fig. 10). Do not press under the front edge of the top section.

ATTACHING THE TOP SECTION TO THE BOTTOM SECTION

1. With the right sides together, pin the unfolded edge of one top section to the cord-trimmed edge of one bottom section. The end seams of the top section should be even with the side edges of the bottom section. Use a zipper foot to stitch along the pinned edge as close as possible to the attached row of cord-edge (fig. 11). Do not catch the side seam allowances in the stitching.

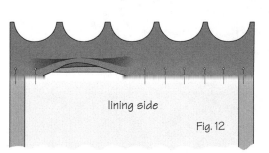

Fig. 11

Stop stitching at
seam allowance.

right side of decorator fabric

lining side

Fig. 12

2. On the wrong side of the curtain, pin the pressed edge of the top section lining to the seam so it just covers the stitching line (fig. 12). From the right side of the curtain, use a zipper foot to

stitch in the ditch flush to the cord, between the cord and the fabric, catching the folded fabric edge under-neath (fig. 13). Do not catch the decorator fabric in your stitching.

Installing and Dressing

1. Handstitch a drapery ring to each point of the top section.

2. Slip the rings over the drapery rod to hang.

Rooms with a View

We think this window treatment would look great in a bedroom, dining room, living room, study, den, or family room.

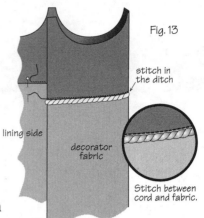

Fig. 13

stitch in the ditch

lining side

decorator fabric

Stitch between cord and fabric.

Adaptations for Wider Windows

Fabric Calculations

See figure 5 for help in planning wider curtains. Add the appropriate number of fabric widths to achieve the required finished width. To determine the cut width, add 6 inches for hems to the finished width measurement. To determine the amount of cord-edge needed, multiply the cut width by 2 for two panels. Add 1/4 yard for ease to this number. To determine the number of drapery rings needed per panel, add one to the number of scoops per panel.

Cutting

For top and bottom sections, join the widths of fabric to achieve the necessary width, matching any repeats. Do this before cutting the fabric to the required cut width. Line up the seams on the top and the bottom section.

14 *Friendly Borders*

DESIGNER TOUCHES
ABOUND. CONTRASTING
CORDING, FABRIC-
COVERED BUTTONS, AND
UNIQUELY STYLED TABS
DETAIL THIS FABULOUS
WINDOW TREATMENT.
COLOR PHOTOGRAPH IS
ON PAGE 121.

Window treatment
can actually contrib-
ute to a sense of peace
and well-being within
your home, surrounding a room with warmth and color.
These bordered panels exude such friendliness—right down
to the cozy buttoned tabs at the very top. And while this
treatment is full of essential details, none are hard to ex-
ecute. To create this design for your own windows, select
two coordinating fabrics and a simple, tasteful cord trim for
the edge. Cover buttons to finish the gathered tabs at the top
of each panel. Each tab seems to be an exclamation point
announcing a warm, welcoming decorating statement.

·············· *Suggested Window Shapes* ··············

This treatment is suitable for single or double windows, bay
windows, bow windows, sliding glass doors, or picture
windows.

······ *Techniques to Know before You Begin* ······

If you need to brush up on your skills in any of these areas,
turn to part III.

- Accurate Measuring
- Usable Fabric Widths
- Fabric Repeats
- Cutting Fabric
- Addressing Take-Up
- Cutting Multiple Fabric Widths

- Installing Rods, Brackets, and Holdbacks
- Stitching Fabric Widths Together
- Matching Repeat Designs
- Advantages of Lining Your Window Treatments
- Hems
- Using Drapery Weights
- Working with Decorative Trims
- Covering Buttons
- Sewing on Buttons

·················· *Materials Needed* ··················

FROM THE FABRIC STORE

- decorator fabric for curtains and tabs (must be at least 48 inches wide)
- coordinating decorator fabric for borders (must be at least 54 inches wide)
- lining fabric (must be at least 54 inches wide)
- thread to match decorator fabrics
- heavy thread such as carpet thread or waxed button thread to attach buttons
- decorative rod, finials, and mounting brackets (also available at department stores)
- four covered drapery weights
- $3/16$- to $1/4$-inch cord-edge (cord with attached lip edge) to separate the center section and the borders (cord should be very pliable)
- $7/8$-inch-diameter (size 36) half-ball cover buttons, one for each tab
- clear backing buttons, one for each tab
- monofilament thread

RECOMMENDED NOTIONS

These are specific notions needed for this project. Also refer to the list of basic notions on page 180.

- size 90/14 universal machine needle
- point turner
- 4- to 6-inch-long doll needle to attach buttons
- zipper foot or special piping foot

Tip

CREATE YOUR OWN ONE-OF-A-KIND BORDER FABRIC FOR THIS WINDOW TREATMENT BY UTILIZING THE BEAUTIFUL DECORATIVE STITCHING PATTERNS AVAILABLE ON EMBROIDERY SEWING MACHINES.

MORE $PLASH THAN ¢ASH

FROM THE HOME IMPROVEMENT CENTER
Refer to the list of basic tools and supplies on page 180.

Suggested Fabrics: Choose medium-weight fabrics, such as jacquard, sateen, linen or linen-like fabric, duck, broadcloth, or denim. We suggest combining fabrics with different size prints, textures, and designs (including plaids) for the borders and center section.

Fabric Calculations

These instructions, as written, will create two curtain panels each with a finished width of approximately 50 inches. When hung on a rod, each panel will cover up to 35 inches. This style of window treatment is considered to be a stationary treatment. That is, it does not open or close easily. This finished size looks nice on windows up to 72 inches wide.

1. Mount the rod brackets 2 to 4 inches above the top edge of the window frame and 2 to 4 inches out from each side of the frame (fig. 1).

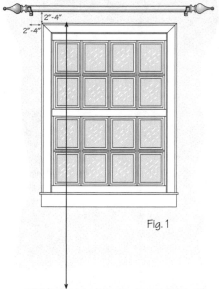

Fig. 1

2. To determine the finished length of the entire curtain, measure from the top edge of the window frame to the floor (fig. 1). Write the number here: _____. This measurement includes the top and bottom borders and the center section.

3. To determine the cut length of the center section, subtract $12^1/2$ inches from the total finished length. Write the number here: _____.

4. To determine the yardage required for the center section, multiply the cut length by 2 to include the second curtain panel. Write the number here: _____. If your fabric has a repeat design, multiply the repeat distance by 2 and add this figure to the total. Write the number here: _____. The extra fabric will allow you to match the panels.

5. Divide this number by 36 and round up to the nearest $1/4$ yard. Add $7/8$ yard for the matching tabs. Write the total here: _____.

6. The borders are cut from a coordinating fabric. The cut length of the side borders is the same as the cut length of the center section (step 3 above). Write the number here: _____. The suggested cutting layout for the borders for two panels ensures that the printed design will all go in the same direction (fig. 2). However, you may have to adjust the spacing so that the borders are identical.

7. The yardage for the top and bottom borders for two curtain panels is 47 inches. To match the borders, you may have to add a full repeat for each horizontal border to this amount. To determine the total yardage, add this number to the total from step 6. Write the number here: _____. Divide this number by 36 and round up to the nearest $1/4$ yard. Write the total here: _____.

8. To determine the yardage required for the lining fabric, add $5^{1}/2$ inches to the finished length of the entire curtain (determined in step 2 above). Multiply this number by 2 (for two curtains). Write the number here: _____. Divide this number by 36 and round up to the nearest $1/4$ yard. Write the total here: _____.

9. To determine the amount of cord-edge, add 58 inches to the finished length of the entire curtain. Write the number here: _____. Multiply this number by 4; then divide by 36 and round up to the nearest $1/4$ yard. Write the number here: _____.

Cutting Instructions

1. Lay the fabric for the center section flat on a large work surface. Use a carpenter's square to mark and cut a straight edge at one end of the decorator fabric. Repeat for the lining.

2. Measure from the straight edge of the decorator fabric to cut one center section to the cut length determined in step 3

Fig. 2

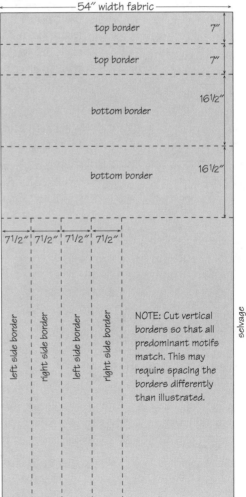

NOTE: Cut vertical borders so that all predominant motifs match. This may require spacing the borders differently than illustrated.

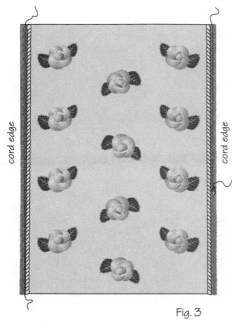

cord edge

cord edge

Fig. 3

above. The cut width is 40 inches. Trim equal amounts of fabric from both side edges to obtain this number. Cut an identical length of decorator fabric for the second curtain.

3. Cut a straight edge on the border fabric as above. Refer to figure 2 to cut the borders. Cut two top borders 7 inches by 54 inches, and cut two bottom borders $16^{1}/2$ inches by 54 inches. Cut four side borders $7^{1}/2$ inches by the cut length of the center section (step 3 above). So that the borders will be positioned correctly on the center section, place a piece of masking tape on each piece to indicate the top edge.

4. Cut the lining 48 inches wide and 3 inches shorter than the finished length of the entire curtain.

5. Cut the tabs from the remaining fabric used for the center section. Cut 16 rectangles 6 inches by 14 inches each.

Construction

Use a $^{1}/2$-inch seam allowance unless otherwise instructed.

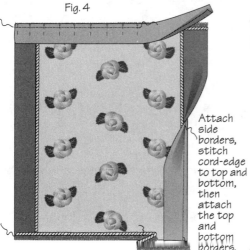

Fig. 4

Attach side borders, stitch cord-edge to top and bottom, then attach the top and bottom borders.

CURTAIN PANEL

1. Prepare the center section first. Pin cord-edge to the side edges on both center sections. Place the cut end of the cord-edge even with the cut edge of the center section (fig. 3). The cord itself should be placed just beyond the $^{1}/2$-inch seam line so your stitching is right against the cord. Use a zipper foot and a long stitch to machine baste as close to the cord as possible. Ease the cord-edge to fit the fabric, working with 3- to 4-inch sections. Trim that has not been eased enough will draw the vertical seams up dramatically.

2. Place the inside cut edges of the side borders and the outside edges of the center section right sides together (fig. 4). To maintain a smooth, even seam, pin the borders to the center section at each end first, then in

the middle. Then ease in the sections between the pins. Using a longer stitch than normal, stitch the borders to the center section on the same stitching line used to attach the cord-edge; use a zipper foot to stitch as close as possible to the cord. Press the cord-edge and fabric seam allowances toward the border.

3. Stitch the cord-edge to the top and bottom edges of the pieced center section as above (fig. 4). Caution: Stitch slowly over the previously stitched cord-edge to avoid breaking a needle.

4. Place the top and bottom borders against the top and bottom edges of the center section, right sides together. Stitch these borders in the same manner as the side borders. Press all seam allowances toward the border (fig. 4).

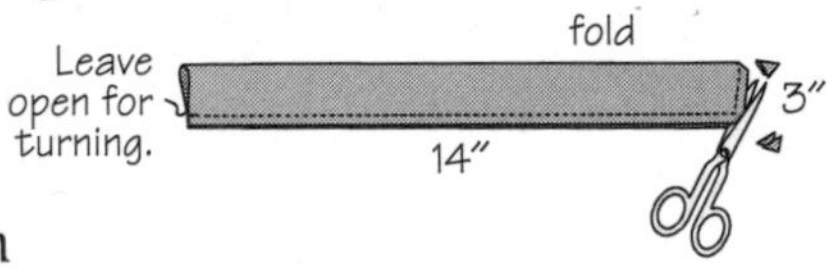

TABS

1. Prepare the tabs by folding each fabric rectangle in half lengthwise with right sides together so each measures 3 inches by 14 inches. Begin at the folded edge and stitch across one short end. Turn the corner and stitch down the length of the strip. Leave the remaining short edge open to turn (fig. 5). Clip the corners diagonally and trim the seam allowances to 1/4 inch to eliminate bulk.

2. Turn the tabs right side out. To create sharp corners, use a point turner to gently push the fabric out from the inside. Press the tabs flat.

3. To determine the exact length for the tabs, drape a strip of fabric over the rod and pin it together at the top edge of the window frame. Mark this position on both layers of the fabric strip. Make another mark 3 inches below the top edge of the window on one layer only (fig. 6). Remove the strip from the rod; measure the distance between the outermost marks and add 1/2 inch. Trim the cut ends of the tabs to this length.

4. Determine the placement of tabs along the top edge of each curtain. The outer edges of the first and last tabs should be 3 inches in from

Fig. 5

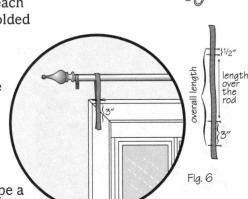

Fig. 6

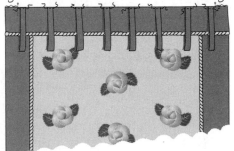

Fig. 7

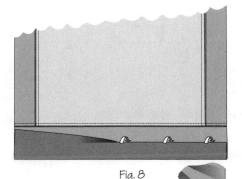

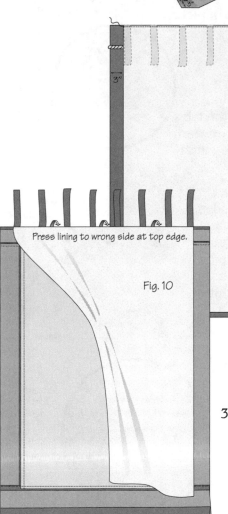

Fig. 8

Fig. 9

3"   3"

1"

Press lining to wrong side at top edge.

Fig. 10

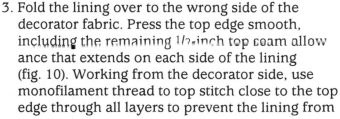

each side edge; the remaining tabs should be evenly spaced between the end tabs. Each curtain has eight tabs total. Pin the tabs to the decorator fabric with the finished ends of the tabs pointing toward the bottom hem (fig. 7).

5. Machine-baste the raw edge of the tabs to the top edge of the decorator fabric so that all raw edges are even.

LINING

1. Hem the lining and curtain panel separately. First hem the curtain panel with a double 4-inch hem. Hand-stitch a drapery weight in each corner about 3 inches from the side cut edge (fig. 8). Stitch the hem. Hem the lining with a double 3-inch hem.

2. Center the lining over the decorator fabric, right sides together. The tabs will be "sandwiched" between the two layers. The border fabric should extend 3 inches beyond each side edge of the lining. Pin, making sure the top edges of the decorator and lining fabrics are even and that the bottom edge of the lining is 1 inch shorter than the decorator fabric. Stitch the fabrics together along the top edge (fig. 9).

3. Fold the lining over to the wrong side of the decorator fabric. Press the top edge smooth, including the remaining 1/2-inch top seam allowance that extends on each side of the lining (fig. 10). Working from the decorator side, use monofilament thread to top stitch close to the top edge through all layers to prevent the lining from

showing on the right side (fig. 11).

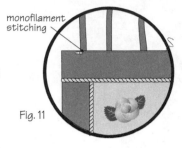

monofilament stitching

Fig. 11

4. Place the curtain on a large work surface. Hem the side edges with a double 1¹/2-inch hem (fig. 12). The top edge seam allowance should remain folded during this process.

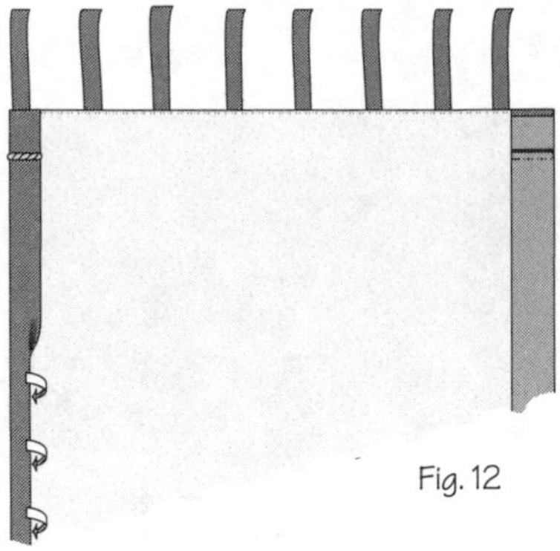

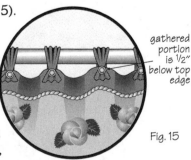

Fig. 12

5. Diagonally fold the bottom edge of the side hem to form a mitered corner (fig. 13). Press. Handstitch in place.

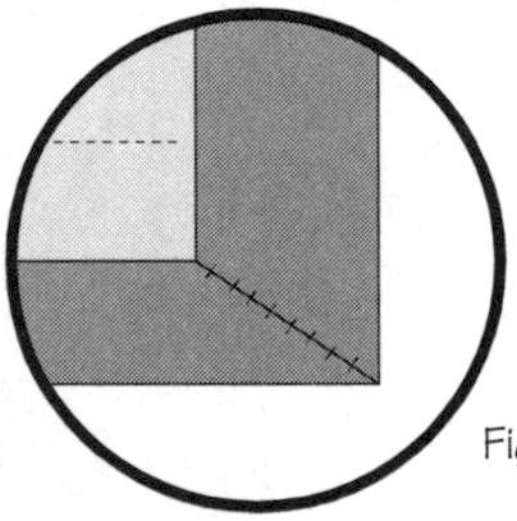

6. Cover the buttons with scraps of the fabric that was used for the borders.

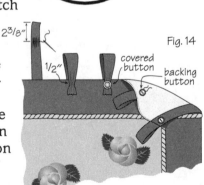

Fig. 13

7. On each tab, measure up from the finished end 2³/8 inches. Pinch the fabric together at this point to form several narrow gathers across the width of the tab (fig. 14). The tab should measure about ¹/2 inch between edges at the gathered line. Handstitch or machine-stitch the gathers to secure them.

2³/8″

Fig. 14

8. Fold the tab over to the front of the curtain so the gathered point is ¹/2 inch below the top finished edge of the curtain. Center a covered button over the gathered portion of each tab. Stitch the button to the tab through all layers. Place a clear backing button on the back of the curtain directly behind the covered button (fig. 14). Stitch through the holes of the backing button as you are stitching the covered button in place.

¹/2″

covered button

backing button

Installing and Dressing

1. Insert the rod through the tabs of the curtains (fig. 15).

2. Place the rod in the brackets.

3. Refer to the photograph and arrange the curtain panels into soft folds.

gathered portion is ¹/2″ below top edge

Rooms with a View

We think this window treatment would look great in a bedroom, living room, family room, dining room, den, study, home office, or sunroom.

Fig. 15

15 Au Provence

CHOOSE TWO FAVORITE
FABRICS TO CREATE
THIS SIMPLY STYLED
VALANCE. COLOR
PHOTOGRAPH IS ON
PAGE 122.

You can feel the warm sun on your face as you transform your window into one from a French villa. The combination of a large, luscious print with a coordinating check will be a daily reminder of the carefree and beautiful lifestyle in the French countryside. Keeping simplicity as the focus, this treatment is mounted to the wall with inexpensive cup hooks that are hidden by stream-lined bows.

············· Suggested Window Shapes ·············

This treatment is suitable for single or double windows, picture windows, or sliding glass doors.

······ Techniques to Know before You Begin ······

If you need to brush up on your skills in any of these areas, turn to part III.

- Accurate Measuring
- Inserting Cup Hooks into a Wall
- Usable Fabric Widths
- Fabric Repeats
- Cutting Fabric
- Cutting Multiple Fabric Widths

Part I – The Projects

- Stitching Fabric Widths Together
- Matching Repeat Designs
- Turning and Cutting Corners and Points

················· *Materials Needed* ·················

FROM THE FABRIC STORE
- decorator fabric
- coordinating decorator fabric for the band and bows
- lining fabric
- thread to match decorator fabric
- paper for patternmaking

RECOMMENDED NOTIONS
These are specific notions needed for this project. Also refer to the list of basic notions on page 180.

- size 90/14 universal machine needle
- point turner
- fabric marker

FROM THE HOME IMPROVEMENT CENTER
These are specific supplies needed for this project. Also refer to the basic list of tools and supplies on page 180.

- 1 1/4-inch cup hooks (one for each bow)

Suggested Fabrics: Choose medium-weight fabrics such as duck, jacquard, sateen, linen or linen-like fabric, denim, broadcloth, or chintz.

Tip

TO SAVE MONEY ON WINDOW HARD-WARE, USE INEXPEN-SIVE WALL HOOKS MOUNTED ABOVE THE WINDOW. THEN HANG THE CURTAIN TABS FROM THE HOOKS.

MORE $PLASH THAN ¢ASH

Fabric Calculations
The instructions are for three mounting points. If you opt to have more mounting points, the calculations need to reflect the additional fullness needed. Allow approximately 3 inches of fullness in step 2 below for each additional mounting point.

1. Install three cup hooks approximately 2 to 4 inches above the top edge of the window frame; place the first and last

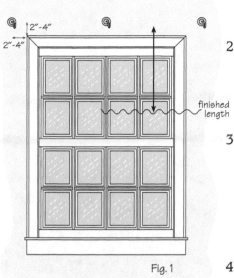

2"-4"

2"-4"

finished length

Fig. 1

hooks 2 to 4 inches out from the sides of the window and one in the exact center (fig. 1).

2. Measure the width of your window from the left cup hook to the right cup hook. Add 6 inches for fullness. Write the number here: _____. This is the top finished width measurement of the trapezoid shape you will be creating.

3. Add 44 inches to the above number for the "tails" on the sides of the valance. Write the number here: _____. This is the bottom finished width measurement of the trapezoid shape. Add 1 inch to the bottom finished width measurement to determine the cut width. Write the number here: _____.

4. To determine the number of fabric widths required to achieve the cut width, divide the bottom cut width by the usable width of the fabric. Round up to the next whole number. Write the number here: _____. Note: If you want to create this window treatment without joining widths of fabric, you can railroad the fabric. Not all fabrics are appropriate for this. Study the fabric closely to make sure the design printed along the selvage does not have a specific direction (e.g., stemmed flowers that appear to be lying on their sides). Purchase enough yardage to equal the bottom cut width measurement.

5. To determine the finished length of the valance, measure from the center cup hook to the desired finished length (fig. 1). Write the measurement here: _____. Add 1 inch to determine the cut length. Write the number here: _____.

6. To calculate the total yardage of the decorator fabric, multiply the cut length measurement by the number of widths needed (determined in step 4). Write the number here: _____. If you need more than one fabric width and the fabric you have selected has a repeat design, multiply the repeat distance by the number of widths and add this figure to the total. The extra fabric will allow you to match the designs.

7. Divide this number by 36 and round up to the nearest 1/4

yard. This is the amount of decorator and lining fabrics needed to construct this window treatment.

8. The fabric bands and bows can be cut from the length-wise or crosswise grain of fabric. To cut from the cross-wise grain, add 9 inches to the cut width of the top edge of the trapezoid. This total must be less than the usable width of the fabric. If this number is less than the usable width of fabric, purchase 5/8 yard of fabric. If the number is greater than the usable width, you must cut the bands from the lengthwise grain of fabric. In this case, purchase the cut width of the top edge plus 9 inches.

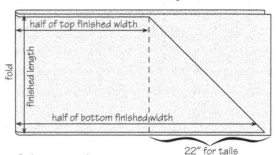

Fig. 2

Creating the Pattern

1. Make a paper pattern of the trapezoid shape. Use a rectangular piece of paper that is at least 1 inch larger all around than the cut width and length of the valance. To determine the exact center of the paper, fold the paper in half crosswise and align the short ends. Refer to step 2 in Fabric Calculations for the measurement of the top edge of the trapezoid. Measure from the fold and mark a point equal to half this amount. Use a carpenter's square to draw a line perpendicular to the fold, extending from the fold to the mark, 1/2 inch down from the top edge (fig. 2).

2. Beginning at the top line, measure down the folded edge a distance equal to the finished length (step 5 of Fabric Calculations). Mark.

3. Starting at this mark, use a carpenter's square to draw a perpendicular line equal to half of the bottom finished width measurement (step 3 of Fabric Calculations).This line should be parallel to the first line drawn.

4. Draw a diagonal line connecting the ends of the top and bottom lines to complete the trapezoid shape.

5. Cut on the lines through both layers of the paper to create the trapezoid pattern.

6. To create a pattern for the contrasting bands, open up the pattern piece and draw a line 2 1/2 inches in from and

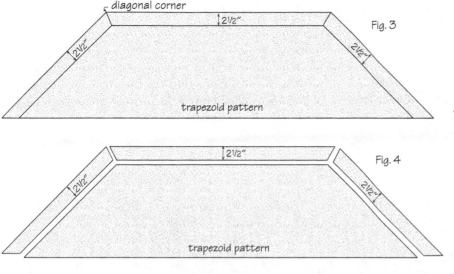

diagonal corner
2½"
2½"
2½"
Fig. 3
trapezoid pattern

2½"
2½"
2½"
Fig. 4
trapezoid pattern

parallel to both diagonal side edges and the top edge (fig. 3).

7. In each upper corner draw a diagonal line from the inside corner to the outside corner of the band lines (fig. 3).

8. Cut along the lines to create the band pattern pieces (fig. 4). Set them aside.

Cutting Instructions

1. Lay the fabric for the trapezoid shape flat on a large work surface. Use a carpenter's square to cut a straight edge at one end of the decorator and lining fabrics.

2. Cut the fabric to the finished length measurement. If you need more than one width to achieve the cut width of your valance, cut additional fabric to the same length, matching motifs. Sew the fabric widths together; make sure the design motifs match at the joined seam. Trim equal amounts of fabric from both side edges to obtain this number. Repeat with the lining fabric.

3. Center the paper pattern on the decorator fabric and pin it in place. Cut one shape

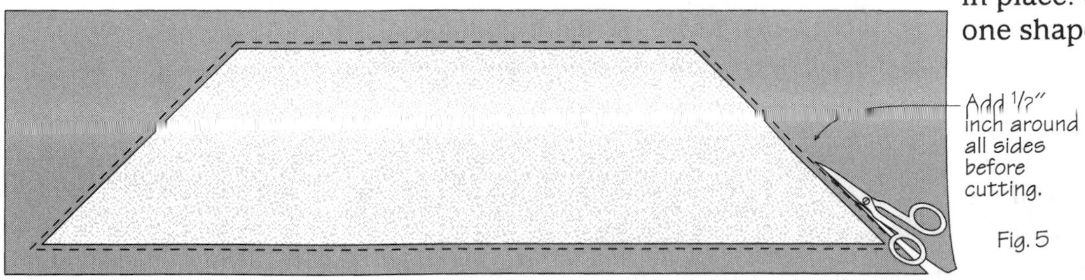

Add ½" inch around all sides before cutting.

Fig. 5

from the decorator fabric. Use a straight edge and fabric marker to mark a 1/2-inch seam allowance to all sides (fig. 5). Cut on this marked line. Do not cut the lining at this time.

4. Pin the band pattern pieces to the fabric, allowing enough space between the pieces for the seam allowance. Use a straight edge and a fabric marker to mark a 1/2-inch seam allowance on all sides. Cut on this marked line.

Construction

Use a 1/2-inch seam allowance unless otherwise instructed.

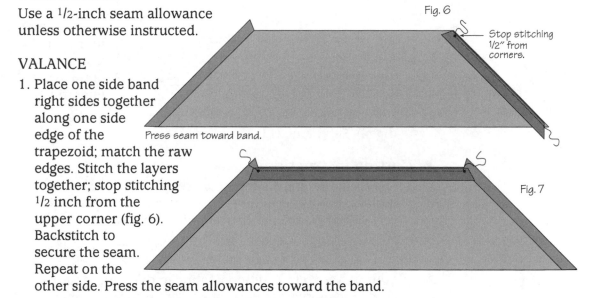

Fig. 6

Stop stitching 1/2" from corners.

Press seam toward band.

Fig. 7

VALANCE

1. Place one side band right sides together along one side edge of the trapezoid; match the raw edges. Stitch the layers together; stop stitching 1/2 inch from the upper corner (fig. 6). Backstitch to secure the seam. Repeat on the other side. Press the seam allowances toward the band.

2. Center and pin the top band to the valance. Stitch the layers together; stop stitching 1/2 inch from each upper corner (fig. 7). Backstitch to secure the seam. Be careful not to catch the adjacent band in your stitching. Press the seam allowances toward the band.

3. Pin the short ends of the bands right sides together at the corners (fig. 8). Pull the valance out of the way so you won't catch anything but the bands in the seam. Begin stitching the bands together at the inside corner and continue toward the outside corner. Be careful not to stretch the band as you stitch. Press this seam open. Trim away the excess fabric tips that extend from the edges of the bands.

Fig. 8

4. Press the valance so all seams lie flat and are smooth.

5. Use this stitched valance as your pattern for the lining fabric. Cut the lining fabric to match the size of the valance exactly.

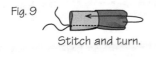

Fig. 9

Stitch and turn.

Fig. 10

Fold in half and stitch.

6. Using scraps of band fabric, make three small loops that will be used to hang the valance from the cup hooks. Cut three strips (one for each cup hook), each 1 1/2 inches by 3 1/4 inches. Fold the strip in half lengthwise, right sides together, and stitch. Turn the strip right side out (fig. 9). Arrange each strip into a loop as shown in figure 10, and stitch along the raw edges to hold the shape.

7. Place the loops along the top edge. Pin one loop in the direct center of the valance and one loop 1/2 inch in from each upper corner. Position the loops so the finished ends point toward the bottom edge of the valance (fig. 11).

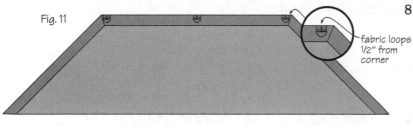

Fig. 11

fabric loops 1/2" from corner

8. Pin the lining and decorator fabrics right sides together. Stitch around the entire shape leaving a 6-inch opening along the bottom edge for turning. Secure the beginning and ending of the stitches with backstitches.

Fig. 12

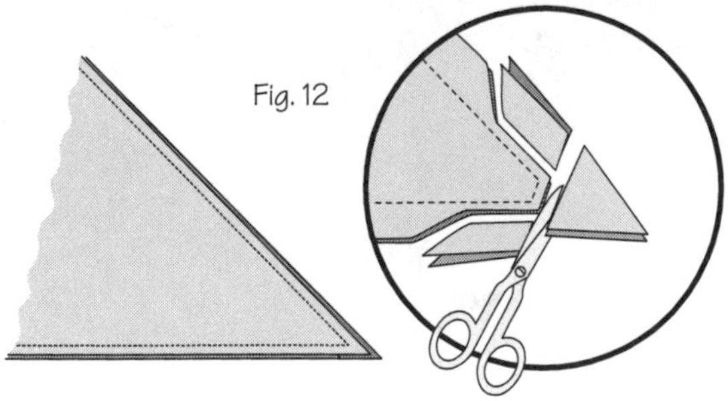

9. To eliminate bulk, clip the corners diagonally (fig. 12).

10. Turn the valance right side out. For sharp corners, use a point turner to gently push the fabric out from the inside. Press the seam so that neither fabric is visible from the opposite side.

11. Handstitch the opening closed.

BOWS

1. For the bows, cut three fabric strips, each measuring 4 by 24 inches. For the knot, cut three fabric strips, each measuring 2 1/2 by 3 1/2 inches.

2. Fold the bow strips in half lengthwise with right sides together so they measure 2 inches by 24 inches. Begin at the folded edge and stitch across one short end. Turn the corner and stitch about halfway down the length of the strip. Leave a 4-inch opening along the long edge, then continue stitching along the edge toward the opposite corner, finishing by stitching across the remaining short end (fig. 13). Clip the corners diagonally and trim the seam allowances to eliminate bulk. Turn the strips right side out. To create sharp corners, use a point turner to gently push the fabric out from the inside. Press each strip flat.

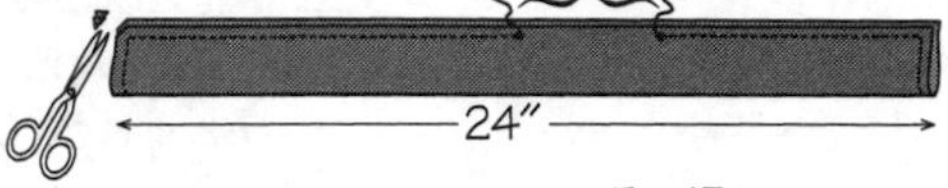

4″ opening for turning

2″

24″

Fig. 13

3. Handstitch the opening closed.

4. Arrange each strip into two loops to create a bow shape. Gather the bows at the center point slightly and stitch by hand or machine to secure (fig. 14).

stitch

Fig. 14

5. Fold a knot strip in half with right sides together so it measures 1 1/4 by 3 1/2 inches. Stitch the long raw edges together using a 1/4-inch seam allowance and press the seam open. Turn the strip right side out to form a tube. Arrange the tube so the seam is in the middle of one side. Wrap the band around the center of the bow so the seam faces inward. Fold under the raw edges and handstitch the ends together at the back of the bow to secure (fig. 15). Repeat for the two other bows.

Fig. 15

Installing and Dressing

1. Place the loops over the cup hooks.

2. Pin or handstitch the bows in place to cover the loops and hooks.

3. Refer to the photograph and arrange the fabric into pleasing folds.

Rooms with a View

We think this window treatment would look great in a bedroom, bathroom, kitchen, home office, or informal dining nook.

16 Skirting the Issue

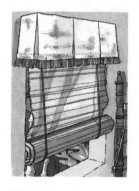

THIS STYLE IS PERFECT OVER BLINDS OR CUR-TAINS BUT IS JUST AS SPECTACULAR STANDING ALONE. COLOR PHOTO-GRAPH IS ON PAGE 122.

This box-pleated valance carries out a casual theme with a bit of structured style. It has the eye-catching sensibilities of fashion without pretension, creating the perfect accessory for your window. The fringe at the skirt hem softens the effect and draws the eye down from the top of the window and into the room. But like any proper skirt, don't make this one too short! The best effect comes from a graceful length. One-third of the window length is best.

Suggested Window Shapes

This treatment is suitable for single or double windows, casement windows, ranch (or strip) windows, window walls, or sliding glass doors.

Techniques to Know before You Begin

If you need to brush up on your skills in any of these areas, turn to part III.

- Accurate Measuring
- Preparing a Mounting Board
- Installing a Mounting Board
- Cutting Multiple Fabric Widths
- Advantages of Lining Your Window Treatments
- Usable Fabric Widths
- Fabric Repeats
- Cutting Fabric
- Hems

Part I - The Projects

- Stitching Fabric Widths Together
- Working with Decorative Trims

················ *Materials Needed* ·················

FROM THE FABRIC STORE

- decorator fabric (must be at least 54 inches wide)
- lining
- 3-inch-long slim bullion or knotted fringe
- thread to match fabric and fringe
- optional: 3/8- to 1/2-inch-diameter filler cord or twisted cord for topknots

RECOMMENDED NOTIONS

These are specific notions needed for this project. Also refer to the list of basic notions on page 180.

- size 90/14 universal machine needle
- zipper foot

FROM THE HOME IMPROVEMENT CENTER

These are specific supplies needed for this project. Also refer to the basic list of tools and supplies on page 180.

- 1-by-6-inch mounting board
- angle brackets, shorter than the projection of the board (at least two plus one for every 36 inches of mounting board)
- screws, 2 inches long (two to four for each bracket)
- heavy-duty staple gun and 1/2-inch long staples

Suggested Fabrics: Choose a linen-like weave, brushed cotton, twill, or duck. We recommend using only fabric with no predominant design that requires exact centering or matching at pleated sections.

Tip

IF YOU ARE LOOKING FOR AN ALTERNATIVE TO EXPENSIVE WINDOW TREATMENTS, AND IF PRIVACY IS NOT A CONCERN, CONSIDER THESE MORE SPLASH THAN CASH OPTIONS. SEARCH YOUR HOME, INCLUDING DRAWERS AND CLOSETS, FOR ITEMS SUCH AS BASKETS, MISMATCHED MITTENS, KITCHEN UTENSILS, HATS, HANKIES, OR DOILIES AND HANG THEM SIDE BY SIDE ACROSS THE TOP OF THE WINDOW FOR A UNIQUE VALANCE.

MORE $PLASH THAN ¢ASH

Planning the Pleat and Seam Positions

This valance needs to be planned before any fabric calculations can be completed. The valance consists of pleats and spaces. Plan to use three spaces (with four pleats) for board lengths of 36 to 50 inches and five spaces (with six pleats) for board lengths of 51 to 60 inches. This treatment can easily be adapted for wider windows by following the worksheet (page 102). Longer boards will require additional pleats and spaces. Always use an odd number of spaces and an even number of pleats, and allow 16 inches for each pleat.

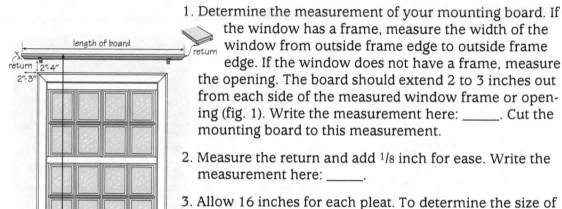

length of board

return

return 2"-4"

2"-3"

Fig. 1

1. Determine the measurement of your mounting board. If the window has a frame, measure the width of the window from outside frame edge to outside frame edge. If the window does not have a frame, measure the opening. The board should extend 2 to 3 inches out from each side of the measured window frame or open- ing (fig. 1). Write the measurement here: _____. Cut the mounting board to this measurement.

2. Measure the return and add $1/8$ inch for ease. Write the measurement here: _____.

3. Allow 16 inches for each pleat. To determine the size of the spaces between the pleats, divide the length of the mounting board (do not include the returns) by the number of spaces (either three or five, or more for treatments wider than 60 inches). Add $1/8$ inch to this measurement for ease. Write the number here: _____. Ideally, the size of each space should be between 10 and 18 inches.

4. Use the diagrams in figures 2 and 3 as a visual guide to complete the worksheet using the above information.

Fabric Calculations

Three widths of 54-inch-wide fabric are required for board lengths of 36 to 50 inches when three spaces (four pleats) are used. Four widths of 54-inch-wide fabric are required for board lengths of 51 to 60 inches when five spaces (six pleats) are used. Additional widths are required for wider treatments or ones with additional pleats and can be calcu- lated by following the worksheet.

DECORATOR FABRIC

1. Place the mounting board 2 to 4 inches above the window

Worksheet for Spaces and Pleats

To use the worksheet, measure your mounting board and calculate the width of the spaces between pleats. Place your measurements in column 4. Start with the usable width for each width of fabric. Subtract the successive amounts shown in gray from the usable width. The gray boxes in Column 4 must add up to the usable fabric width or less for each width of fabric. To determine the cut width of each piece of fabric, add up the numbers placed in the gray boxes.

WORKSHEET FOR 36- TO 50-INCH-WIDE WINDOW WITH THREE SPACES AND FOUR PLEATS—Our example (column 3) uses a 45-inch-long board with a return of 4 inches.

COLUMN 1 Pleat Number	COLUMN 2 Valance Sections	COLUMN 3 Our Example	COLUMN 4 Your Measurements	COLUMN 5 Your Cut Width	Cut Width Example
Start with a usable fabric width		53"			
	Side hem	2"	2"	First Fabric Width	Example: By adding up the gray boxes in column 3, we determine that the cut width will be the entire 53" of usable fabric width.
	Measured return	4"		Add up the numbers in gray boxes from column 4 to determine cut size of first width of fabric.	
Pleat #1, corner pleat	16" pleat	16"	16"		
	Space measurement	15"			
	Remaining fabric width (Ex: 53" less 37" = 16")	16"			
	Less 1/2" seam allowance to join the next fabric width	1/2"	1/2"	Write no. here: _____.	
Pleat #2	The entire remaining amount of fabric will be part of the next 16" pleat.	15 1/2"		Seam here	
Start again with the usable fabric width		53"		Seam here Second Fabric Width	Example: By adding up the gray boxes in column 3, we determine that the cut width will again be the entire 53" of usable fabric width.
	1/2" seam allowance to join widths	1/2"	1/2"		
Pleat #2	Balance of the 16" pleat (Ex: 16" less 15 1/2" = 1/2")	1/2"		Add up the numbers in gray boxes from column 4 to determine cut size of second width of fabric.	
	Space measurement	15"			
Pleat #3	16" pleat*	16"	16"		
	Space measurement	15"			
	Remaining fabric width (Ex: 53" less 47" = 6")	6"		Write no. here: _____.	
	Less 1/2" seam allowance to join the next fabric width	1/2"	1/2"		
Pleat #4, corner pleat	The entire remaining amount of fabric will be part of the corner 16" pleat.	5 1/2"		Seam here	
Start again with the usable fabric width		53"		Seam here Third Fabric Width	Example: By adding up the gray boxes in column 3, we determine that the cut width will be 17".
	1/2" seam allowance to join widths	1/2"	1/2"		
Pleat #4 corner pleat	Balance of the 16" pleat (Ex: 16" less 5 1/2" = 10 1/2")	10 1/2"		Add up the numbers in gray boxes from column 4 to determine cut size of third width of fabric.	
	Measured return	4"			
	Side hem	2"	2"		
	Any fabric remaining is extra fabric. Cut off remaining fabric.	36"		Write no. here: _____.	

Double check all measurements before cutting fabric widths by pin-marking your fabric at hems, returns, seams, spaces and pleats. Pin fabric together at seams and pleats. The measurement of the pinned fabric (excluding pleats) between side hem marks should equal the finished width of the valance.

*If you are using fabric that is less than 54 inches wide, additional seams and widths of fabric may be necessary. Create your own worksheet following the one above adding seams where required.

For board lengths of 51 inches and wider, create your own worksheet using the above worksheet as your guide. Pleat #4 will not be positioned at the corner: instead, it will be one of your front pleats. Continue by adding width as necessary to achieve your required finished width.

like a shelf; mark the position of the angle brackets. Screw the angle brackets to the wall. Place the board on top of the brackets, but do not attach it at this time (fig. 1).

2. To determine the finished length of the fabric portion of the valance, measure from the top of the mounting board to the top of the window sill and divide this number by 3. Subtract the visible length of your fringe from this number. Write the number here: _____.

3. To determine the cut length of the valance, add the amount of one board return plus 3/4 inch to the finished length. Write the number here: _____.

4. To determine the finished width of the valance, multiply the measured return by 2 and add it to the length of the mounting board (steps 1 and 2, Planning the Pleat and Seam Positions). Write the number here: _____.

5. The total cut width of the valance is determined by the worksheet on page 102. Add together the cut fabric widths determined by the worksheet and subtract the 1/2-inch seam allowance where indicated. After completing the worksheet, write the total cut width here: _____. Refer to figures 2 and 3.

6. To calculate the total yardage, multiply the cut length by the number of fabric widths needed. Write the number here: _____. Divide this number by 36 and round up to the nearest 1/4 yard. Write the number here: _____.

7. If you choose to cover the mounting board with fabric, you will also need a piece of fabric measuring 14 inches

Fig. 2   *Write your measurements for the returns and the spaces between the pleats.

2" hem   16" pleat   16" pleat   16" pleat   16" pleat   2" hem

return | 16" corner pleat | space 1 | space 2 | space 3 | 16" corner pleat | return

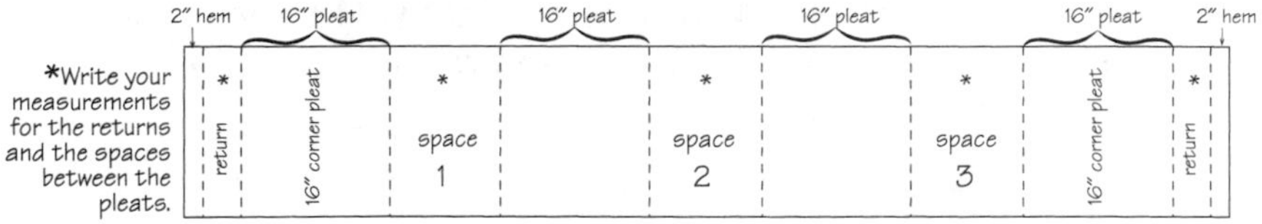

3 spaces, 4 pleats

Fig. 3

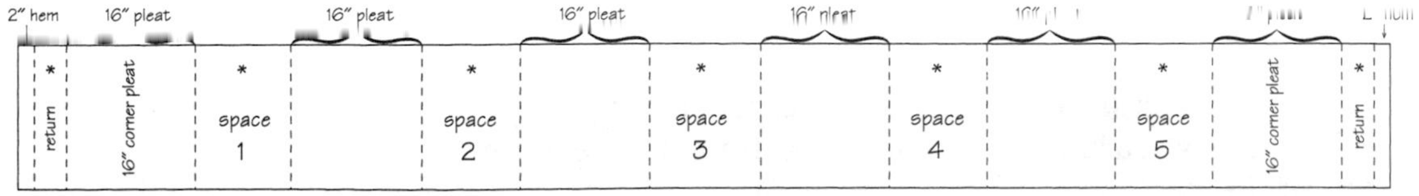

2" hem   16" pleat   16" pleat   16" pleat   16" pleat   16" pleat   16" pleat   2" hem

return | 16" corner pleat | space 1 | space 2 | space 3 | space 4 | space 5 | 16" corner pleat | return

5 spaces, 6 pleats

by the board length plus 3 inches. Add this amount to the above total. Write the total yardage required here: _____.

8. The amount of fringe required is equal to the cut width of the valance (step 5 above) plus $1/8$ yard for the ease. Divide the total by 36 and round up to the nearest $1/4$ yard. Write the number here: _____.

9. Optional topknots: Plan for one knot per pleat (including corner pleats). Each knot uses 27 inches of fabric-covered cord. Purchase double this amount of filler cord for each knot. Also purchase $1/2$ yard of additional fabric to cover the cord. For an Asian flair, use $3/8$-inch twisted cord instead of fabric-covered cord to create the knots. This cord should match the fringe in color.

LINING

1. To determine the cut width of the lining, add 12 inches for the two corner pleats and seam allowances to the finished width of the valance (step 4, Decorator Fabric). Write the number here: _____.

2. To determine the number of fabric widths required, divide the cut width of the lining by the width of the lining fabric. Round up to the nearest whole number. Write the number here: _____.

3. To determine the cut length of the lining, add 3 inches for the bottom hem to the cut length of the valance (step 3, Decorator Fabric). Write the number here: _____.

4. To calculate the amount of lining fabric required, multiply the number of fabric widths (step 2 above) by the cut length (step 3 above). Divide by 36 and round up to the nearest $1/4$ yard. Write the number here: _____.

Construction

Use a $1/2$-inch seam allowance unless otherwise instructed.

CUTTING

1. Lay the fabric flat on a large work surface. Use a carpenter's square to mark and cut a straight edge at one end of the decorator fabric.

2. Cut the fabric to the cut length measurement. If you need more than one fabric width to achieve the cut width of the valance, cut additional fabric to the same length, matching design repeats.

3. The fabric widths must be cut to different measurements so that the seams will fall within the pleats. Before cutting, refer to the worksheet to determine the measurement for each width of fabric. We suggest that you place the fabric widths side by side on a large work surface and pin-mark the pleat and seam positions. Once you are sure the measurements are correct, cut the fabric to size and stitch the widths together. It may not be possible to match the design motifs exactly at the joined seams. However, line up any predominant horizontal patterns when stitching. Press the seams open.

4. If your fabric has a tendency to ravel, serge or zigzag the bottom and top cut edges of the decorator fabric before continuing. (Be sure to move the pins used to mark your pleats away from the edge to be serged!)

FRINGE

MORE $PLASH THAN ¢ASH · *Tip* WATCH FOR DECORATOR OUTLET SALES IN YOUR AREA. INTERIOR DESIGN FIRMS OFTEN END UP WITH EXTRA FABRIC FROM LARGE COMMERCIAL JOBS. THIS FABRIC WILL TRULY BE A MORE SPLASH THAN CASH FIND!

1. Place the fringe along the bottom edge of the valance right sides together. Position the cut end of the fringe 2 inches from the cut side edge of the valance. Place the fringe so the header edge just covers the edge of the fabric and the fringe ends point toward the center of the fabric.

Fig. 4

right side of decorator fabric

2"

(The edge of the fabric should not be visible beyond the header edge of the fringe.) Use a zipper foot to stitch, working with 3 to 4 inches of fringe at a time, easing the fringe to fit the fabric. Stitch along the innermost row of fringe stitching. Stop stitching about 3 inches from the opposite end with the needle in the down position. Cut the fringe so it ends 2 inches from the side edge. Continue stitching over the cut fringe end; reinforce with extra stitching to finish (fig. 4).

2. Press the seam allowance and the header edge of the fringe toward the wrong side of the fabric. The fringe will

now hang away from the fabric. Working from the right side, stitch 3/8 inch from the seam through all layers. Start at the edge of the fabric and continue to the opposite edge, catching the header edge of the fringe on the underside (fig. 5).

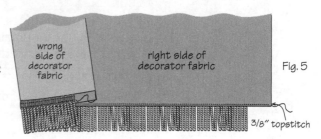

Fig. 5

wrong side of decorator fabric

right side of decorator fabric

3/8" topstitch

PLEATS

1. Place the valance right side up on your work surface. Pin-mark your pleat and space measurements (from the worksheet) along the top edge and the fringed edge of the valance, using figure 2 or 3 as your guide.

2. To form pleats, bring the marks at each side of the 16-inch pleat section right sides together, keeping the top and bottom edges even (fig. 6). Stitch the pleats together from the top cut edge to a distance equal to the amount of one return. Arrange the fabric so a deep pleat folds equally on each side of the stitching. Pin the pleats at the top and bottom edges. Press.

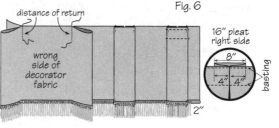

Fig. 6

distance of return

wrong side of decorator fabric

16" pleat right side

8"

4" 4"

basting

2"

3. Machine-baste the pleats in place along the top edge. Stitch a second row of basting below the first at a distance equal to one return from the top edge (fig. 6).

LINING

1. Cut the lining fabric as determined in Fabric Calculations, Lining. Stitch the seams to join. Press them open.

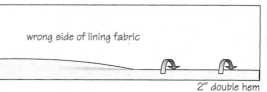

Fig. 7

wrong side of lining fabric

2" double hem

2. At the bottom edge of the lining fabric, fold under and press 4 inches toward the wrong side. Tuck under the top edge of the hem 2 inches to meet the fold (fig. 7). Stitch the hem.

3. The lining has only two pleats—one at each corner. Measure in from each end of the lining a distance equal to one return less 1 inch and place a mark for the beginning of the corner pleat. Place another mark 8 inches away for the opposite side of the pleat. Bring the 8-inch marks

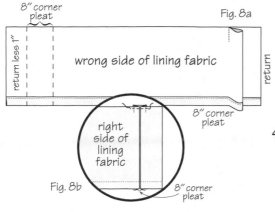

Fig. 8a

8" corner pleat

return less 1"

wrong side of lining fabric

return

right side of lining fabric

8" corner pleat

Fig. 8b

8" corner pleat

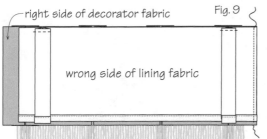

right side of decorator fabric

Fig. 9

wrong side of lining fabric

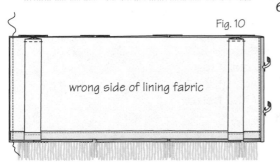

Fig. 10

wrong side of lining fabric

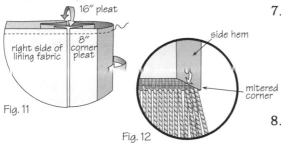

Align center pleats.

16" pleat

right side of lining fabric

8" corner pleat

side hem

mitered corner

Fig. 11

Fig. 12

together to form the pleats. Stitch the pleats together from the top cut edge a distance equal to the amount of one return (fig. 8a). Arrange the fabric so a pleat folds equally on each side of the stitching. Machine-baste the pleats along the top edge of the lining (fig. 8b).

4. Place the decorator fabric and lining right sides together and pin along one side seam. Make sure the top edges of the decorator fabric and lining fabric are even and that the bottom edge of the lining is 1/2 inch shorter than the hem of the decorator fabric. Stitch one side seam together (fig. 9). Press the seam toward the decorator fabric.

5. Gently pull the lining over to meet the other side of the decorator fabric. Pin this side seam together and stitch. Press the seam toward the decorator fabric (fig. 10).

6. Turn the valance right side out. Place the valance, lining side up, on a large work surface. Arrange the valance so the decorator fabric "wraps" around to the back equally on each side from the top of the valance to the fringed hem. The centers of the corner pleats should line up. The fringe should end at each hemmed side. Press the side edges. Machine-baste the lining and decorator fabric together along the top edge, from side to side (fig. 11).

7. For a custom hem finish, create mitered corners at the bottom of the decorator fabric. With the lining side facing you, diagonally fold under the bottom edge of the side hem until no raw edges are visible. Press. Handstitch in place (fig. 12).

8. To ensure that each pleat maintains its shape, diagonally stitch the inside fold at

Part I – The Projects

the bottom of each pleat on both the lining and
decorator fabrics (fig. 13).

Fig. 13

OPTIONAL TOPKNOTS

1. For topknots made of fabric-covered cord, cut
   and stitch bias strips of decorator fabric to
   cover the cord. Cover the cord as instructed in
   Fabric-Covered Cording (page 224).

2. About 27 inches of cord is required for each knot. Follow
   figure 14 to make each knot. Pull the cord evenly as
   you tie it so that the knot is uniform and untwisted. The
   knot is most attractive when it is tied loosely with some
   open space remaining between the loops. When the knot
   is completed, cut the cord ends so they extend about
   2$^{1}/_{2}$ inches beyond the knot. At each cord end, slide the
   end of the casing back; then pull out and cut off 1 inch of

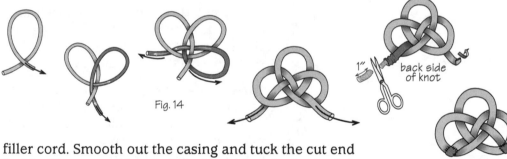

Fig. 14

back side
of knot

back side
of knot

filler cord. Smooth out the casing and tuck the cut end
inside. Flatten and handstitch the end to the back of the
knot. If using twisted cord, leave the tape (attached before
cutting the cord) on the ends to complete the knot.

3. To evenly position the knots on the valance,
   remove the mounting board from the brackets
   and place it on your work surface. Place the
   valance so it is centered against the mounting
   board, with the lower row of basting stitches just
   above the top edge of the board and with a pleat at
   each front corner. Use pushpins to temporarily hold
   the valance in place. Using straight pins, pin one knot
   to each pleat, 1 inch below the lower row of basting
   stitches. The center loop of the knot can be on the top or
   the bottom, but all knots should be uniformly positioned
   across the valance (fig. 15).

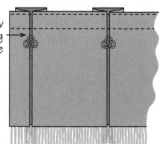

1" below
basting
line

Fig. 15

4. To pin the corner knots, slide the board to the edge of your table so the corner fabric hangs straight down. Bend each corner knot so it evenly folds around the corner pleat and pin it in place. Remove the valance from the board.

5. Loosely hand stitch the top outer edge of each knot to the valance. Tight stitching will pucker the valance. The corner knots will appear to be arched but will hug the corner when the valance is mounted.

Installing and Dressing

1. Prepare the mounting board by painting it to match the wall color or by covering it with decorator fabric.

2. Place the valance so it is centered against the board, with a pleat at each front corner as in step 3, Optional Top-knots. The fabric edge should be flush to the back edge of the board. Use pushpins to hold the valance as you position it. Staple the valance to the board, working from the center toward the side edges (fig. 16).

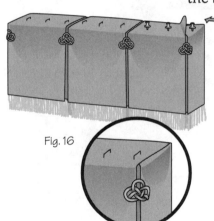

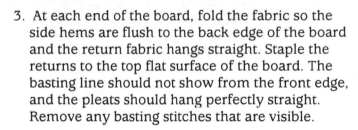

Fig. 16

3. At each end of the board, fold the fabric so the side hems are flush to the back edge of the board and the return fabric hangs straight. Staple the returns to the top flat surface of the board. The basting line should not show from the front edge, and the pleats should hang perfectly straight. Remove any basting stitches that are visible.

4. Replace the mounting board on the brackets and screw it into position.

Rooms with a View

We think this window treatment would look great in a living room, dining room, office, study, bathroom, or family room.

17 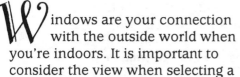Inside Outlook

Windows are your connection with the outside world when you're indoors. It is important to consider the view when selecting a window treatment because the view, in a sense, becomes part of the treatment. This inside-out awning is the perfect transitional component between the inside and outside environments. This design is simple in both concept and construction and is the perfect complement to your room when you want to be enveloped by nature. The fabric we selected is a nature-inspired toile. We added trim and tassels for the perfect finishing touches.

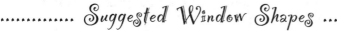

Suggested Window Shapes

This treatment is suitable for single or double windows, corner windows (where the windows do not meet in the corner), sliding glass doors, window walls, or ranch windows.

Techniques to Know before You Begin

If you need to brush up on your skills in any of these areas, turn to part III.

- Accurate Measuring
- Preparing a Mounting Board
- Installing a Mounting Board
- Matching Repeats

- Usable Fabric Widths
- Fabric Repeats
- Cutting Fabric
- Hems

COVERED BUTTONS, TRIM, AND TASSELS SET THIS DESIGN ABOVE ALL OTHERS. COLOR PHOTOGRAPH IS ON PAGE 122.

- Cutting Multiple Fabric Widths
- Covering Buttons
- Stitching Fabric Widths Together
- Sewing on Buttons
- Advantages of Lining Your Window Treatments
- Turning and Cutting Corners and Points
- Working with Decorative Trims

·*Tip*·

MORE $PLASH THAN ¢ASH ·

MAKE YOUR OWN TASSELS BY CUTTING A PIECE OF CARD- BOARD TO THE LENGTH OF THE TASSEL. WRAP EMBROIDERY FLOSS AROUND THE CARD- BOARD TO ACHIEVE THE DESIRED THICK- NESS. TO MAKE THE TASSEL HEAD, GATHER THE FLOSS AT ONE EDGE OF THE CARD- BOARD AND TIE IT TOGETHER WITH MATCHING FLOSS. REMOVE THE CARD- BOARD AND TIE ANOTHER PIECE OF FLOSS 1/2 INCH TO 1 INCH BELOW THE KNOTTED END. CUT THE FLOSS LOOPS TO CREATE THE TASSEL TAILS

Materials Needed

FROM THE FABRIC STORE

- decorator fabric
- 1/2 to 1 yard (depending on the size of windows) of con- trasting fabric for the rod sleeve and covered buttons
- lining fabric
- thread to match decorator fabrics
- 3/16- to 1/4-inch cord-edge (cord with attached lip edge), enough to go around three sides but not the top of the valance
- 3-inch tassels (one for each point)
- 2 1/2-inch-diameter half-ball cover buttons (one for each point)
- standard flat rod with a 6- to 8-inch return
- paper for patternmaking

RECOMMENDED NOTIONS

These are specific notions needed for this project. Also refer to the list of basic notions on page 180.

- point turner
- zipper foot
- size 90/14 universal machine needle

FROM THE HOME IMPROVEMENT CENTER

These are specific supplies needed for this project. Also refer to the basic list of tools and supplies on page 180.

- 1-by-2-inch board
- screws, 2 inches long (at least two, plus one for every 36 inches of board length)
- heavy-duty staple gun with 1/2-inch long staples

Suggested Fabrics: Choose medium-weight fabrics, such as duck, jacquard, sateen, linen or linen-like fabric, denim, broadcloth, or chintz.

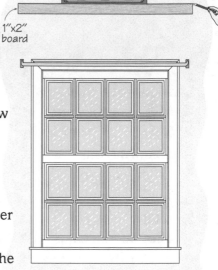

1"x2" board

Fabric Calculations

1. Determine the length of your mounting board. If the window has a frame, measure the width of the window from outside frame edge to outside frame edge. If the window does not have a frame, measure the opening. The board should extend 2 to 4 inches out from each side of the measured window frame or opening. The length of the board is also the finished width of the valance. Add 1 inch for the cut width. Write the number here: _____.

2. Place the mounting board flat against the wall above the window. It can be placed anywhere from 2 to 4 inches above the window to the ceiling. Make a light pencil mark on the wall at the top edge of the board (fig. 1). Use a level when positioning the board. Do not permanently attach the board to the wall at this time.

Fig. 1

3. Install the standard flat rod even with or below the top of the window frame and 2 to 4 inches out from the sides of the window frame (the same distance as the board) (fig. 1).

4. Using a yardstick, measure from the mark on the wall to the top of the installed rod (fig. 2).

5. Add $11\frac{1}{4}$ inches to the above measurement for the cut length of the fabric. Write the measurement here: _____.

6. To determine the number of fabric widths required to achieve the cut width, divide the cut width by the usable width of the fabric. Round up to the next whole number. Write the number here: _____.

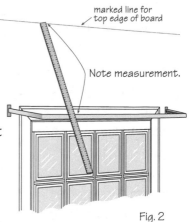

marked line for top edge of board

Note measurement.

Fig. 2

7. To calculate the total yardage of the decorator and lining fabrics, multiply the cut length measurement by the number of widths needed. Write the number here: _____. If your fabric has a repeat design, multiply the repeat

distance by the number of widths and add this figure to the total. The extra fabric will allow you to match the designs.

8. Divide this number by 36 and round up to the nearest 1/4 yard. Write the number here: _____. This is the amount of decorator and lining fabrics that you need. Note: You'll need extra fabric if you decide to cover the mounting board with the decorator fabric.

9. For the rod sleeves, measure the length of the rod (including returns). Multiply this number by two for the necessary fullness. Write the measurement here: _____. Divide this number by the width of the fabric and round up to the next whole number. Write the number here: _____. The cut length is 4 inches. Multiply the cut length measurement by the number of widths needed. Write the number here: _____. Divide by 36 and round up to the nearest 1/4 yard. Write the number here: _____. Add 1/8 yard to the final amount for the covered buttons.

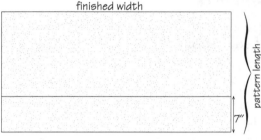

finished width

pattern length

7″

Fig. 3

Creating the Pattern

1. Using a carpenter's square, make a rectangular paper pattern using the finished width and the pattern length (step 5, Fabric Calculations). Measure and mark a line 7 inches above and parallel to the bottom edge (fig. 3).

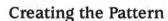

3 points

7″

2. Determine how many points you would like on your valance. This should be an odd number. Multiply the number of points by 2 and add 1. Divide the finished width by this number. Write the number here: _____ Mark these increments on the line you drew.

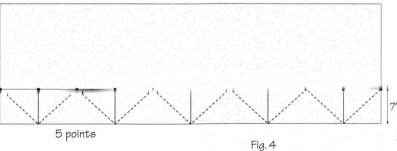

5 points

7″

Fig. 4

3. Starting at the first mark, draw a vertical

line from every other mark connecting the horizontal line to the bottom edge of the paper. Then draw diagonal lines to form the points (fig. 4).

4. Cut on the diagonal lines to form the points. Before cutting the fabric, tape the paper pattern in position to the wall and to the rod with the drawn horizontal line about 1 inch below the top edge of the rod. The paper pattern will extend beyond the light pencil line you drew on the wall in step 2, Fabric Calculations. This excess is for finishing and should be no more than 2$^1/4$ inches. Adjust if necessary.

Construction

Use a $^1/2$-inch seam allowance unless otherwise instructed.

1. Lay the fabric flat on a large work surface. Use a carpenter's square to mark and cut a straight edge at one end of the decorator and lining fabrics.

2. Cut the fabric to the cut length measurement. If you need more than one width to achieve the cut width of your valance, cut additional fabric widths matching motifs.

Fig. 5

Sew the fabric widths together, making sure the design motifs match at the joined seam. Trim equal amounts of fabric from both side edges to obtain the cut width. Do the same with the lining fabric.

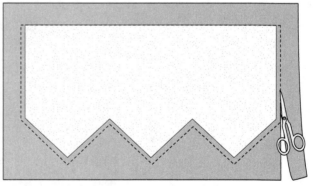

3. Center and pin the paper pattern on the fabric. Use a straightedge and a fabric marker to mark a $^1/2$-inch seam allowance to each side edge and along the pointed bottom edge (fig. 5). Do not add a seam allowance to the top edge. Cut on this marked line. Repeat the process for the lining fabric.

4. Serge or zigzag stitch along the top edge of the fabric for a clean finish.

5. Starting at the top cut edge pin the cord-edge to the right side of the decorator fabric along one side edge. The cord itself should be placed just beyond the $^1/2$-inch seam line so your stitching is right against the cord. Using a zipper

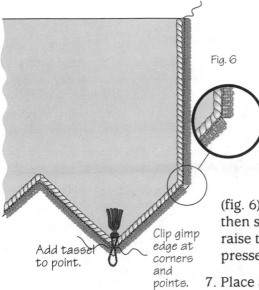

Fig. 6

Add tassel to point.

Clip gimp edge at corners and points.

foot, stitch as close to the cord as possible easing the cord to fit the fabric and working in 3- to 4-inch increments (fig. 6).

6. At each corner or point, stitch to within 1 inch of the corner or point and stop with the needle in the down position. This will allow you to pivot the cord-edge to create a sharp corner or point. Clip the lip edge to, but not through, the innermost row of trim stitching exactly at the corner or point (fig. 6). Continue stitching to the corner or point, then stop with the needle in the down position, raise the presser foot, pivot the fabric, lower the presser foot, and continue stitching.

7. Place a tassel at each point with the head of the tassel touching the cord and the cut ends pointing toward the center of the fabric. Baste the loop of the tassel at the point (fig. 6).

8. Pin the decorator and lining fabrics right sides together. Stitch around three sides on the same stitching line used to attach the cord-edge. Leave the top edges open for turning (fig. 7).

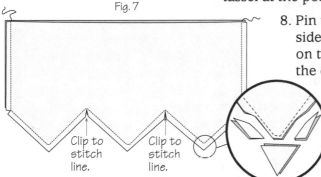

Fig. 7

Clip to stitch line.

Clip to stitch line.

9. To eliminate bulk, clip the corners and points diagonally. Taper the seam allowances away from the corners and points. Clip the seam allowance to the stitching line at the inside corners between the points (fig. 7).

10. Turn the valance right side out. For sharp corners, use a point turner to gently push the fabric out from the inside. Press the seam so neither fabric is visible from the opposite side.

11. Cover buttons with contrasting fabric.

12. Make a rod sleeve from the contrasting fabric by cutting enough 4-inch-wide strips to equal two times the length (including the returns) of the standard flat rod. If

necessary, stitch strips together end to end for the needed
length. At each end, fold under and stitch a double
1/2-inch hem. Then fold the entire
strip right sides together and stitch
the long side. Press the seam open
and turn the strip right side out to create a tube (fig. 8).

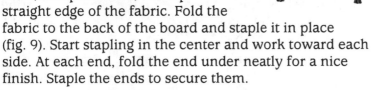

Fig. 8

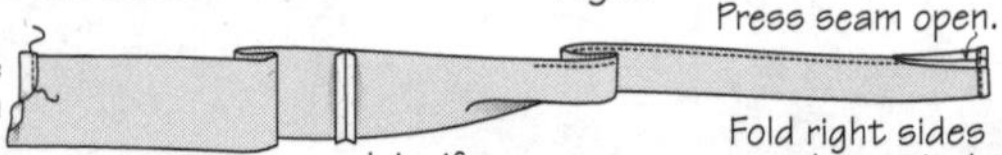

double 1/2" hem

Join, if necessary.

Press seam open.

Fold right sides together; stitch.

Installing and Dressing

1. Prepare the mounting
   board by covering
   it with the decorator fabric.

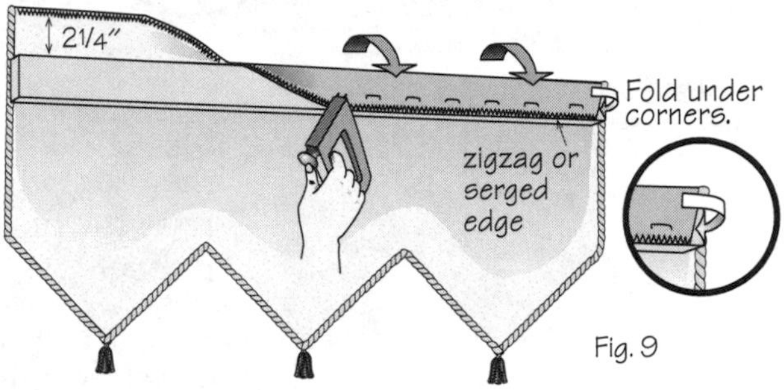

2. Place the valance on the work
   surface, wrong side up. Center
   the mounting board on the valance so the long edge is 2 1/4 inches
   from, and parallel to, the top
   straight edge of the fabric. Fold the
   fabric to the back of the board and staple it in place
   (fig. 9). Start stapling in the center and work toward each
   side. At each end, fold the end under neatly for a nice
   finish. Staple the ends to secure them.

Bring to back and staple.

2 1/4"

Fold under corners.

zigzag or serged edge

Fig. 9

3. Refer to the photograph and handstitch the covered
   buttons along the top edge of the valance.

4. Insert the flat rod into the rod sleeve and gather the sleeve
   evenly along the entire length of the rod. Replace the rod
   in the brackets.

5. Position the mounting board at the mark you made in
   step 2 of Fabric Calculations. Use a level when positioning
   the board. Secure the board to the wall with screws.

6. Refer to the photograph and drape the fabric over the
   sleeved rod. If the valance slips, use double-stick carpet
   tape to hold it in place.

Rooms with a View

We think this window treatment would look great in a
bedroom, bathroom, kitchen, home office, informal dining
area, living room, or sunroom.

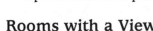

Window Projects
Color Photos

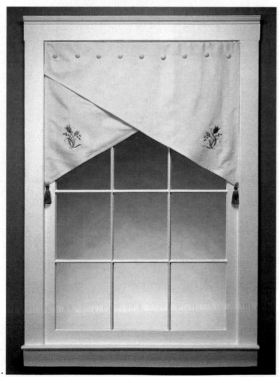

1.

2.

3.

4.

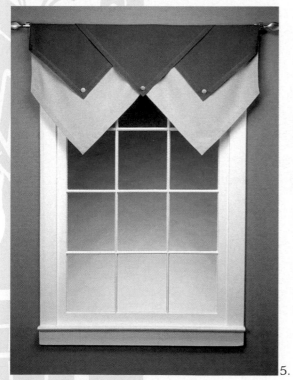

5.

6.

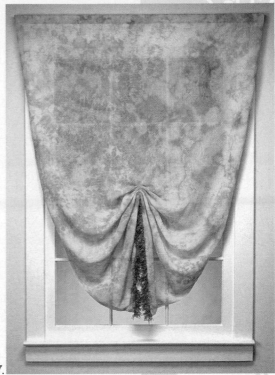

7.

Sheer Illusions

8.

9.

10.

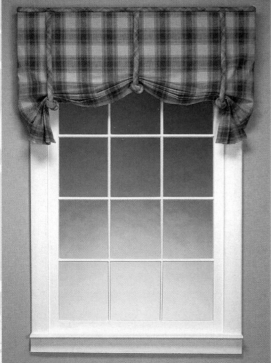

11.

Simply Sensational

9. Leaf Motif –
page 49

10. Tying the Knot –
page 53

Classic Choices

11. Knot Sew – page 60

12.

13.

Classic Choices
(continued):

12. The Envelope,
    Please – page 67

13. Beaucoup Scoops
    – page 75

14. Friendly Borders – page 83

14.

15.

16.

Classic Choices
(continued):

15. Au Provence – page 91

16. Skirting the Issue – page 99

Tradition With a Twist

17. Inside Outlook – page 110

17.

18.

19.

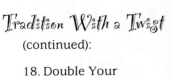

Tradition With a Twist

(continued):

18. Double Your
Pleasure – page 125

19. Regal Simplicity –
page 133

20. Walk on the Wild Side –
page 143

20.

21.

22.

23.

Just for Fun

21. Cancan Valance –
    page 150

22. Flutterby –
    page 155

23. Pointed in the
    Right Direction –
    page 161

18 Double Your Pleasure

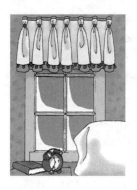

TRADITIONAL TECH-
NIQUES COMBINE
WITH CONTEMPORARY
STYLING TO CREATE
THIS VERSATILE
VALANCE. COLOR
PHOTOGRAPH IS ON
PAGE 123.

Perky describes this treatment best. Playful fringe dances along layered hems. Crisp pleats are punctuated with matching buttons. The great detail in this project gives satisfaction—but it's not hard to construct. You can create a masterpiece—and a perky one at that!

Suggested Window Shapes

This treatment is suitable for single or double windows, casement windows, sliding glass doors, picture windows, ranch windows, or bay windows.

Techniques to Know before You Begin

If you need to brush up on your skills in any of these areas, turn to part III.

- Accurate Measuring
- Preparing a Mounting Board
- Installing a Mounting Board
- Cutting Multiple Fabric Widths
- Stitching Fabric Widths Together
- Matching Repeat Designs
- Advantages of Lining Your Window Treatments

- Fabric Repeats
- Cutting Fabric
- Usable Fabric Widths
- Addressing Take-Up
- Covering Buttons
- Sewing on Buttons

Part I – The Projects

- Turning and Cutting Corners and Points
- Working with Decorative Trims

················· *Materials Needed* ·····················

FROM THE FABRIC STORE
- decorator fabric for the top layer (print recommended)
- decorator fabric for the bottom layer (solid recommended)
- lining fabric for both bottom and top layers
- novelty fringe (ball fringe or tassel fringe) in a color to contrast with the bottom layer
- thread to match the decorator fabric
- heavy button thread (preferably waxed)
- 3/4-inch-diameter (size 30) half-ball cover buttons (one for each pleat)

RECOMMENDED NOTIONS
These are specific notions needed for this project. Also refer to the list of basic notions on page 180.

- point turner   • zipper foot
- 4- to 6-inch doll needle to sew buttons

FROM THE HOME IMPROVEMENT CENTER
These are specific supplies needed for this project. Also refer to the basic list of tools and supplies on page 180.

- 1-by-4- or 1-by-6-inch board
- angle brackets, shorter than the projection of the board (at least two plus one for every 36 inches of board length)
- 2-inch long screws, two to four per bracket
- heavy-duty staple gun and 1/2-inch long staples
- level

Suggested Fabrics: For the top layer choose cotton duck, chintz, sateen, or cotton sheeting. This layer is ideal for border prints (which must be railroaded). For the bottom layer choose twill, chintz, duck, sateen, or cotton sheeting.

Tip

TO CREATE AN UNUSUALLY SHAPED COVERED BUTTON SUCH AS A TRIANGLE OR SQUARE, CUT TWO TO THREE LAYERS OF CHIPBOARD (USE THE BACK OF A DISCARDED WRITING TABLET) TO THE DESIRED SHAPE AND SIZE. GLUE THE LAYERS TOGETHER SECURELY. COVER THE SHAPE NEATLY WITH FABRIC, FOLD THE FABRIC TO THE BACK, AND GATHER THE EDGES TOGETHER TO FORM A SHORT SHANK (NO LONGER THAN 1/8 TO 1/4 INCH). TRIM AWAY EXCESS FABRIC. HANDSTITCH THE BUTTON TO THE PROJECT.

Fabric Calculations

This treatment has two separate layers of decorator fabric, individually lined.

1. Determine the length of your mounting board. If the window has a frame, measure the width of the window from outside frame edge to outside frame edge (fig. 1). If the window does not have a frame, measure the opening. The board should extend 2 to 4 inches out from each side of the window. This is the length of your mounting board. Write the measurement here: _____. Cut the mounting board to this measurement.

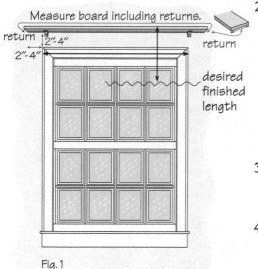

Measure board including returns.

return

2"-4"

2"-4"

return

desired finished length

Fig. 1

2. Place the mounting board 2 to 4 inches above the window like a shelf; mark the position of the angle brackets. When positioning the board, keep in mind that the valance will extend $1^1/2$ inches above the top edge of the board. Screw the angle brackets to the wall. Place the board on top of the brackets, but do not permanently attach it at this time.

3. Measure the return of the mounting board (fig. 1). Multiply this by 2. Write the measurement here: _____.

4. Add this measurement to the length of the mounting board. Multiply the total by 2 and add $4^1/2$ inches for ease. Round up any fraction to the nearest whole number. Write the number here: _____. This is the finished width of both layers of the valance.

5. To determine the cut width of the decorator and lining fabrics for both layers, add 1 inch to the finished width. Write the number here: _____.

6. To determine the number of widths of the lining and each decorator fabric needed to achieve this cut width, divide the cut width of the valance by the usable fabric width of each fabric. Round each up to the nearest whole number. Write the numbers here: top layer _____, bottom layer _____, lining _____. Note: If you want to create this

window treatment without joining widths of fabric, you can railroad the fabric. Not all fabrics are appropriate for this. Study the fabric closely to make sure the design printed along the selvage does not have a specific direction (e.g., stemmed flowers that appear to be lying on their sides). Purchase enough yardage to equal the bottom cut width measurement.

7. Measure from the top of the mounting board to the desired finished length of the bottom layer (fig. 1). To determine the finished length of the bottom layer, add 2 inches to this number for the top extension. Write the number here: _____. Add 5 inches for hems and seam allowance for the cut length. Write the number here: _____.

8. Cut the lining for the bottom layer 8 inches shorter than the cut length measurement for the decorator fabric (step 7). Write the number here: _____.

9. The decorator fabric and lining for the top layer are cut the same size. Cut the top layer 7 inches shorter than the cut length of the decorator fabric for the bottom layer (step 7). Write the number here: _____.

10. To determine the required yardage of the lining and both decorator fabrics, multiply the cut length of each by the number of widths required. If your fabric has a repeat design, multiply the repeat distance by the number of widths and add this figure to the total. The extra fabric will allow you to match the designs. Add the lining yardage for each layer together. Write the numbers here: top layer _____, bottom layer _____, lining _____.

11. Divide each number by 36 and round up to the nearest 1/4 yard. Write the required yardage here: top layer _____, bottom layer _____, lining _____. If the fabric for any layer is railroaded, purchase enough fabric to equal the cut width. You'll need extra fabric if you decide to cover the mounting board with the decorator fabric.

12. The amount of trim required is equal to the cut width of the top layer of the valance plus 1/8 yard for ease.

13. To determine the number of covered buttons required, divide the length of the mounting board by 4 and add 3 to this number. Disregard any fraction. Write the quantity here: _____.

Construction

Use a 1/2-inch seam allowance unless otherwise instructed.

BOTTOM LAYER

1. Lay the fabric flat on a large work surface. Use a carpenter's square to mark and cut a straight edge at one end of the decorator fabric and lining for the bottom layer. Measure from this straight edge and cut both fabrics to the cut width and length determined in Fabric Calculations. Save scraps of the fabric to cover the buttons.

2. If you need more than one width of fabric to achieve the cut width, cut additional fabric widths to the same length, matching repeats. Sew the fabric widths together; make sure the designs match at the seams. Press the seams open. Trim equal amounts of fabric from both side edges to obtain the cut width. Repeat for the lining fabric.

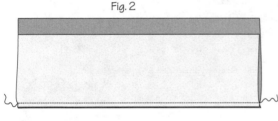

Fig. 2

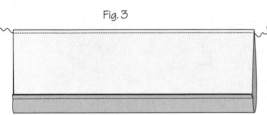

Fig. 3

3. Place the decorator and lining fabrics for the bottom layer right sides together so the side edges of the two fabrics are even. Pin along the bottom edge. Stitch together along the bottom edge (fig. 2). Press the seam toward the lining fabric.

4. Gently pull the lining to meet the top edge of the decorator fabric. Pin this seam together and stitch (fig. 3). Press the seam toward the lining fabric.

5. With the decorator fabric and lining fabric still right sides together, place the valance on a large surface. Arrange the valance so the decorator fabric "wraps" around to the lining side, about 3 inches at the bottom edge and about 1 inch at the top edge. Pin.

6. Pin both layers together along the side edges. Stitch from the top folded edge to the bottom folded edge on

each side leaving a 10-inch opening along one side edge
for turning. To eliminate bulk, clip the corners diagonally
(fig. 4). Turn the valance right side out. For sharp corners,
use a point turner to gently push the fabric out from the
inside. Make sure the
top and bottom hems
are even. Handstitch the
opening closed. Press.

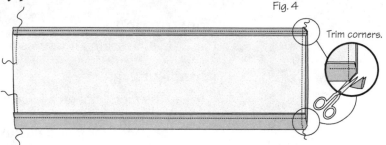

Fig. 4

Trim corners.

TOP LAYER

1. Repeat steps 1 and 2
   from Bottom Layer.

2. Pin the novelty fringe to the right side of the bottom edge
   of the decorator fabric so the
   innermost edge of the gimp edge
   falls on the 1/2-inch seam line and
   the balls/tassels point toward the
   center of the fabric. Use a zipper
   foot to stitch on the seam line,
   along the innermost edge of the gimp edge. Ease the
   fringe to fit the fabric 3 to 4 inches at a time. Begin
   and end by extending the gimp edge into the side seam
   (fig. 5). Trim off any fringe that may extend into the side
   seam allowance.

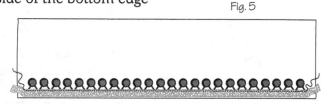

Fig. 5

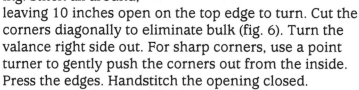

Fig. 6

3. Pin the lining to the
   decorator fabric, right
   sides together, with
   the cut edges match-
   ing. Stitch all around,
   leaving 10 inches open on the top edge to turn. Cut the
   corners diagonally to eliminate bulk (fig. 6). Turn the
   valance right side out. For sharp corners, use a point
   turner to gently push the corners out from the inside.
   Press the edges. Handstitch the opening closed.

CONNECTING THE LAYERS

1. Place the two valances together on a
   large work surface with the lining side
   of the top layer against the right side
   of the bottom layer. The layers should

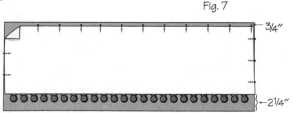

Fig. 7

3/4"

2¼"

align at the side seams. The top layer is be 3/4 inch below the upper edge of the bottom layer and 2 1/4 inches above its lower edge (fig. 7). Pin both layers together at the sides and upper edge. Treat the two layers as one.

2. To determine the number of pleats, divide the length of the mounting board by 4 and add 3. Disregard any fraction.

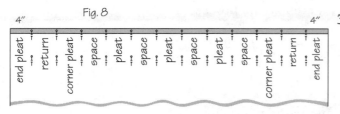

Fig. 8

4″　　　　　　　　　　　　　　　　　　　　　　　　　　　　　　　　4″

end pleat | return | corner pleat | space | pleat | space | pleat | space | pleat | space | corner pleat | return | end pleat

3. Working along the top edge of the valance, place a pin mark 4 inches from each end. Then measure and pin-mark the distance of one return on each side. Divide the remaining section into approximately 4-inch spaces. You must have an odd number of spaces. Distribute any difference equally (added to or subtracted from) the spaces. Place a second row of corresponding pins 3 inches below the top edge of the valance (fig. 8).

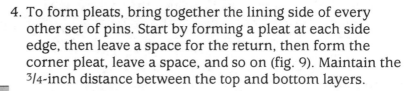

Fig. 9

4. To form pleats, bring together the lining side of every other set of pins. Start by forming a pleat at each side edge, then leave a space for the return, then form the corner pleat, leave a space, and so on (fig. 9). Maintain the 3/4-inch distance between the top and bottom layers.

5. Machine-stitch each pleat from the lower pin mark to the upper edge of the valance (fig. 9). Backstitch at each end to secure the stitching. Test the fit of the valance to the board size. Adjust the pleat size if necessary.

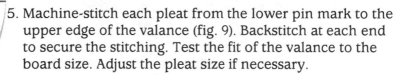

2½″

Fig. 10

6. Flatten each pleat so equal portions extend on each side of the pleat seam. Pin to hold. Use a fabric marker to mark the center of each pleat 2 1/2 inches below the top of the valance (fig. 10).

7. Pinch the front of each pleat together at the marked point. Handstitch to gather the fullness (fig. 11). The stitches will be concealed by the covered buttons.

ATTACHING THE BUTTONS

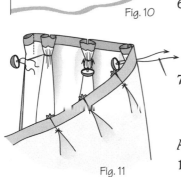

Fig. 11

1. Cover the buttons with scraps of decorator fabric from the bottom layer, following the package directions.

2. Cut a 16- to 18-inch piece of heavy thread and tie the middle of the thread to the shank of each button. Insert one thread end only through a long needle.

3. To attach each button, pass the needle through all layers of fabric from the front to the back at the marked center of each pleat. Unthread the needle, leaving the first thread end loose on the back of the valance. Thread the needle with the remaining strand and repeat the process 1/8-inch above the first stitch (fig. 11). Knot the thread ends securely at the back of the valance. Clip the excess thread.

Installing and Dressing

1. Prepare the mounting board by either painting it to match the wall color or by covering it with one of the decorator fabrics.

2. Place the mounting board on a large flat surface. Staple the valance to the mounting board so the top edge of the valance extends 2 inches above the top edge of the board. Each return should touch the back edge of the board. The first pleat should be on the front edge flush to the corner.

Fig. 12

3. Place one staple on each side of each pleat, flush to the seam (fig. 12). The fullness of the pleat will hide the staple.

Staple each side of pleat to board.

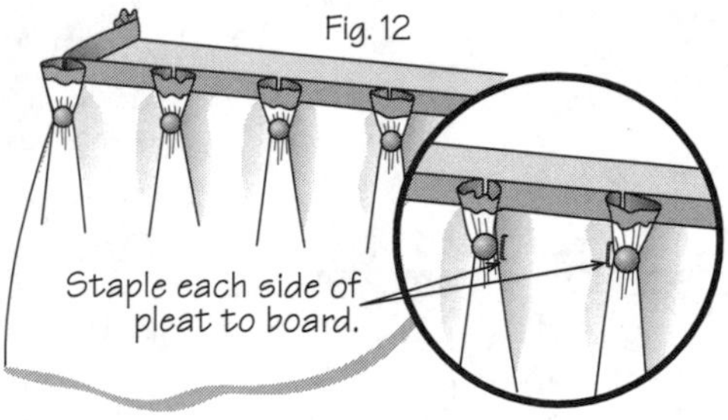

Rooms with a View

We think this window treatment would look great in a kitchen, bathroom, bedroom, office, library, sunroom, or family room.

19 Regal Simplicity

CORD-COVERED
BUTTONS ARE THE
EXTRA TOUCH THAT
MAKES THIS DESIGN
SO APPEALING.
COLOR PHOTOGRAPH
IS ON PAGE 123.

If a window could select its own wardrobe, this simple treatment would certainly be high on its list of favorites. It frames the window without overpowering it and lets the outside light pour in. The purpose of a window, after all, is to allow light to enter a room while framing the view beyond. The optional swag between fabric columns helps to visually create this frame, but it may be eliminated for use around a door. If privacy is not an issue, this regal design may be just the outfit for your window.

Suggested Window Shapes

This treatment is suitable for single windows or beside French doors. The recommended maximum window width per swag is 50 inches.

Techniques to Know before You Begin

If you need to brush up on your skills in any of these areas, turn to part III.

- Accurate Measuring
- Usable Fabric Widths
- Cutting Fabric
- Installing Rods, Brackets, and Holdbacks
- Fabric Repeats
- Covering Buttons
- Matching Repeat Designs
- Stitching Fabric Widths Together

- Cutting Multiple Fabric Widths
- Turning and Cutting Corners and Points
- Working with Decorative Trims

.... *Materials Needed* ....

FROM THE FABRIC STORE

- decorator fabric*
- lining fabric for the swag
- 1 3/4 yards of muslin for swag pattern
- 3/16- to 1/4-inch-diameter cord-edge (cord with attached lip edge) for swag
- 5 yards of 3/16- to 1/4-inch-diameter cord for rosettes
- 1 3/4 yards of 3/8-inch-diameter cord for swag and side panels
- four tassels, 3 inches long with 1/2-inch top loops for rosettes
- 7/8 yard of 3-inch-long bullion fringe
- matching thread
- heavy thread to attach rosette cord
- 1/8 yard of heavyweight iron-on interfacing
- four 1 7/8-inch-diameter (size 75) half-ball cover buttons for rosettes

RECOMMENDED NOTIONS

These are specific notions needed for this project. Also refer to the list of basic notions on page 180.

- point turner
- epoxy glue
- zipper foot
- clear plastic grid-marked ruler with angle markings

FROM THE LINEN STORE

- two large medallion-style holdbacks (may also be available from a fabric store)

FROM THE HOME IMPROVEMENT CENTER

Refer to the list of basic tools and supplies on page 180.

* For best results, select a fabric that is at least 54 inches wide.

Suggested Fabrics: Choose brocade, duck, heavy twill, linen or linen-like fabric, sateen, jacquard, heavy silk, or damask. Choose an overall design that does not need to be centered.

●●

Fabric Calculations

SIDE PANELS

1. Mount the holdbacks 2 to 3 inches above the top outside edge of your window or door frame and 2 to 4 inches out from the side edges of the frame.

2. The cut width of each side panel is 27 inches. This piece is folded in half lengthwise to create a self-lined panel that has a finished width of 13 inches.

3. For simplicity's sake, we strongly urge you to use fabric at least 54 inches wide for this treatment. Only one width is required of decorator fabric that is 54 inches wide or wider. It is cut in half lengthwise, with each half used for a panel. To determine the number of widths needed if the fabric is less than 54 inches wide, divide the total cut width (54 inches) by the usable width of the fabric. Round up to the nearest whole number.

4. To determine the finished length of the side panels, measure from the bottom of the holdback medallion (not the bracket) to the desired finished length (fig. 1). Write the number here: _____. This measurement is also used for the cut length. It takes into account the drop of the rosette cording.

5. To determine the amount of fabric required for the side panels only, multiply the cut length by the number of fabric widths required. Divide this number by 36 and round up to the nearest 1/4 yard. Write the total yardage here: _____.

SWAG

1. The swag is made from a trapezoid-shaped piece of fabric. Some simple calculations will determine the size of your swag. Measure the distance between holdback medallions (fig. 1). Subtract 1 inch to

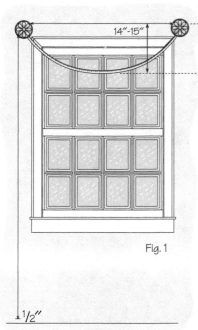

14"-15"

Fig. 1

1/2"

determine the cut width of the top edge of the swag (Measurement A in fig. 2). Write the number here: _____.

2. Tape a tape measure to the inside edge of one medallion. Drape the tape measure between medallions to simulate the bottom curve of the swag (fig. 1). The bottom of the tape measure curve should be 14 to 15 inches below the top edge of the window frame. This is the finished drop of the swag at the center and lowest point of the swag. Note the measurement where the tape measure touches the inside edge of the opposite medallion. Add 1 inch for seam allowances. Write the number here: _____. This is the cut width at the bottom edge of the swag (Measurement B in fig. 2). Measurement C in figure 2 is 21¹/₂ inches.

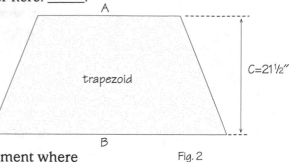

Fig. 2

3. To create a muslin pattern for the swag, draw the trapezoid from figure 2 with the measurements determined above on a rectangle of muslin. The bottom corners need to be slightly curved. To curve the corners, measure along the diagonal sides from each bottom corner a distance of 3 inches and make a mark. Measure 8¹/₂ inches along the bottom edge of the same corners and mark. Use a large bowl or plate to help you to draw a gentle curve between the marks at each corner (fig. 3). Both corners must match exactly. Cut out the muslin pattern on the marked lines.

Fig. 3

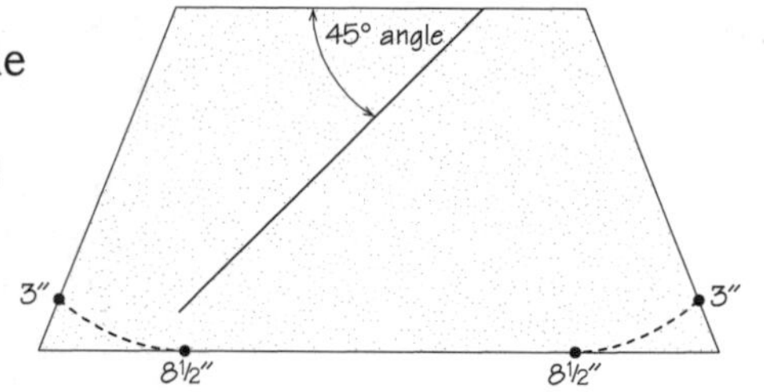

4. Mark a 45-degree angled line from the top edge to the bottom edge of the pattern (fig. 3). (This line will be used as a guide to position the muslin pattern correctly on the decorator fabric.)

5. The easiest way to determine the yardage required is to take the muslin pattern with you to the fabric store. To determine the amount of fabric needed, place the pattern on the decorator fabric so the 45-degree line is parallel to the selvages and the top corner is near the top cut edge of the fabric

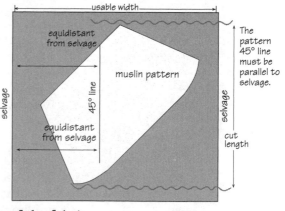

Fig. 4

(fig. 4). The distance between the uppermost point on the fabric to the lowermost point is the cut length of the decorator and lining fabrics for the swag. Write the number here: _____.

6. If the pattern is wider than the usable width of the fabric, you will need additional fabric to achieve the cut width.

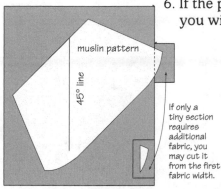

muslin pattern

45° line

If only a tiny section requires additional fabric, you may cut it from the first fabric width.

Fig. 5

The area of the pattern extending beyond the muslin pattern will be the additional amount required (fig. 5). Since we have suggested a maximum window width of 50 inches for this design, the size of this joined section should be minimal. You may be able to cut a section from the remaining fabric around the pattern to use for joining. Consider the fabric design when making this decision.

7. To calculate the total amount of decorator fabric required for the side panels and the swag, add the determined yardage for the side panels (see Fabric Calculations, Side Panels, step 5) to the determined yardage for the swag (see Fabric Calculations, Swag, step 5). Write the number here: _____.

8. Divide this number by 36 and round up to the nearest 1/4 yard. This is the total amount of fabric required to make this window treatment.

9. The cut length determined in step 5 above is the amount of lining fabric required.

10. To determine the amount of cord-edge required for the swag, add up the swag measurements (A + B) and add 1/4 yard for ease. Write the number here: _____.

Construction

SIDE PANELS

Use a 1/2-inch seam allowance unless otherwise instructed.

Fig. 6

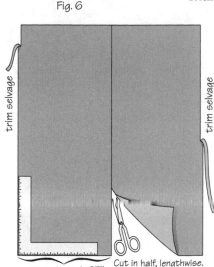

trim selvage

trim selvage

approximately 27"   Cut in half, lengthwise.

1. Lay the fabric flat on a large work surface. Use a carpenter's square to mark and cut a straight edge at one end of the decorator fabric. Measure from this straight edge to cut the fabric

length for the side panels as determined in Fabric Calculations. Trim the selvages from the fabric. Cut this piece of fabric in half lengthwise so that each half measures approximately 27 inches (fig. 6).

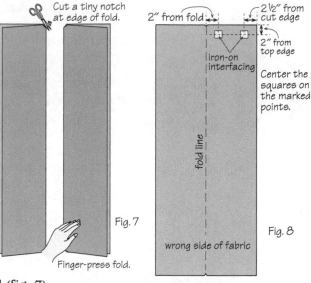

Fig. 7

Fig. 8

2. Each fabric panel is self-lined. Fold each piece of fabric in half lengthwise with the wrong sides together. Choose the side of each panel that will face the room. This is the front of each panel. Finger-press the fold line at the top and bottom of each panel. Cut a tiny notch in the fold at the top and bottom edges of each panel (fig. 7).

3. Open up the folded fabric so it is wrong side up. On the selected front section of each panel, measure and make a mark 2 inches down and 2^1/2 inches in from the top corner, and make another mark 2 inches down and 2 inches in from the center fold line. Cut 4 pieces of iron-on interfacing, each 2^1/2 inches square. Center one piece on each marked position on each side panel, adhesive side down, against the wrong side of the fabric (fig. 8). Press to fuse, following the manufacturer's directions.

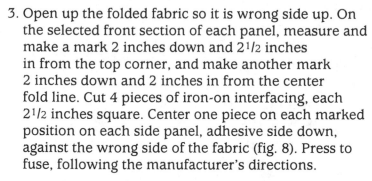

Fig. 9

4. Turn the fabric right side up. Cut the fringe into two equal pieces. Pin the fringe along the bottom edge of the front portion of each panel, between the notch and the 1/2-inch side seam allowance. Align the fringe so the header edge is even with the cut edge of the fabric and the fringe ends point toward the center of the fabric. Ease the fringe to fit. Starting at the side seam allowance, use a zipper foot to stitch along the innermost row of fringe stitching, stopping at the notched fold (fig. 9).

5. Fold each fabric panel in half lengthwise, right sides together. Stitch across the bottom edge, along the side edge, and across the top edge, leaving 6 inches open at the center of the top or side edges to turn. Trim the

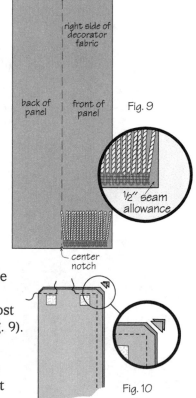

Fig. 10

corners diagonally to remove bulk (fig. 10). Turn the panel right side out. For sharp corners, use a point turner to gently push the corners out from the inside. Press the edges. Handstitch the opening closed.

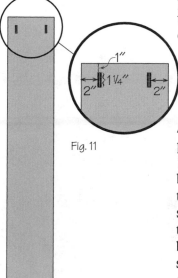

Fig. 11

6. Before stitching the final buttonholes in each panel, do a test buttonhole on a scrap of fabric using the measurements below to insure that the knotted 3/8-inch rosette cord will fit through the buttonhole. Adjust the length of the buttonhole if needed. On each panel place a pin mark 2 inches in from each side and 1 inch down from the top edge to mark the top of each buttonhole. Place another pin mark 1 1/4 inches below for the bottom of the buttonholes. Working from the front side of each panel, follow your sewing machine instructions to stitch a vertical buttonhole at each position between the pin marks (fig. 11). The buttonholes will be stitched through the interfaced section of each panel. Cut open the buttonholes and set the side panels aside.

SWAG

1. Lay the fabric on a large work surface. Use the muslin pattern created in Fabric Calculations to cut one swag from the decorator fabric and one swag from the lining fabric. If additional widths are required to achieve the total cut width of the swag, join the widths before cutting the swag (fig. 12).

Fig. 12   This is a common seam placement for fabric less than 54" wide.

2. Stitch cord-edge to the right side of the decorator fabric along the top and bottom edges. Starting at the side seam allowances, bend the cord perpendicular to the long edge so the cut end extends off the long cut edge of the fabric. The cord itself should be placed just beyond the 1/2-inch seam line so your stitching will be right against the cord. Use a zipper foot to stitch over the cord; then continue to stitch as close to the cord as possible. Working with a 3- to 4-inch section, ease the cord-edge to fit the fabric. Since the seams will be on the bias, be careful not to stretch or to pucker the fabric as you sew. Clip the cord-edge every 1/2 inch along the curves. End the cord-edge the same way you started (fig. 13).

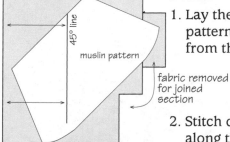

Fig. 13   1/2" seam allowance

decorator fabric

clip   clip

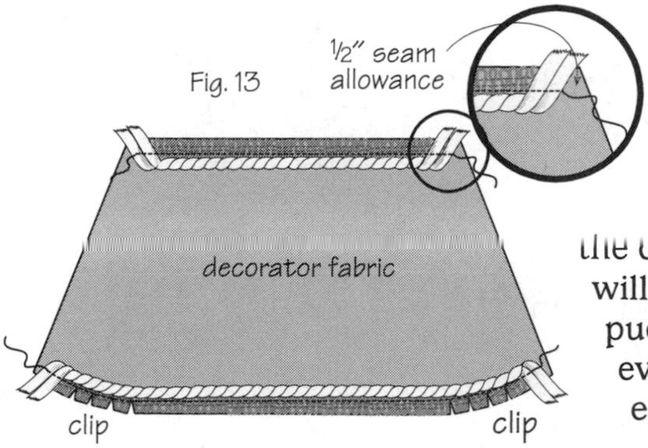

3. Pin the lining to the decorator fabric right sides together. Use a zipper foot to stitch both layers together along the top and bottom edges directly over the previous stitching. Turn the swag right side out. Press the cord-trimmed edges so the lining does not roll out to the right side.

4. Machine-baste the diagonal sides of the lining and the decorator fabric together.

5. Mark the spacing for the pleats along the diagonal sides. Use straight pins to mark seven equal spaces (approximately $2^1/_2$ inches each) on each side (fig. 14). Since the finished width of the swag will vary according to your window measurements, the length of the diagonal line will also vary slightly. Divide any difference evenly among the spaces.

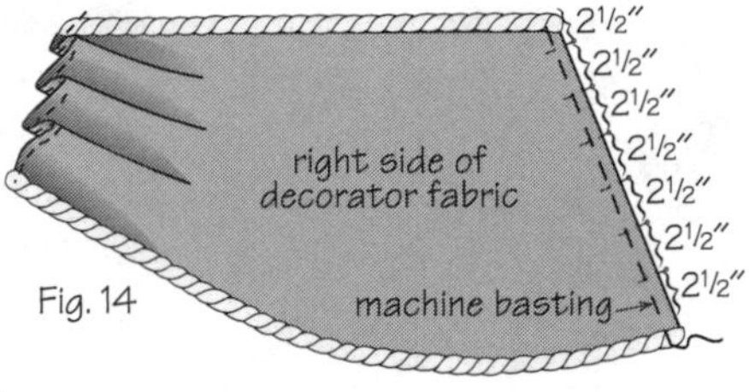

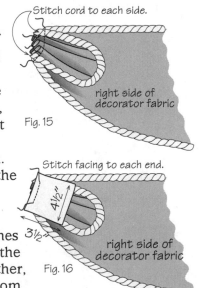

Fig. 14

right side of decorator fabric

machine basting→

$2^1/_2$"
$2^1/_2$"
$2^1/_2$"
$2^1/_2$"
$2^1/_2$"
$2^1/_2$"
$2^1/_2$"

6. Starting at the bottom edge, fold the decorator fabric at each side along the marked pleat lines. Arrange the pleats as shown in figure 14. The bottom edge should be in front and folded down. The top edge should be at the back and folded up. The sides should be even with the cut edges lined up. For a less bulky seam, place the top edge of each successive pleat $1/_8$ inch above the one before it.

7. Machine-baste the pleated edges together (fig. 15).

Stitch cord to each side.

Fig. 15

right side of decorator fabric

8. Tape and cut two pieces of $3/_8$-inch-diameter cord 10 inches long. To form a cord loop on each pleated side edge, pin one cord to each side of the swag. Position one end of the cord in each corner, flush to the top and bottom seams. Line up the cut cord end with the edge of the fabric (fig. 15). Carefully stitch over the cord ends to secure them. Remove the tape from the cord ends, and flatten the cord twists into the seam allowance to eliminate bulk. Repeat for the opposite side.

Stitch facing to each end.

$4^1/_2$"

$3^1/_2$

Fig. 16

right side of decorator fabric

9. Cut two facings measuring $4^1/_2$ inches by $3^1/_2$ inches from scrap swag fabric. Pin one $4^1/_2$-inch edge of the facing to each pleated swag edge, right sides together, so an equal amount of seam allowance extends from each end (fig. 16). Stitch.

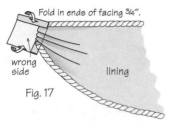

Fold in ends of facing ¾".

wrong side

lining

Fig. 17

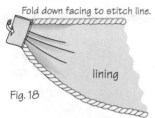

Fold down facing to stitch line.

lining

Fig. 18

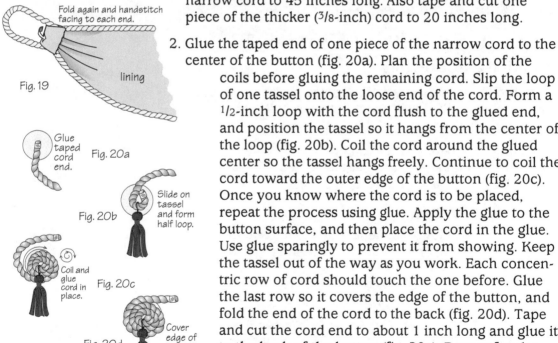

Fold again and handstitch facing to each end.

lining

Fig. 19

Glue taped cord end.

Fig. 20a

Slide on tassel and form half loop.

Fig. 20b

Coil and glue cord in place.

Fig. 20c

Cover edge of button with

Fig. 20d

Fold cord end to back and glue.

Fig. 20e

10. Lay the swag on your work surface with the lining side up. Fold and press the 3½-inch edges toward the lining side, encasing the cut corners of the swag (fig. 17). Fold and press the unstitched 4½-inch edge toward the lining side so the cut edge lines up with the stitch line (fig. 18). At the stitch line, fold the doubled facing toward the lining again until it is smooth and flat. Pin. Handstitch the facing in place (fig. 19). Repeat for the opposite side of the swag.

ROSETTES

1. Each side panel hangs from two rosettes connected with a cord loop. For each panel you will need two buttons covered with decorator fabric and two tassels that have a ½-inch loop at the top. Tape and cut two pieces of the narrow cord to 45 inches long. Also tape and cut one piece of the thicker (⅜-inch) cord to 20 inches long.

2. Glue the taped end of one piece of the narrow cord to the center of the button (fig. 20a). Plan the position of the coils before gluing the remaining cord. Slip the loop of one tassel onto the loose end of the cord. Form a ½-inch loop with the cord flush to the glued end, and position the tassel so it hangs from the center of the loop (fig. 20b). Coil the cord around the glued center so the tassel hangs freely. Continue to coil the cord toward the outer edge of the button (fig. 20c). Once you know where the cord is to be placed, repeat the process using glue. Apply the glue to the button surface, and then place the cord in the glue. Use glue sparingly to prevent it from showing. Keep the tassel out of the way as you work. Each concentric row of cord should touch the one before. Glue the last row so it covers the edge of the button, and fold the end of the cord to the back (fig. 20d). Tape and cut the cord end to about 1 inch long and glue it to the back of the button (fig. 20e). Repeat for the second button.

3. Tie a tight knot at one end of the ⅜-inch cord. To keep the knot from untying, place a drop of glue in the folds of the knot. Allow the glue to dry. Cut off excess cord flush to the knot.

4. Use heavy thread to stitch the knotted cord end to the shank of one rosette button (fig. 21).

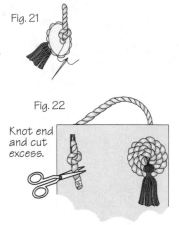

Fig. 21

Fig. 22

Knot end and cut excess.

5. Place one side panel on a flat work surface, front side up. Pass the unknotted end of the cord through a buttonhole from the front to the back and then through the second buttonhole from the back to the front (fig. 22). This will form a loop. Knot the end of the cord on the front side of the panel so that the looped portion of the cord measures 10 inches from knot to knot. The knot should sit on the front side of the buttonhole. Place a drop of glue in the knot to prevent it from untying. Be careful not to get the glue on the decorator fabric. Cut off any excess cord close to the knot.

6. Use heavy thread to stitch the unattached knot to the shank of the remaining covered button. Pull the finished knots to the back side of the buttonhole.

7. Repeat steps 1 through 6 for the second side panel.

Installing and Dressing

1. Slip the loops at the ends of the swag over the holdback medallions so the swag hangs between. Refer to the photograph to adjust the folds of the swag.

2. Slip the rosette loop at the top of one side panel over one medallion. Adjust the fabric at the center so it hangs smoothly. Repeat for the second panel.

Rooms with a View

We think this window treatment would look great in a living room, dining room, or bedroom that doesn't require privacy.

Pucker-Free Seams

It is very easy to accidentally pucker a bias seam when attaching a trim. Forcing too much trim along the seam will stretch the fabric. Pulling will develop spoon-like puckers. Ease the trim slightly to fit the edge, pinning it to the bias edge of the swag before stitching. Machine-baste; then check the edge you have just stitched. If puckering is minimal, leave it alone. It should press out. If it is extreme, however, remove the basting and rebaste. When the appearance is satisfactory, stitch permanently. (This is one of those times when sewing requires patience.)

20 Walk on the Wild Side

*T*his window treatment can pull together dissimilar elements of an eclectic decorating style and still have plenty of personality to compete with all the components of a room. Two coordinating fabrics can offer enough pizzazz to tie together all of your decorating efforts. How do you choose the fabrics and the colors to accent a room? One way is to start with the trimming. Select a beautiful trim in colors that you absolutely love. Then repeat those colors in the rest of the window treatment. Design coordination like this will make you look like a pro!

ANIMAL-SKIN-INSPIRED FABRICS AND NOVELTY TRIM GIVE THIS TAB CURTAIN DYNAMIC STYLE. HOWEVER, A TAMER FABRIC SELECTION IS JUST AS POWERFUL A CHOICE. COLOR PHOTOGRAPH IS ON PAGE 123.

.... Suggested Window Shapes ....

This treatment is suitable for single or double windows, bay windows, sliding glass doors, or picture windows. For best results, windows should be at least 36 inches wide for this treatment.

...... Techniques to Know before You Begin ......

If you need to brush up on your skills in any of these areas, turn to part III.

- Accurate Measuring
- Installing Rods, Brackets, and Holdbacks
- Usable Fabric Widths

Part I – The Projects

- Fabric Repeats
- Addressing Take-Up
- Using Drapery Weights
- Cutting Multiple Fabric Widths
- Stitching Fabric Widths Together
- Advantages of Lining Your Window Treatments
- Working with Decorative Trims
- Cutting Fabric
- Hems
- Matching Repeat Designs

················ *Materials Needed* ················

All fabrics for this window treatment must be at least 54 inches wide (including the lining).

- decorator fabric for the curtains
- decorator fabric for the top section and tabs
- lining fabric
- thread to match decorator fabrics
- decorative rod, finials, and mounting brackets (also available at department stores)
- four covered drapery weights
- novelty trim or 3/16- to 1/4-inch cord-edge (cord with attached lip edge) to separate the top and bottom sections
- monofilament thread

RECOMMENDED NOTIONS

These are specific notions needed for this project. Also refer to the list of basic notions on page 180.

- size 90/14 universal machine needle
- zipper foot or piping foot

FROM THE HOME IMPROVEMENT CENTER

Refer to the list of basic tools and supplies on page 180.

Suggested Fabrics: Choose medium-weight fabrics, such as jacquard, sateen, linen or linen-like fabric, duck, denim, or broadcloth. We suggest combining fabrics with different size prints, textures, and designs, including plaids and stripes, for a look all your own.

Tip

TABS OFTEN CATCH ON THE ROD AND DO NOT SLIDE EASILY. TO AID IN THE SIDE-TO-SIDE MOVEMENT WHEN CURTAINS ARE OPENED AND CLOSED, CAREFULLY HAND-STITCH A 1-INCH LENGTH OF BALL CHAIN (AVAILABLE IN HOME IMPROVEMENT CENTERS) TO THE TOP INSIDE CENTER OF EACH TAB. THE BALL CHAIN SHOULD BE ABOUT 1/8 INCH IN DIAMETER.

Fabric Calculations

These instructions, as written, will create two curtain panels, each with a finished width of approximately 50 inches. When hung on a rod, each curtain will cover approximately 25 to 40 inches. This style of window treatment is considered to be a stationary treatment. That is, it does not open and close easily for privacy. This finished size looks nice on windows up to 72 inches wide.

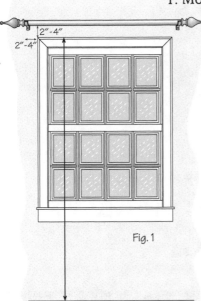

Fig. 1

1. Mount the rod brackets 2 to 4 inches above the top edge of the window frame and 2 to 4 inches out from each side of the frame (fig. 1).

2. To determine the finished length of the entire curtain, measure from the top edge of the window frame to the floor. Write the number here: _____. The finished length includes the top and bottom sections (fig. 1).

3. To determine the visible length of the top section, divide the above measurement by 3 to 5. Write the measurement here: _____. Add 1 inch for the cut length. Write the number here: _____.

4. To determine the visible length of the bottom section, subtract the visible length of the top section from the finished length of the entire curtain. Write the number here: _____. Add $8^1/2$ inches for the cut length. Write the number here: _____.

5. To determine the yardage for the top section, multiply the cut length by 2 (for two curtain panels). Add $5/8$ yard for matching tabs. Write the number here: _____. If you are using a print fabric that has a repeat design, multiply the repeat distance by 2 and add this figure to the total. Write the number here: _____. The extra fabric will allow you to match the panels. Divide the number by 36 and round up to the nearest $1/4$ yard to get the total yardage. Write the number here: _____.

6. To determine the yardage for the bottom section, multiply the cut length by 2 (for two curtain panels). Write the number here: _____. If you are using a print fabric that has a repeat design, multiply the repeat distance by 2 and

add this figure to the total. Write the number here: _____.
The extra fabric will allow you to match the panels.
Divide the number by 36 and round up to the nearest
$1/4$ yard to get the total yardage. Write the number here:

_____.

7. To determine the yardage required for the lining fabric,
   add $5^{1}/2$ inches for the hem and seam allowance to the
   finished length of the entire curtain (determined in step 2
   above). Multiply this number by 2 (for two curtain panels). Write the number here: _____. Divide this number by
   36 and round up to the nearest $1/4$ yard to get the total
   yardage. Write the number here: _____.

8. Purchase $3^{1}/4$ yards of cord-edge or novelty trim for the
   two curtain panels.

Cutting Instructions

1. Lay the fabric for the top section flat on a large work
   surface. Use a carpenter's square to mark and cut a
   straight edge at one end of the fabric. Measure from this
   straight edge to cut one top section to the cut length
   determined in step 3 above. Cut an identical length for
   the second curtain.

2. From the remaining top section fabric, cut 16 rectangles,
   each 5 inches by 10 inches, for the tabs.

Fig. 2

3. Cut a straight edge on the fabric for the bottom
   section as above. Cut two identical lengths to
   the cut length measurement for the bottom
   section determined in step 4 of Fabric Calculations.

4. Cut the lining 6 inches narrower than the cut
   width of the top and bottom sections and
   $5^{1}/2$ inches longer than the finished length of
   the entire curtain.

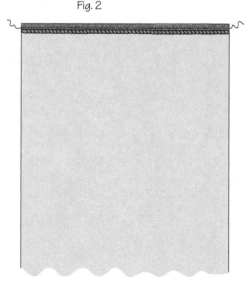

Construction

Use a $1/2$-inch seam allowance unless otherwise
instructed.

1. Pin the decorative trim to the top edge of the

Fig. 3

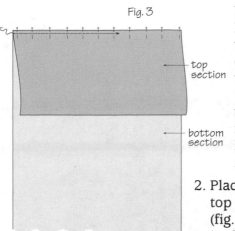

top section

bottom section

bottom section from side to side. Place it so the lip or header edge of the cord or the top edge of the trim is along the top cut edge of the fabric (fig. 2). The cord itself or the innermost row of trim stitching should be placed just beyond the 1/2-inch seam line so your stitching is right against the decorative portion of the trim. Use a zipper foot to stitch the trim to the fabric on the seam line. Ease the trim to fit the fabric, working in 3- to 4-inch increments.

2. Place the bottom edge of the top section against the top edge of the bottom section right sides together (fig. 3). Pin the layers together at each end and then in the middle. Pin the remaining top edge so all the layers are smooth and even. Stitch together with a zipper foot so that you can stitch on the same stitch line used to attach the trim. Press the seam allowances toward the top section.

3. Hem the lining and curtain panel separately. First hem the curtain panel with a double 4-inch hem. Handstitch a drapery weight in each corner about 3 inches from the side cut edge (fig. 4). Stitch the hem. Hem the lining with a double 3-inch hem.

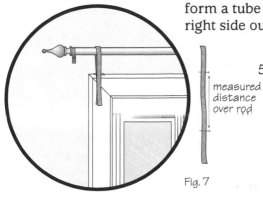

Fig. 4   Fig. 5   Fig. 6

4. Prepare each 5-by-10-inch tab by folding it in half lengthwise with the right sides together so it measures 2 1/2 inches by 10 inches. Stitch along the 10-inch edge to form a tube (fig. 5). Press the seam open. Turn each tab right side out and arrange it so the seam is in the middle of the tab (fig. 6). Press the tabs flat.

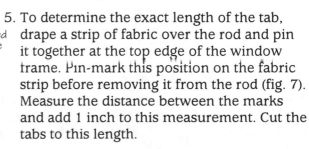

measured distance over rod

5. To determine the exact length of the tab, drape a strip of fabric over the rod and pin it together at the top edge of the window frame. Pin-mark this position on the fabric strip before removing it from the rod (fig. 7). Measure the distance between the marks and add 1 inch to this measurement. Cut the tabs to this length.

Fig. 7

6. Fold each tab in half crosswise, with the seam inside the fold, and line up the cut edges. Pin the tab together at the cut edges.

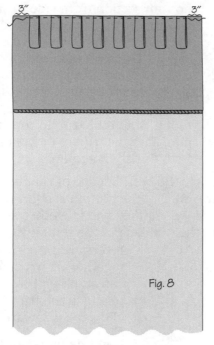

Fig. 8

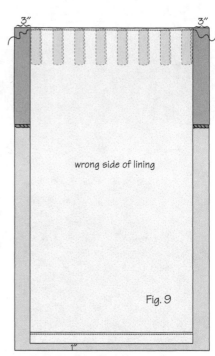

wrong side of lining

Fig. 9

7. Determine the placement of the tabs along the top edge of each curtain. The outer edges of the first and last tabs should be 3 inches in from each side edge; the remaining tabs should be evenly spaced between the end tabs (fig. 8). Each curtain has eight tabs total.

8. Pin the tabs to the top edge of the curtain panel with the folded ends of the tabs pointing toward the bottom hem and the raw edges lined up with the top edge of the fabric (fig. 8). Machine-baste the raw edge of the tabs to the top edge of the front section only.

9. Center the lining over the decorator fabric right sides together. The tabs will be "sandwiched" between the two layers. The decorator fabric should extend 3 inches from each side edge of the lining. Pin, making sure the top edges of the decorator and lining fabrics are even and that the bottom edge of the lining is 1 inch shorter than the decorator fabric. Stitch the fabrics together along the top edge (fig. 9).

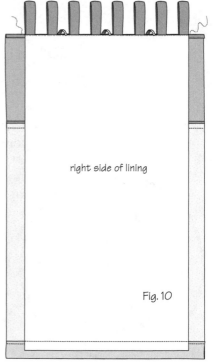

right side of lining

Fig. 10

10. Fold the lining over to the wrong side of the decorator fabric. Press the top edge smooth, including the remaining 1/2-inch top seam allow-

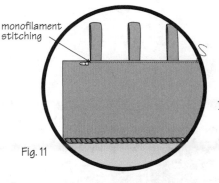

monofilament stitching

Fig. 11

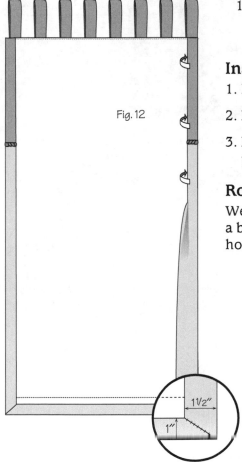

Fig. 12

1 1/2"

1"

ance that extends on each side of the lining (fig. 10). Working from the decorator side, use monofilament thread to top stitch close to the top edge through all layers to prevent the lining from showing on the right side (fig. 11).

11. Place the curtain on a large work surface. Hem the side edges with a double 1 1/2-inch hem (fig. 12). The top edge seam allowance should remain folded during this process. Slipstitch this edge in place.

12. Diagonally fold the bottom edge of the side hem to form a mitered corner (fig. 12). Press. Handstitch in place.

Installing and Dressing

1. Insert the rod through the tabs of the curtains.

2. Place the rod in the brackets.

3. Refer to the photograph and arrange the curtain panels into soft folds.

Rooms with a View

We think this window treatment would look great in a bedroom, living room, family room, den, study, home office, dining room, or sunroom.

21 Cancan Valance

The essence of the cancan is captured in this sassy window treatment by the wavy curls of fabric dancing along the bottom edge.

These topsy-turvy edges seem to create a flurry of movement across the window. Actually, they are held firm, restrained by the inexpensive curtain rod hidden within the rod pocket at the top edge. Capture the energy of high-spirited dancers by creating this valance for your own window.

·············· Suggested Window Shapes ··············

This treatment is suitable for single or double windows, picture windows, corner windows, casement windows, or sliding glass doors.

······ Techniques to Know before You Begin ······

If you need to brush up on your skills in any of these areas, turn to part III.

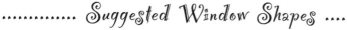

- Accurate Measuring
- Cutting Multiple Fabric Widths
- Installing Rods, Brackets, and Holdbacks
- Matching Repeat Designs
- Working with Decorative Trims

- Usable Fabric Widths
- Fabric Repeats
- Stitching Fabric Widths Together
- Cutting Fabric
- Hems

GATHERED ON AN INEXPENSIVE ROD, THIS WINDOW TREATMENT IS SURE TO KICK UP ITS HEELS. COLOR PHOTOGRAPH IS ON PAGE 124.

Tip

CHECK THE "FLAT FOLDS" IN YOUR FABRIC STORE FOR GREAT SAVINGS. FLAT FOLDS ARE FABRICS THAT ARE SOLD IN BULK TO THE STORE AND ARE DISPLAYED AS FOLDED FABRICS STACKED FLAT ON A TABLE (AS COMPARED TO ROLLS OR BOLTS). DEPENDING ON THE FABRIC STORE, THE FLAT FOLDS ARE SOLD BY THE PIECE OR BY THE YARD. IF YOU HAVE TO BUY THE ENTIRE PIECE, YOU MAY END UP WITH EXTRA YARDAGE, BUT THE COST SAVINGS ARE WORTH IT. USE THE LEFTOVER FABRIC FOR ACCESSORIES.

MORE $PLASH THAN ¢ASH

* Purchase ready-made welting or make your own. To make your own, purchase filler cord plus 1/2 yard of a contrasting decorator fabric to make bias strips for covering the cord.

.... Materials Needed ....

FROM THE FABRIC STORE
- decorator fabric for the top layer
- decorator fabric for the bottom layer
- thread to match fabrics
- ready-to-use welting ($5/32$ inch or $1/4$ inch)*
- standard white flat rod (also available at department stores)

RECOMMENDED NOTIONS
These are specific notions needed for this project. Also refer to the list of basic notions on page 180.

- size 90/14 universal machine needle
- zipper foot or piping foot   - fabric marker

FROM THE HOME IMPROVEMENT CENTER
Refer to the list of basic tools and supplies on page 180.

Suggested Fabrics: Choose medium-weight fabrics, such as duck, jacquard, sateen, linen or linen-like fabric, denim, ticking, or broadcloth.

Fabric Calculations
Two fabrics are used to construct the two layers of this valance. Use the same calculations for both fabrics.

1. Mount the rod brackets 2 to 4 inches above the top edge of the window frame and 2 to 4 inches out from each side of the frame (fig. 1). Place the rod on the brackets.

2. To determine the finished width, measure the length of the rod including the returns. Write the measurement here: _____. Multiply this number by $2^1/2$ for fullness and add 6 inches for hems and seam allowances. Write the total here: _____. This is the cut width of the valance.

3. To determine the amount of welting you need for the top and bottom edges, multiply the cut width by 2 and add

1/4 yard for ease. Divide by 36 and round up to the nearest 1/4 yard. Write the number here: _____.

4. To determine the number of fabric widths you need to achieve the cut width, divide the cut width by the usable width of the fabric. Round up to the next whole number. Write the number here: _____.

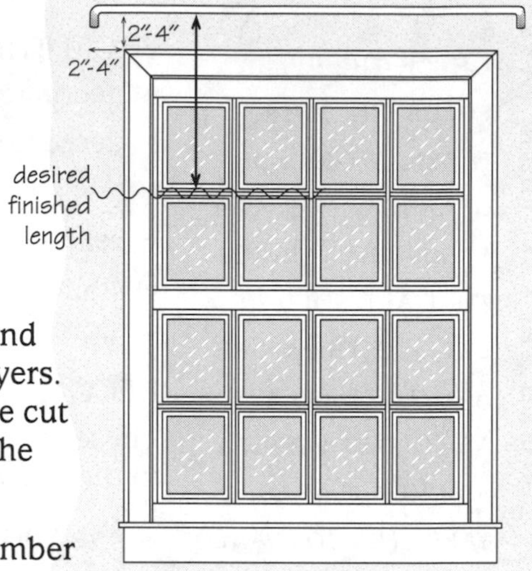

5. Measure from the bottom edge of the mounted rod to the desired finished length of the valance (fig. 1). Multiply this number by 2 and add 1 1/2 inches for the finished length of the layers. Write the number here: _____. To determine the cut length, add 1 inch for seam allowances. Write the measurement here: _____.

6. Multiply the cut length measurement by the number of widths needed (determined in step 4). Write the number here: _____. If you need more than one fabric width and the fabric you have selected has a repeat design, multiply the repeat distance by the number of widths and add this figure to the total. The extra fabric will allow you to match the designs.

7. To determine the yardage needed, divide this number by 36 and round up to the nearest 1/4 yard to get the total yardage. Write the number here: _____. This is the amount of one decorator fabric needed to construct this window treatment. The yardage of the second fabric may differ slightly if the repeat distance is different. Write the yardage of the second fabric here: _____.

Fig. 1

Construction

1. Lay the fabric flat on a large work surface. Use a carpenter's square to cut a straight edge at one end of each decorator fabric.

2. Cut the fabric for the top layer to the cut length measurement. If you need more than one width to achieve the cut width, cut additional fabric to the same length, matching motifs. Sew the fabric widths together, making sure the design motifs match at the joined seam. Do the same with the decorator fabric being used for the bottom layer. Trim

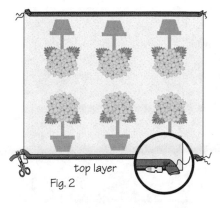

top layer

Fig. 2

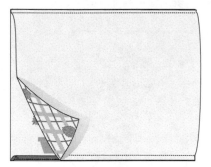

Fig. 3

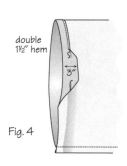

double
1½" hem

3"

Fig. 4

equal amounts of fabric from both side edges to obtain the cut width.

3. Cover the filler cord if you are not using ready-made welting.

4. Pin the welting to the right side of either decorator fabric along the bottom and top cut edges. To begin, extend the welting 1/2 inch beyond the edge of the fabric. Open the casing of the welting and snip out 1 inch of filler cord. Manipulate the welting, curving it slightly, so the filler cord stops at the seam line with the casing fabric flattened into the top or bottom seam allowance. Stitch the welting to the fabric using a zipper foot or piping foot (fig. 2).

5. Study the prints of both layers of fabrics to determine if they have a direction. If so, arrange the layers so the design on the top layer points up and the design on the bottom layer points down.

6. Pin the rectangles right sides together; maintain the direction of the prints as described above. Stitch along the top and bottom edges and leave the side edges open to create a tube (fig. 3).

7. Open the ends of the tube. Make a double 1 1/2-inch hem around the entire circumference at each end of the tube (fig. 4). Stitch the hem.

8. Turn the valance right side out.

9. Arrange the valance on a large work surface with the bottom layer of fabric facing up and the bottom edge closest to you. Press the valance smooth and flat at the center and along the edges.

10. To create the rod pocket, measure up from the bottom seam edge of the bottom layer of fabric to the desired finished length measurement determined in step 5 of Fabric Calculations. (Do not include the thickness of the welting in this measurement.) Pin to mark. Do this several times across the width of the valance. Connect the pin marks by drawing a line with a fabric marker. Measure up from this line 1 1/2 inches and draw a parallel

line across the entire width of the valance. Topstitch through both fabric layers directly over the two drawn lines (fig. 5). The section above the stitching should be 1½ inches shorter than the finished length (not including the welting).

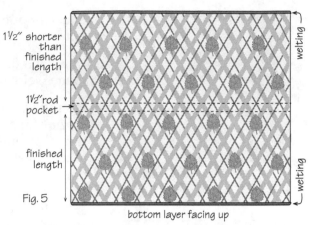

1½" shorter than finished length

1½" rod pocket

finished length

welting

welting

Fig. 5

bottom layer facing up

Installing and Dressing

1. Insert the rod into the rod pocket. Arrange the valance evenly across the rod. Make sure the top edge of the stitched rod pocket is at the top edge of the back of the rod (fig. 6). This will insure that the front layer is 1½ inches shorter than the back layer.

2. Refer to the photograph and arrange the fabric into even waves across the bottom edge.

Rooms with a View

We think this window treatment would look great in a bedroom, bathroom, child's room, nursery, kitchen, or informal dining nook.

Fig. 6

22 *Flutterby*

LIKE A BEAUTIFUL
BUTTERFLY, THIS
VALANCE FLITS AND
FLUTTERS AT THE TOP
OF YOUR WINDOWS.
COLOR PHOTOGRAPH
IS ON PAGE **124.**

This flirty style will have you smiling the moment you finish it. You may recognize the trapezoid shape from high-school geometry class. Remember asking yourself, "Why do I have to learn geometry? When will I ever use it?" This is your chance. Geometry is the basis for great shapes in design, and the trapezoid is the perfect shape for creating this wispy valance. Little bows hold the valance in place on inexpensive cup hooks. Welting added to the lower edge accentuates the soft wavy bottom curves. Flirty and fabulous!

·············· *Suggested Window Shapes* ··············

This treatment is suitable for single or double windows, picture windows, bay windows, bow windows, corner windows, casement windows, or sliding glass doors.

······ *Techniques to Know before You Begin* ······

If you need to brush up on your skills in any of these areas, turn to part III.

- Accurate Measuring
- Inserting Cup Hooks into a Wall
- Cutting Fabric
- Fabric Repeats
- Cutting Multiple Fabric Widths
- Usable Fabric Widths

Part I – The Projects

- Stitching Fabric Widths Together
- Matching Repeat Designs
- Turning and Cutting Corners and Points
- Working with Decorative Trims

················· *Materials Needed* ·················

FROM THE FABRIC STORE
- decorator fabric
- decorator fabric for lining
- thread to match decorator fabrics
- ready-to-use welting (5/32 inch or 1/4 inch)*
- paper for patternmaking

RECOMMENDED NOTIONS
These are specific notions needed for this project. Also refer to the list of basic notions on page 180.

- size 90/14 universal machine needle
- point turner
- zipper foot or piping foot

FROM THE HOME IMPROVEMENT CENTER
These are specific supplies needed for this project. Also refer to the basic list of tools and supplies on page 180.

- cup hooks—one for each tie (make sure the hook portion clears the top edge of the window frame)

Suggested Fabrics: Choose medium-weight fabrics, such as duck, jacquard, sateen, linen or linen-like fabrics, denim, ticking, or broadcloth.

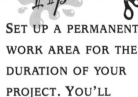

· *Tip* · ···

SET UP A PERMANENT WORK AREA FOR THE DURATION OF YOUR PROJECT. YOU'LL LOSE TIME AND MOMENTUM IF YOU HAVE TO BREAK DOWN YOUR WORK AREA AFTER YOU FINISH EACH DAY. TIME IS MONEY!

MORE $PLASH THAN ¢ASH

Fabric Calculations

1. Install the cup hooks approximately 2 to 4 inches above the top edge of the window frame with the first and last hooks 2 to 4 inches out from each side of the window. To determine the exact placement of additional cup hooks, measure the distance between the two outside cup hooks

* Purchase ready-made welting or make your own. To make your own, purchase filler cord plus 1/2 yard of a contrasting decorator fabric to make bias strips for covering the cord.

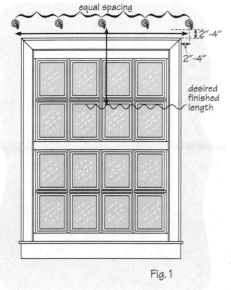

equal spacing

2"-4"

2"-4"

desired
finished
length

Fig. 1

(fig. 1). Divide this measurement by an odd number (3, 5, 7, and so on) until the space between the hooks falls between 8 and 15 inches. Mark this spacing, and install a cup hook at each marked point.

2. Multiply the distance between the two outside cup hooks by 2 for the necessary fullness and add 1 inch for seam allowances. Write the number here: _____. This is the top measurement of the trapezoid shape you will be creating. Add 20 inches for the "tails." Write the number here: _____. This is the bottom measurement of the trapezoid and the cut width of the fabric.

3. The amount of welting required is equal to the bottom cut width of the fabric plus $1/8$ yard for ease. Write the number here: _____.

4. To determine the finished length of the valance, measure from the center cup hook to the desired finished length (fig. 1). The recommended length is 14 to 16 inches. Add 1 inch for seam allowances. Write the measurement here: _____. This is the cut length. Note: The shorter the valance, the "flirtier" the look.

5. To determine the number of fabric widths required to achieve the cut width, divide the cut width by the usable width of the fabric. Round up to the next whole number. Write the number here: _____.

6. To calculate the total yardage of the decorator fabric, multiply the cut length measurement by the number of widths needed. Write the number here: _____. If you need more than one fabric width and the fabric you have selected has a repeat design, multiply the repeat distance by the number of widths and add this figure to the total. The extra fabric will allow you to match the designs.

7. To determine the yardage needed, divide this number by 36 and round up to the nearest $1/4$ yard to get the total yardage. Write the number here: _____. This is the amount of decorator and lining fabrics needed to construct this window treatment.

Creating the Pattern

1. Make a paper pattern of the trapezoid shape. Use a rectangular piece of paper that is at least 1 inch larger all around than the cut width and length measurements of the valance. To determine the exact center of the paper, fold the paper in half crosswise and align the short ends. Refer to step 2 in Fabric Calculations for the measurement of the top edge of the trapezoid. Measure from the fold and mark a point equal to half this amount. Use a carpenter's square to draw a line perpendicular to the fold, extending from the fold to the mark, 1/2 inch down from the top edge (fig. 2).

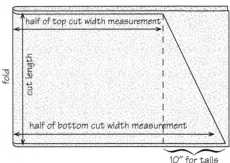

Fig. 2

2. Beginning at the top line, measure down the folded edge a distance equal to the cut length (step 4 of Fabric Calculations). Mark.

3. Starting at this new mark, use a carpenter's square to draw a perpendicular line equal to half of the bottom cut width measurement (step 2 of Fabric Calculations).This line should be parallel to the first line drawn.

4. Draw a diagonal line connecting the ends of the top and bottom lines to complete the trapezoid shape (fig. 2).

5. Cut on the lines through both layers of the paper to create the trapezoid pattern.

Cutting Instructions

1. Lay the fabric flat on a large work surface. Use a carpenter's square to cut a straight edge at one end of the fabric.

2. Cut the fabric to the cut length measurement. If you need more than one width to achieve the cut width of your valance, cut additional fabric to the same length, matching motifs. Sew the fabric widths together, making sure the design motifs match at the joined seam. Trim equal amounts of fabric from both side edges to obtain the cut width. Repeat with the lining fabric.

3. Unfold the paper pattern. Center the pattern on the fabric and pin it in place. Cut one shape from the decorator fabric and one shape from the lining fabric.

4. Determine and mark the placement of the ties along the top edge of the valance. The first and last sets of ties should be ¹/2 inch from the side edges with a third set in the exact center. Divide the remaining area into the same number of spaces determined for cup hook placement. Note: The space between the ties is larger than the space between the cup hooks.

5. Prepare the fabric tie sets. For each set of ties cut two strips, each 1¹/4 by 20 inches. Fold one short end of each strip under ¹/2 inch toward the wrong side. Then fold both long sides ¹/2 inch toward the wrong side. Then fold the entire tie in half lengthwise with the wrong sides together, matching all folded edges. Stitch each tie through all layers along the folded edges (fig. 3). Set aside.

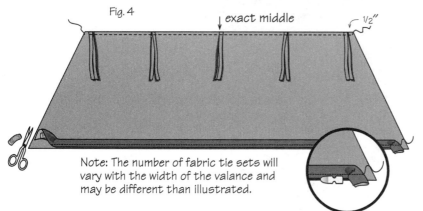

Fig. 3

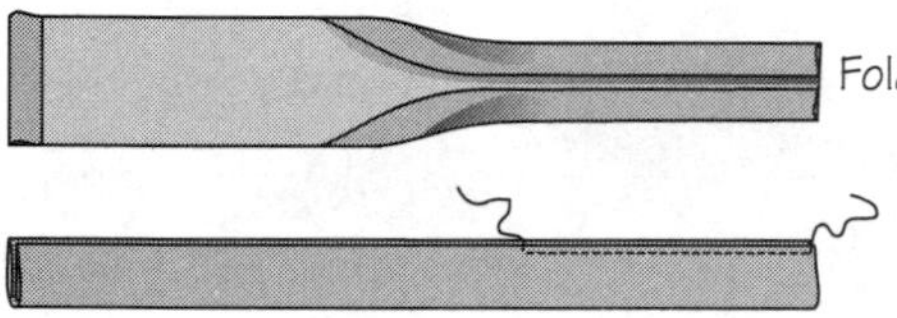

Fold over ¹/2".

Construction

Use a ¹/2-inch seam allowance unless otherwise instructed.

1. Pin the welting to the right side of the decorator fabric along the bottom cut edge. To begin, extend the welting ¹/2 inch beyond the edge of the fabric. Open the casing and snip out 1 inch of filler cord. Manipulate the welting, curving it slightly, so the filler cord stops at the seam line with the casing fabric flattened into the seam allowance of the bottom seam. Stitch the welting to the fabric using a zipper foot or piping foot (fig. 4).

Fig. 4

exact middle

¹/2"

Note: The number of fabric tie sets will vary with the width of the valance and may be different than illustrated.

2. Pin two ties to each marked point (one on top of the other) along the top edge with the first and last sets ¹/2 inch in from the side edges. Position the ties with the cut ends touching the top edge of the fabric and the finished ends pointing toward the bottom edge (fig. 4). Baste in place.

3. Pin the lining and decorator fabrics right sides together. Stitch around the entire shape, leaving a 6-inch opening along the top edge for turning (fig. 5).

4. To eliminate bulk, clip the corners diagonally. Next, taper the seam allowances away from the corner (fig. 5).

5. Turn the valance right side out. For sharp corners, use a point turner to gently push the fabric out from the inside. Press the seam so neither fabric is visible from the opposite side.

6. Handstitch the opening closed.

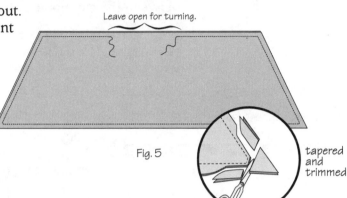

Leave open for turning.

Fig. 5

tapered and trimmed

Installing and Dressing

Tie the ties into a bow at each cup hook. Refer to the photograph and arrange the fabric into pleasing folds.

Rooms with a View

We think this window treatment would look great in a bedroom, bathroom, child's room, nursery, kitchen, or informal dining nook.

23 Pointed in the Right Direction

ANY COMBINATION OF FABRICS WORKS FOR THIS VALANCE, INCLUDING A TRENDY COMBINATION OF DENIM AND A COLORFUL HAWAIIAN PRINT AS SHOWN IN THE COLOR PHOTOGRAPH ON PAGE 124.

We wanted to create a design that could be used almost anywhere. A simple treatment with lots of possibilities is a big order to fill, but this design fits the bill. Almost any decorator fabric will work, as well as lots of nontraditional fabrics. Pick a festive print for a child's room and use a different color for each tab to replicate flags celebrating a special event. Create tabs with one or two layers and contrast or match the buttons with the valance fabric. Use the valance alone or place it over an existing treatment to point your decorating in a brand new direction.

Suggested Window Shapes

This treatment is suitable for single or double windows, casement windows, ranch windows, window walls, or sliding glass doors.

Techniques to Know before You Begin

If you need to brush up on your skills in any of these areas, turn to part III.

• Accurate Measuring
• Enlarging Patterns from Gridded Designs
• Installing Rods, Brackets, and Holdbacks
• Usable Fabric Widths

- Cutting Fabric
- Turning and Cutting Corners and Points
- Covering Buttons
- Sewing on Buttons

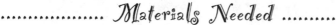 *Materials Needed*

FROM THE FABRIC STORE

- decorator fabric for valance
- lining fabric for valance
- contrasting decorator fabrics for tabs (two different fabrics, one for each layer)*
- medium-weight iron-on interfacing for tabs
- matching thread
- heavy thread such as carpet thread or waxed button thread
- 4- to 6-inch-long doll needle to attach buttons
- 1 1/8-inch-diameter (size 45) half-ball cover buttons, one for each tab
- clear backing buttons, one for each tab
- pattern paper with preprinted 1-inch grid
- optional: contrasting thread for topstitching

RECOMMENDED NOTIONS

This is a specific notion needed for this project. Also refer to the list of basic notions on page 180.

- point turner

FROM THE HOME IMPROVEMENT CENTER

These are specific supplies needed for this project. Also refer to the basic list of tools and supplies on page 180.

- decorator rod with brackets and finials**
- 3 feet of bell wire (Ask for it by name; it's the wire used in doorbells.)
- wire snips or old scissors to cut wire
- fishing line

Tip

COPPER PIPING MAKES AN INEXPENSIVE CURTAIN ROD. IT'S AVAILABLE AT YOUR LOCAL HARDWARE STORE AND CAN BE CUT TO THE EXACT LENGTH YOU NEED.

MORE $PLASH THAN ¢ASH

---

* Whereas heavier-weight fabrics (such as duck and denim) present a desirable finished appearance, they may offer more sewing challenges than lighter-weight fabrics when creating sharp points.

**If you are planning to mount this valance over an existing treatment, pay close attention to the distance the rod bracket extends from the wall. The decorative rod for this valance must clear the existing one so it does not obstruct the working mechanism of the existing curtains. However, plan the width so it is as close as possible to the sides of the existing treatment.

Suggested Fabric: Choose medium-weight fabrics, such as denim, cotton ticking, duck, sateen, chintz, or twill. For windows that measure wider than the usable width of the fabric, plan to railroad the fabric so that no seams are required to obtain the finished width. To do this, choose a fabric with a nondirectional design that looks as good sideways as it does up and down. Study the fabric closely to make sure that the design does not have a specific direction. (You don't want stemmed flowers to appear to be lying on their sides.)

• •

Fabric Calculations

1. Mount the rod brackets 3 to 4 inches above and 2 to 4 inches out from the sides of the window frame. If you are mounting the valance over an existing treatment, mount the brackets 3 to 4 inches above and 1 to 2 inches out from the existing brackets. Make sure that the rod for the valance clears the existing rod by at least 2 inches.

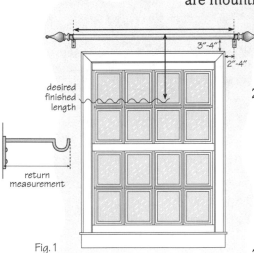
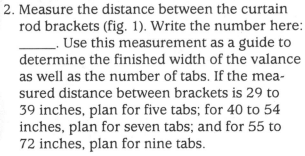

desired finished length

return measurement

3"-4"

2"-4"

Fig. 1

2. Measure the distance between the curtain rod brackets (fig. 1). Write the number here: _____. Use this measurement as a guide to determine the finished width of the valance as well as the number of tabs. If the measured distance between brackets is 29 to 39 inches, plan for five tabs; for 40 to 54 inches, plan for seven tabs; and for 55 to 72 inches, plan for nine tabs.

3. Measure the distance from the front of the rod to the wall for the return (fig. 1). Multiply this measurement by 2 for two returns. Write the number here: _____.

4. Sketch your window treatment on a piece of paper to determine the tab placement. To the measured distance between the rod brackets, add 1 inch for ease. Add the doubled return measurement to this number to determine the finished width of the valance. Write the number here: _____.

5. To determine the cut width of the decorator and lining fabrics, add 1 inch for seam allowances to this number. Write the number here: _____.

6. Measure the distance from the top of the rod to the desired finished length (fig. 1). We suggest a length of about one-third of the distance from the top of the rod to the sill. Subtract $3^{1}/_{2}$ inches to allow for the tabs. This is the finished length of the valance. Write the number here: _____. Add 2 inches for seam allowances to determine the cut length of the deco-rator fabric. The cut length of the lining is equal to the finished length of the valance. Write the num-bers here: decorator fabric _____, lining fabric _____.

7. To determine the amount of lining and decorator fabric needed for the valance, compare the cut width to the usable width of the fabric. If the usable width is equal to or wider than the cut width, purchase only the cut length of the valance. If the usable width is less than the cut width, plan to railroad your fabric. For railroaded fabric, divide the cut width by 36 and round up to the nearest $1/4$ yard. Write the number here: _____.

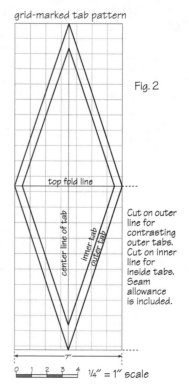

grid-marked tab pattern

Fig. 2

top fold line

center line of tab

inner tab

outer tab

Cut on outer line for contrasting outer tabs. Cut on inner line for inside tabs. Seam allowance is included.

7"

0 1 2 3 4 $1/4'' = 1''$ scale

8. For the smaller top tabs, you will need $7/8$ yard of 45- to 54-inch-wide fabric for nine tabs. For the larger under tabs, you will need 1 yard of 45- to 54-inch wide fabric for nine tabs.

9. Purchase enough iron-on interfacing to cover one side of each tab for each layer. Take the tab pattern to the store for the most accurate measurement.

10. You will need one covered button and one backing button for every tab.

Making the Pattern for the Tabs

1. Using the grid-marked pattern paper, transfer the tab pattern (fig. 2). This pattern will be used for both layers of the tab. The cut measurement of the larger under tab is $21^{1}/_{4}$ inches by 7 inches, and the smaller top tab mea-sures 18 inches by 6 inches. A $1/2$-inch seam allowance is included in each measurement.

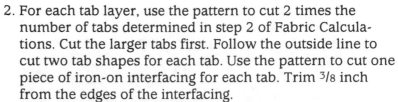

2. For each tab layer, use the pattern to cut 2 times the number of tabs determined in step 2 of Fabric Calculations. Cut the larger tabs first. Follow the outside line to cut two tab shapes for each tab. Use the pattern to cut one piece of iron-on interfacing for each tab. Trim 3/8 inch from the edges of the interfacing.

3. Next, cut the smaller tabs following the inside line. Cut two tab shapes for each tab. Use the pattern to cut one piece of iron-on interfacing for each tab. Trim 3/8 inch from the cut edges.

Construction

Use a 1/2-inch seam allowance unless otherwise instructed.

VALANCE

1. Lay the fabric flat on a large work surface. Use a carpenter's square to mark and cut a straight edge at one end of both the decorator and lining fabrics.

2. Cut the decorator fabric to the cut width and length determined in Fabric Calculations. For fabric that is railroaded, the cut width should be measured along the lengthwise grain of the fabric.

MORE $PLASH THAN ¢ASH · Tip

INSTEAD OF USING TRADITIONAL DRAPERY HARDWARE, MAKE YOUR OWN CURTAIN RODS FROM TWIGS, BOAT OARS, FISHING POLES, TENNIS RACKETS, HOCKEY STICKS, RAKES, OR FIREPLACE TOOLS.

Fig. 3

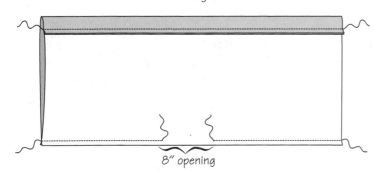

8" opening

3. Pin the decorator and lining fabrics right sides together along the top edges. Stitch. Gently pull the lining to meet the bottom edge. Pin this seam together and stitch, leaving an 8-inch opening for turning (fig. 3).

4. Attaching bell wire to the valance will allow you to bend the valance fabric at the corners to form a rigid return. Cut the bell wire into four equal pieces. Make a small, closed loop at each end of the wire to keep the wire from poking through the fabric. Lay the wire in the seam allowance close to the stitching line of the top and bottom edges of the valance so it ends 1/8 inch short of the side seam allowances. Set

the machine to a wide zigzag stitch with a medium length and stitch carefully over the wire. As the stitch swings left, it should just touch the stitching line but not go over it (fig. 4). Press the seam allowance toward the lining.

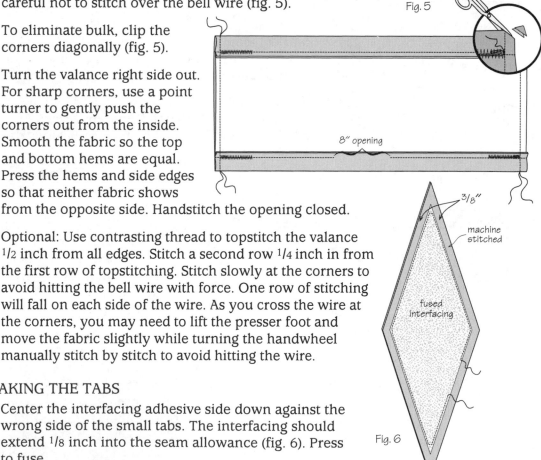

Fig. 4

bell wire

8" opening

Fig. 5

8" opening

5. Place the valance lining side up on a large surface. Arrange the valance so the decorator fabric "wraps" around to the lining side equally on the top and bottom edges. Pin the layers together at the sides. Stitch side seams together, being careful not to stitch over the bell wire (fig. 5).

6. To eliminate bulk, clip the corners diagonally (fig. 5).

7. Turn the valance right side out. For sharp corners, use a point turner to gently push the corners out from the inside. Smooth the fabric so the top and bottom hems are equal. Press the hems and side edges so that neither fabric shows from the opposite side. Handstitch the opening closed.

8. Optional: Use contrasting thread to topstitch the valance 1/2 inch from all edges. Stitch a second row 1/4 inch in from the first row of topstitching. Stitch slowly at the corners to avoid hitting the bell wire with force. One row of stitching will fall on each side of the wire. As you cross the wire at the corners, you may need to lift the presser foot and move the fabric slightly while turning the handwheel manually stitch by stitch to avoid hitting the wire.

3/8"

machine stitched

fused interfacing

Fig. 6

MAKING THE TABS

1. Center the interfacing adhesive side down against the wrong side of the small tabs. The interfacing should extend 1/8 inch into the seam allowance (fig. 6). Press to fuse.

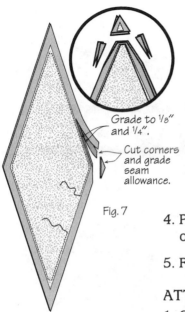

Grade to 1/8"
and 1/4".

Cut corners
and grade
seam
allowance.

Fig. 7

2. Pin one interfaced tab to one lining tab, right sides together. Using a 3/8-inch seam allowance, stitch around all four sides, leaving 5 inches unstitched along one side to turn (fig. 6).

3. Grade the seam allowances of the tabs by trimming the side with no interfacing to 1/8 inch and the side with interfacing to 1/4 inch. Cut off the seam allowance at the points. Then trim the seam allowance diagonally at each point (fig. 7). Turn the tabs right side out. For sharp points, use a point turner to gently push out the point from the inside.

4. Press the tabs so that neither fabric is visible from the opposite side. Handstitch the opening closed on each tab.

5. Repeat steps 1 through 4 for the large tabs.

ATTACHING THE TABS

1. Cover the buttons with scraps of decorator fabric to match or contrast with the valance. Cover one button for each tab. Set aside.

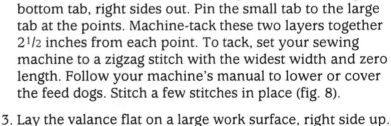

Fig. 8

2½"

2. Fold the tabs so the long points match and the interfaced side faces out. Center one small top tab over one large bottom tab, right sides out. Pin the small tab to the large tab at the points. Machine-tack these two layers together 2½ inches from each point. To tack, set your sewing machine to a zigzag stitch with the widest width and zero length. Follow your machine's manual to lower or cover the feed dogs. Stitch a few stitches in place (fig. 8).

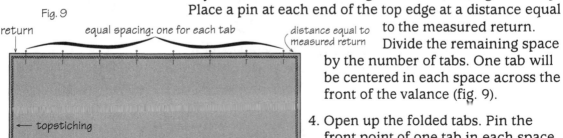

Fig. 9

return

equal spacing: one for each tab

distance equal to
measured return

← topstiching

3. Lay the valance flat on a large work surface, right side up. Place a pin at each end of the top edge at a distance equal to the measured return. Divide the remaining space by the number of tabs. One tab will be centered in each space across the front of the valance (fig. 9).

4. Open up the folded tabs. Pin the front point of one tab in each space so the tip of the large tab is about 5½ inches below the top edge of the

valance. Make sure each tab point is an equal distance from the bottom of the valance. Tack the tab to the valance as in step 2 above (fig. 10).

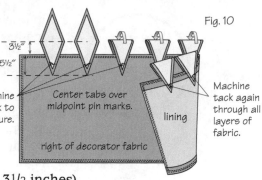

Fig. 10

5. Refold the tabs so the back points fold over to the lining side of the valance. The back points should line up with the front points. However, it is more important that the tabs line up visually from the front side and that the distance to the fold (about 3¹/₂ inches) is equal. Pin. Carefully machine-tack the tab through all layers as above (fig. 10).

6. Use heavy thread and a large needle to stitch a covered button to the stitch-marked point at the front of each tab. Connect the stitch to a backing button at the corresponding point on the back of each tab (fig. 11). Knot the thread between the backing button and the tab. Clip the thread ends.

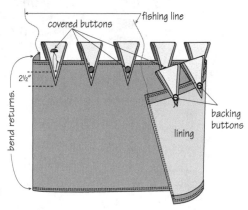

Fig. 11

7. Cut two pieces of fishing line about 12 inches long. Use a large needle to attach one piece to the top edge of each return (fig. 11).

8. Bend each wired corner of the valance toward the wrong side at a 90-degree angle to form the returns (fig. 11).

Installing and Dressing

1. Slide the tabs over the rod. Adjust the returns so they are perpendicular to the wall.

2. Arrange the tabs evenly across the rod so ease is distributed equally between the tabs.

3. Tie the fishing line to the rod brackets to ensure that the returns hang straight with the back edges flush to the wall. Clip off any excess fishing line.

Rooms with a View

We think this valance would look great in a kitchen, den, study, home office, bathroom, family room, child's room, nursery, or bedroom.

Part II: Sketchbook

Gone are the days when windows could only be covered with pleats of fabric or plain roller shades. Today everything from bottles to plants to teapots can adorn the windows of your world.

❋ Scatter rubber stamp designs across a large solid-colored sheet with fabric paint. Place decorative hooks above your window and attach a ribbon or metal eyelet at corresponding points on the sheet and hang from the hooks.

❋ Some scrolled wire garden borders are simply too beautiful for outside use only. Hang the border upside down inside a window from small cup hooks. Add dried flowers or ivy to complete this indoor-outdoor transition.

❋ Turn white or off-white Battenburg lace doilies into colorful appliques with fabric dye. Scatter them across the front of a ready-made curtain panel. Hand tack to secure.

❋ Hang an assortment of men's ties or women's silk scarves from a rod above the window. Tie the ties and scarves as you would around a neck. Visit a thrift store for great bargains on these accessories.

❋ Create an open design on a ready-made curtain by creating geometric shapes using different size grommets and eyelets. For a touch of color, paint them with car touch-up paint before inserting.

❋ Tack matching woven rugs across the top of the window. Roll the rugs to the desired height and secure them with ties of your choosing (similar to On A Roll). The same can be done with a long runner-styled rug. Consider using a quilt rack to hold the rug in place or use a decorative rod with clips.

❂ Tie a ready-made window scarf with a tieback in a loopy bow at the center of a curtain rod. Pull the two halves to the sides of the window and drape them gracefully behind the holdbacks.

❂ Embroider a collection of designs randomly over a ready-made curtain or in a planned fashion across the top, down the leading edge, or around the entire perimeter.

❂ A plain ready-made sheer curtain can be given new life by stamping a large design evenly over the entire surface. Create a checkerboard by alternating the stamped image in two different colors.

❂ Insert a rod through belt loops of denim skirts or cut off jeans and hang as a valance or a café curtain (pin or stitch the waist together first).

❂ Cut different colors of sandpaper into a planned geometric pattern to fit around the outside of the window frame. Use upholstery tacks to attach them to the wall and to add dimension.

❂ Insert cut-off jean legs onto a curtain rod and scrunch them together—the more the better! For some added color, scatter some colorful bandanas across the rod as well.

❂ Attach glass shelves inside a deep window and display a group of objects or a collection of plants, colored glass, teapots, etc.

❂ Incorporate overall buckles into your tab design. Mimic overalls by attaching the buckle to a loose end of a tab and the buttons to the top edge of the curtain.

❂ Sew sheer fabric pockets onto a ready-made curtain and fill with seasonal items such as seashells for the summer, colored leaves for the fall, snowflakes for the winter, and silk flower heads for the spring.

❂ Cut a length of picket fence to fit the top of a window. Mount it (points down) and embellish with dried or silk flowers.

❂ Personalize plain and drab ready-mades with written words, sayings, or poems painted or stenciled directly onto the fabric surface. And, if you are really confident, free-hand your messages with a fabric paint pen.

❂ Embellish tabs (or the entire curtain) with colorful ribbon, lots of buttons, faux jewels, metal studs, costume jewelry, or feathers. Pin, stitch, or glue in place to secure.

❂ Throw beach towels over a curtain rod, creating a short flip-over valance at the top. To secure in place, stitch buttons to the valance to create a rod pocket (similar to Crisscross).

❂ Hand paint designs onto each window pane with water-based or tempera paints. To change these temporary designs, simply scrape off the old design and repaint. Perfect for seasonal decorating!

❂ Train a potted ivy plant to climb up and around a window frame; use clear tacks to help guide the vine.

❂ Fold a square tablecloth over a rod and cinch each end with a coordinating ribbon at each side to create a swagged effect.

❂ Mount a thin wire across the width of the window and suspend glass prisms from the wire. Use small screw eyes to hold the wire in place.

❂ Use printed and solid-colored ready-made sheer curtains on the same rod. Place the printed sheers toward the center of the window with the solid-colored sheers to the outside edges (or vice-versa).

❂ Drape multitudes of threaded beads (Christmas garlands are perfect!) over an existing window treatment for a sparkling topper.

❂ Embellish your windows with elements from nature such as grapevine wreaths, pine cones, straw, willows, seashells, or sprays of wheat.

❂ Paper fans of all sizes (found in party stores or Asian shops around the country and abroad) can be attached to the top edge of the window frame with a few discreet nails.

Sketchbook

Window treatments don't have to be traditional in design, nor does fabric always have to be used. This section is a compilation of quick and easy treatments that are fun to make. For many of these designs, you don't even have to sew a stitch!

The Great Frame-Up

Include favorite photographs in your window décor. Hang small, framed prints of similar size across the top of your window from ribbons or decorative chains. Hang the frames from small nails placed in the top of the window molding. Conceal the nails by twisting wire-edge ribbon (about 2 times the measured width of the window) around the nails as you pass it through the ribbon or chain that suspends the frame.

Treasured Keepsakes

For a whimsical valance that is sure to charm, tie treasured items, such as shells, charms, mini teacups, or beads, to colorful ribbons. Paint the rod a color that coordinates with the ribbons. Tie the ribbons to the rod, leaving 1 to 2 inches between items. Staggering the ribbon lengths will create even more dimension in this treasured window treatment.

Knotted Lattice

The intrigue of lattice is due to not only the simple crisscross design but also the ability to gaze beyond the design. Cut beautiful cord 4 to 5 times the desired finished length and secure it to cup hooks spaced about 6 inches apart. Knot the cords together two at a time with square knots. Alternate the knot position in succeeding rows to create an open-weave design. Stop knotting 4 inches above the desired finished length. Untwist the cord ends and trim evenly.

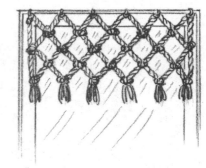

Ring Toss

Decorator scarf rings or towel rings offer a novel and simple way to hang sheer fabric. Use enough fabric or ready-made window scarves (available in 6-yard lengths at linen or department stores) to cover 2 1/2 times the width and length of the window plus about 24 inches to puddle. If using fabric, cut it into two equal lengths and hem each end first with iron-on adhesive. Fold the entire length of fabric accordion-style and temporarily tie it with string. Drape the tied fabric through rings that have been mounted 2 to 4 inches above the window frame or opening. Then untie the string and adjust the fabric into pleasing folds for a stunning treatment that will soften the shape of any window.

Bohemian Delight

For a window treatment that is certain to satisfy any nonconformist urge, tie a printed scarf or sari to a curtain rod with narrow ribbon. For added appeal, string multicolored beads on beading thread or fishing line. Tie one strand to the rod at each side of the scarf for a true bohemian touch!

Wizardry

Invite the stars, sun, and moon to dance across the window with cutout iron-on appliqués. Apply

iron-on adhesive to the cutout shapes. Attach the shapes to felt pennants cut 12 to 15 inches wide by 20 inches long. Fold the top edge of each pennant to the wrong side and use iron-on adhesive along the edge to create a rod pocket. Trim the rod pocket edges so they are not visible from the right side. Star-shaped finials complete the magic. This treatment is designed especially for the little wizards in your house!

Knot Going to Believe It

Swags and tails do not need to be complicated. Use a half hitch knot to secure a length of fabric to the center of a rod.

Flip the fabric ends over the rod on each side to create a swag with tails. You will need a long ready-made window scarf (available in 6-yard lengths in department stores) or a length of sheer fabric measuring 2 times the width and side drop of the window. If you purchase fabric, hem the cut edges first with iron-on adhesive. Fold the entire length of fabric accordion-style and secure it with ribbons or rubber bands in several places. Keep the fabric folded and tied until the knot and swag have been created.

Daisy Delight

You can be a quick-change artist for parties or holiday fun by cutting out felt flowers and tying them to your tab tops. For each tab, cut a 6-inch-diameter flower, a 2- to 2 1/2-inch-diameter contrasting center, and a 1-by-15-inch felt tie. Cut two 1-inch-long slits, 1 inch apart, at the center of the flower and thread the tie through the slits with the ends at the back. Use iron-on adhesive to attach the round center to the front of the flower, concealing the tie.

Waterfall

Difficulty is definitely not the benchmark of a great window treatment. This is one of the quickest and easiest treatments we know. Choose a fabric that is the same on both sides and is solid or has a nondirectional print. The fabric must be as wide or wider than the rod. Purchase 2 times the measured length of the window from the top of the rod to the floor plus about 24 inches to puddle. Trim the cut edges evenly, and hem them with iron-on adhesive. Fold the fabric evenly over the rod so the width of the fabric covers the rod and any returns. Place a piece of double-stick carpet tape on the rod at each side to keep the fabric from slipping. Place one holdback at each side of the window. Pull the front layer of fabric to one side and the back layer to the opposite side and secure them behind the holdbacks. Large tassels or dried flowers make great accents for the pulled-back sides.

Draped to Perfection

Update an existing tab-top curtain by adding some matching bullion fringe to the leading edge (the edge closest to the center of the window). The fringe can be stitched or glued, whatever is your preference. For added emphasis, gather the curtain to one side and secure it with a tieback made from dried flowers and ribbons.

Your Number Is Up

Address numbers from your local home improvement center can be turned into simple hardware for a unique window treatment. Select numbers that have two holes to secure them in place. Attach the numbers directly to the frame of the window using the top hole only. Hem all sides of a piece of fabric

that measures 1 1/2 times the width of the window. Insert grommets (one for each number) into the upper edge of the fabric. Insert a 12-inch length of 1/8-inch-wide ribbon into the bottom hole of each number and then through one grommet. Tie the ribbon into bows.

Trés Chic

Some windows are just too pretty to cover up. To add some softness without disturbing the architectural beauty, insert a large cup hook in the center of the arch and two others evenly placed at the sides of the window. Determine the center of a length of fabric or a prehemmed window scarf (available in 6-yard lengths at department stores) and attach it to the highest hook. Then drape the ends to the sides and secure them in place with cord. Add some dried or silk flowers for the perfect finishing touch.

Three's Company

Three (or more) large scarves or squares of fabric (at least 28 inches) are used to create this whimsical valance. Mount a decorative rod or cup hooks. Fold the squares in half diagonally and tie them together with knots and then knot them to the rods or hooks. Trim the front edges with some wonderful fringe and you have a spectacular window treatment.

Someone's in the Kitchen

The great array of decorative kitchen towels and matching potholders are hard to resist. Buy enough dishtowels so that the total width is equal to at least 1 1/2 times the length of the rod. Handstitch some colorful ribbons to the corners of the towels and tie them to the rod. For the valance, mix and match square potholders with mitts, and throw in a utensil or two for additional personality!

Victorian Splendor

Have you ever noticed a Victorian house with lots and lots of gingerbread trim on the front porch? This trim is readily available in home centers and is an interesting way to add some texture and interest to inside windows. Place corner pieces on the inside of the window frame and secure them in place with nails or screws.

Cutting the Apron Strings

Vintage aprons are all the rage. You may be able to find a treasured apron in your grandmother's attic, or search for them at flea markets and yard sales. Cut the apron ties from each side and use them to create tabs that are evenly spaced along the waistband. The tabs need to be long enough to allow the rod to slide through them. Hand-tack or machine-stitch them in place.

Babes in Toyland

Decorating a nursery is always a fun project to undertake. For a unique and inexpensive window treatment, make a valance from assorted wooden baby blocks and large colorful beads. Drill a small hole through the blocks. Then thread the blocks and beads onto a thin wire or monofilament (fishing line), alternating the blocks with several beads. Leave some wire or fishing line at the top for hanging. You can hang the block valance from kitchen knobs or wrap the wire around a decorative rod. (For safety's sake, make sure the valance is well out of the reach of your children.)

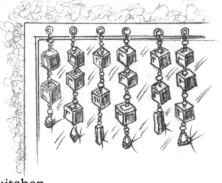

Runners Up

Yes, you guessed it. This window treatment is created from premade table runners. Use as many as you need to fill the width of your window. Just cut them in half, fold over the cut edge to make a rod pocket large enough for your rod to slide through, and stitch it in place (either by hand or machine). Add buttons along the top edge and a little fringe to the diagonal edges for a stunning alternative to a traditional window treatment.

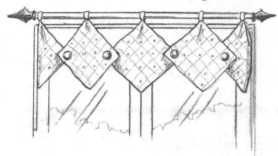

Point Well Taken

Gather a selection of same-size napkins for this window treatment. Arrange the napkins "on point" and overlap them at the side corners. Secure all the layers together with buttons that are handstitched in place. At each top point, stitch a ribbon loop that is large enough to slide your rod through. No one will ever know these are napkins!

Wooden It Be Nice?

Use wooden letters from craft stores to create a word for the room you are decorating. Spell out "Dance" for your little ballerina or "Paris" if that's your favorite city. Attach the letters directly to the frame of the window with screws. Select the thickest possible letters and screw a cup hook at the same place on the back of each letter or directly into the window frame. Gather and tie fabric to these hooks with a length of ribbon or cording.

Double Vision

This creative window treatment is truly no-sew. All you need are two pairs of matching or coordinating rod pocket curtains, an inexpensive double rod (available at department stores), and a pair of holdbacks. Place one pair of curtains on each rod and place the rods in the brackets. Mount the holdbacks to the wall at each side. Drape only the top pair of curtains over the two holdbacks.

Down by the Sea

She sells seashells down by the seashore. Put the seashells you brought home from your summer vacation to good use. Attach them to the hemline of a ready-made window treatment. Stitch or glue them in place. If you plan to stitch the shells in place, you will need to drill a hole into the top of each shell. Use a special drill bit designed to drill tile and pottery. Regular drill bits will heat the shells too much and will cause them to disintegrate.

Zig and Zag

Jazz up a ready-made curtain with fused designs. You can use a zigzag as shown, but any geometric shape works well. To create the zigzag, first fuse a fabric border in a bright color to the front of the curtain. Then apply the adhesive to another bright-colored fabric and cut your shape. Center the shape within the border and fuse it in place. It's as simple as can be, but what an impact!

Fit to Be Tied

Laced cord makes this treatment ideal for nautical themes or casual summer décor. It is a very simple design and is actually a combination of Au Provence and Flutterby. Refer to the Au Provence instructions (see page 91) to draft the pattern, but add only a top band. The fullness is different as well—the top edge of the trapezoid is actually $1 1/2$ times the width of the window. Select two fabrics and add cord-edge between the band and the main body of the valance. Then add grommets to the top edge and attach the valance to the rod by looping cording through the grommets and over the rod.

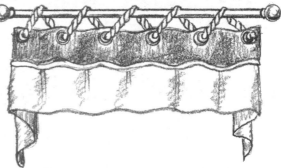

Clothesline

Do you hate the thought of discarding those cute clothes that your child has outgrown? Give them a new life as a fun and inexpensive valance. Use a decorative rod and slide it through the sleeves of your child's favorite sweaters, dresses, or overalls. Try to use sets of clothes in coordinating colors. This is also a great idea for old sports jerseys for the ultimate in recycling.

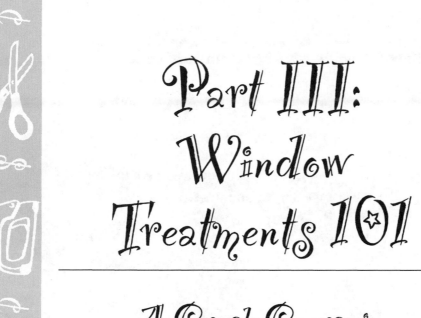

Part III: Window Treatments 101

A Crash Course in Sewing without Pulling Your Hair Out

Since we promised you that you don't have to know how to sew to create beautiful window treatments, we have compiled lots of information we want to share with you to insure your success.

Tool Time

We have assumed that you have these basic tools and notions handy. We have listed anything else you need with each project.

Notions

Fabric marker

Handsewing needles

Loop turner

Machine needles in various sizes for different types of fabric

Point turner

Press cloth

Seam gauge

Seam ripper

Straight pins (extra long) with large heads (normally used for quilting)

Tape measure

Tweezers (sewing tweezers are best)

Yardstick (see-through ones are great)

Tools

Awl

Carpenter's square

Drill and assorted drill bits

Hammer

Hand steamer

Iron

Large, flat ironing surface

Level

Retractable metal measuring tape

Scissors (embroidery)

Screwdrivers (Phillips head and flat head)

Sewing machine with zigzag stitch capabilities

Shears (large bent handle)

Staple gun

Straightedge (ruler or yardstick)

Supplies

Masking tape

Wall anchors, assorted types

1 – Planning for Success

Planning Your Window Treatment

When selecting a window treatment style and fabric for a room, ask yourself some questions. Your answers will give you the direction you need to choose what will work best. Do you need to have an easy-care treatment? Do you need to prevent bright sunlight from streaming into the room? Do you need to make the room feel more cozy? Do you live on a noisy street and need the window treatment to act as a noise buffer? Do you need the window treatment to provide privacy? Do you need to hide an unattractive view without blocking the daylight? Do you have a specific decorating style in mind?

With the above questions answered, you are ready to begin.

☀ Selecting fabric is the most exciting part of planning your window treatment. We suggest that you go to the fabric store with an open mind. Wander leisurely though the aisles. When you spot a fabric that you instantly fall in love with, pay attention. This might be the one to purchase. If you absolutely love the fabric today, you will most likely love it five years from now.

☀ Some fabric stores have a policy that allows you to "check out" an entire bolt of fabric to see how it looks in your home. If your store does, hang or drape the fabric over your curtain rod and live with your choice for at least 24 hours. Look at the fabric in the morning, afternoon, and evening. Decide if you like it with the different sun exposures and with your furniture and other décor. If checking out an entire bolt is not possible, purchase at least 1 yard. This small investment may save you money in the long run; you may change your mind about the fabric once you get it home. Also, by buying a small amount of fabric, you can do a test run to see how the fabric sews, presses, and drapes.

☀ Don't skimp on fullness. An expensive fabric will lose its impact if the treatment is not full enough. On the other hand, an inexpensive fabric will look rich if the fullness is abundant and if the window treatment is lined.

☀ It is perfectly acceptable (if necessary) to use different window treatments in the same room as long as they are compatible in style and fabric.

☀ Headings and hems should not be visible from outside the window if at all possible. When deciding on hardware placement, make sure the rod is far enough above the window opening to hide the heading and that the hems of curtains (not including valances, of course) fall below the window sill.

☀ To help you determine the perfect finished length of a valance, make a paper pattern to the length you think you want and tape it to the mounted hardware. Stand back and examine the proportion and length. Trust your eye when doing this. If your eye tells you that the valance should be a smidgen shorter or longer, make appropriate adjustments and then rehang the pattern. Do not proceed further until you like what you see.

☀ To aid in choosing a length for your valance, consider the ratio used by decorating workrooms as the suggested finished length for most valances—$1/5$ or $1/6$ of the measurement from the top of the rod to the floor.

☀ Do as the professionals do when planning the finished lengths of longer window treatments. These lengths are considered acceptable according to workroom standards:

- Floor length: Curtains should be $1/2$ inch above the floor so they do not drag.

- Sill length: The bottom edge of the curtain should "kiss" the top of the window sill. This length is usually for inside-mounted window treatments.

- Apron length: The bottom edge of the curtain should be 2 to 3 inches longer than the bottom edge of the apron (the flat piece of wooden trim that is placed below the window sill).

- Puddling: In this novelty length, the curtains should extend at least a foot (or more) past the floor; the excess fabric is bunched together in a pile on the floor (hence, it "puddles").

- Baseboard heaters: The hemline should fall above baseboard heaters to prevent the fabric from coming in direct contact with a heat source and possibly ignite. The fiber content of most fabrics is very combustible. For safety purposes, choose a treatment that looks good in a shorter length.

Fabric Considerations

A window treatment will most likely be a part of your life for many years. Therefore, you will want to be happy living with your fabric selection. The fabric you select can also contribute to the ease with which the project is completed. The following tips will aid you in choosing and handling decorator fabrics.

☀ Consider a window treatment as a transition between indoors and outdoors. The fabric you select should harmonize not only with the room you are decorating but also with the view from the window.

☀ Select the best quality fabric you can afford; the finished project will last longer and look better. To stretch your budget, consider using "seconds," a term that implies "second quality." Sometimes, however, fabric is classified as a second simply because the color is slightly different from the manufacturer's standard. A knowledgeable salesperson can tell you why a second is classified as such.

☀ Use a fabric that is specially manufactured for home furnishings. The printed or woven design of such fabrics is planned so that the motifs along the selvage edge will match when fabric widths are stitched together. Matching motifs is very important when making window treatments for a much more pleasing and professional visual appearance. Fabrics used for crafts, quilts, and dressmaking do not have this feature.

☀ Before cutting the fabric, check the entire yardage for flaws. If you find a flaw (such as a pulled thread) and you can't cut around it, try to incorporate it into the hem. If there is no way of working around it, return the fabric to where you purchased it to see if the store will replace it.

❋ Buy all the fabric you need for your project at the same time. Fabric is dyed in lots, and dye lots can vary in color significantly. If you run short of fabric, you may be able to find more but not necessarily of the same dye lot.

❋ Look for decorator fabrics grouped together in a separate department in a fabric store. These fabrics are specifically designed for home décor projects and are usually 54 inches wide. Many special finishes are applied to the fabrics to resist wrinkles, mildew, soiling, fading, and overall deterioration, to name a few. These finishes make these fabrics more expensive but are very beneficial characteristics when making home décor projects. Fabrics typically used for crafts, quilts, and dressmaking do not have these finishes.

❋ If you know the window treatment will get unusually dirty, as in a kitchen or in a room with a wood stove, select a fabric that's machine washable. In this case, you may not want to choose a decorator fabric as most of these are dry-clean only.

❋ If you plan to clean a window treatment on a regular basis, consider preshrinking the fabric before beginning your project. To preshrink the fabric, use the same method you will use to clean your project when it's finished. For example, if you plan to launder the curtains, then launder the fabric. If you plan to dry-clean your curtains (as we recommend), then have a dry cleaner preshrink the fabric. Also preshrink the lining fabric. However, keep in mind that any cleaning process, including preshrinking, can remove some protective fabric finishes. See Care and Cleaning of Window Treatments for more information.

❋ Choose a thread color that is slightly darker than the predominant color in the fabric (it sews in lighter). Remember, you may need more than a single spool of thread for a large project.

❁ If you are selecting a sheer fabric, be conscious that the color of the fabric will appear more intense on the roll or bolt. Unwrap the fabric and hold it up to the light to get a better idea of how the color will actually appear.

Care and Cleaning of Window Treatments

It's understandable that you would like to be able to just throw your curtains in your washer and dryer for easy cleaning. It will seemingly save you so much money on dry cleaning. But think about it a minute. After you have invested your time and effort into creating the perfect window treatment, do you really want to throw it into the washing machine? All of your hard work may literally go down the drain. Manufacturers of home decorating fabrics recommend dry cleaning to maintain the fabric finish, as do most trim manufacturers. For these reasons, we recommend dry cleaning. However, if you insist on using your washing machine, always test the fabric by washing a sample before sewing. Choose care-compatible lining and decorative trims. Here are some steps you can take to keep your window treatment clean and fresh looking so that you do not have to dry-clean it often.

❁ Always work with clean hands during the construction process.

❁ Regularly vacuum your window treatments to remove dust and pollen. Pay particular attention to pleats and gathers, where dust collects.

❁ Hang your window treatments outside on a dry breezy day to help keep the fabrics clean and fresh. Alternatively, place a curtain panel and a damp—not wet—cloth into the dryer. Turn the dryer on "air fluff" (with no heat) and tumble for about 15 minutes. The tumbling action shakes the dirt and dust free, and the cloth absorbs these impurities.

❁ If the window treatments in the same room are the same size, rotate them periodically from window to window. Because different windows get different sun exposures, this prevents one treatment from wearing out or fading before another.

❀ If you take your curtains to the dry cleaner, be aware that some of the protective fabric finishes may be removed even during this recommended cleaning process. This may result in the fabrics being less crisp and losing some protection against stains or sun. Check with friends or a local decorator for recommendations for dry cleaners. Keep a record of the finished size of the treatment and its fabric finishes, fiber content, and manufacturer's care instructions, and provide your dry cleaner with this information. Some dry cleaners will measure the curtains themselves before the cleaning process begins and have additional procedures to avoid excessive shrinkage.

❀ For the care of decorative trims, refer to Choosing Trims, page 213, and Caring for Your Trims, page 216.

2 – The Basics

Working Efficiently

Before diving into a project, spend some time planning your work area (even if it is only temporary). An efficient work area will make creating window treatments a more pleasurable experience. Try to incorporate as many of these suggestions as possible.

❀ Set up a permanent work area for the duration of your project. Time and momentum are lost when you have to break down your work area after you finish each day.

❀ Work on as large a surface as possible. If you're using the dining room table, extend the table to its maximum size. Large, inexpensive cardboard cutting surfaces (40 inches by 72 inches) are available in fabric stores and make great temporary work surfaces. Of course, if all else fails, move the furniture and use the floor!

❀ Make sure you have a good light source in your work area.

❀ Wind several bobbins before you start a project; you will always have a spare at your fingertips.

☀ Keep all of your tools orderly and within reach.

☀ When sewing large volumes of fabric, keep the weight of the fabric from pulling on the needle by positioning a chair behind the sewing table to catch the fabric as you sew. Also have a chair beside you to hold the fabric before it goes into the machine.

☀ Needles become dull through use, so start each project with a new sewing machine needle. Select a needle that is compatible with the weight of your fabric. (The needle package will provide you with this information.) Needles break, so always have extras on hand.

☀ The amount of fabric required to make some window treatments can be cumbersome. If a traditional ironing board is too small to accommodate the amount of fabric you're using, create your own surface. Rest a door or a sheet of plywood on two sawhorses. Cut a piece of muslin that's a foot or so larger on all sides than the surface. Place several wool or cotton blankets (no polyester) on the surface and cover them with the muslin. Pull the muslin taut, and secure the edges of it to the underside of the door or plywood with staples. Voilà! You have a large ironing surface that is perfect for large projects such as window treatments!

☀ Avoid eating and drinking in your work area. Spills and stains can be the downfall of any sewing project.

☀ Tidy up at the end of each workday; it's easier to get going again when everything is in its place.

Pressing Matters

When making professional-looking window treatments, using the correct pressing techniques is just as important as taking accurate measurements.

☀ Give your iron a thorough cleaning before starting your project. Special iron-cleaning creams are available in the notions department of your fabric store.

☀ To prevent scorching and a shiny ironed surface, use a press cloth (available at fabric stores) when ironing. A specially coated soleplate protector will also prevent pressing disasters.

☀ To achieve crisp edges when pressing a curtain that is lined to the edges, first press the seam open and turn the panel right side out. Then arrange the panel so that the lining and decorator fabrics are equally divided at the seam line and neither shows on the opposite side. Press again if necessary.

☀ Press by lifting the iron up and down. Sweeping the iron back and forth may stretch bias edges and seams.

☀ Press on the wrong side of the fabric when possible. If you must press on the right side of the fabric, always use a press cloth.

☀ To prevent seam edges from appearing on the surface of the fabric, place a strip of brown kraft paper between the seam allowance and the fabric before pressing. Remove the paper after the seams are pressed.

☀ Turn off the iron before you leave the room. Many irons today have automatic shutoff devices to prevent fires. But cautionary tales about the dangers of a hot iron are as timely today as they were years ago.

☀ Heat can create a professional finish or it can scorch, discolor, or even melt some fabrics. Cottons require a hot temperature setting, while synthetics require a cool setting. Blends need a setting somewhere in between. If you are unsure about the safest heat setting for your fabric, test a range of temperatures on scraps of fabric before ironing the actual project. When changing iron temperatures, be sure to allow enough time for the iron to reach the desired temperature.

☀ Should you use steam when making window treatments? The answer depends on the fabric. Use a scrap piece of the fabric you are using for your project to test it for the perfect temperature, with and without steam. Check to see if there are press marks or any shrinkage. If the finish is damaged or if water spots are visible, make a temperature adjustment. Determine if you get better results with a dry iron and a moist press cloth or a steam iron and a dry press cloth. If you're using a steam iron, do not overfill it—unwanted splashes on fabric can be disastrous.

Accurate Measuring

The axiom "measure twice, cut once" is aptly applied to making window treatments. Accurate measurements are integral to every step of the process and are well worth the extra time.

❀ Ideally, mount the hardware before taking any measurements.

❀ Whenever possible, hang all treatments in the same room from the same height. If window heights vary a few inches, use the highest window as the standard measurement. Raise the placement of the rods on the lower windows so that the window treatments are uniform in height.

❀ Windows in the same room may all look the same size, but often they are not. Measure each one and record its location.

❀ Floors can be uneven and windows out of plumb, so measure for the finished length of floor-length curtains in several places across the width of the window. Use the shortest measurement as the finished length so the curtain doesn't buckle on the bottom edge. If the floor is carpeted, lay a piece of cardboard over the carpet to get more accurate measurements.

❀ If the distance between side-by-side windows is 12 inches or less, treat the area as one large window.

❀ For accurate measurements, use a stepladder to reach the top of the window. Use a retractable metal tape measure, not a cloth or plastic one (which stretches). Have someone else hold one end of the tape measure in position when you're taking measurements.

❀ Write down all measurements as you determine them so these figures are always close at hand. Check every measurement twice before cutting the fabric!

Enlarging Patterns from Gridded Diagrams

Follow a grid-marked pattern to easily reproduce intricate shapes and designs. A copy machine may be a timesaver for small jobs, but it is not efficient for large designs and may distort shapes. Follow these easy steps when enlarging a pattern from the book.

1. Look for preprinted 1-inch grid paper at fabric stores, art supply stores, and some office supply stores. This saves lots of time! If you can't find this paper, use a large piece of tracing paper (available in office supply stores), and draw a grid of squares that are equal in dimension to the grid size indicated on the small diagrams (usually 1 inch). Carefully copy the pattern, one square at a time, onto the large grid. The result should be a full-size paper pattern.

2. Follow the specific project instructions for adding seam allowances.

3 – Hardware

Hardware for Your Windows

Think of hardware as the bone structure of your window treatment. The correct hardware will aid in the proper fit and overall shape of the finished treatment.

❀ Buy good-quality hardware from a reputable manufacturer. Don't try to save money by buying bargain brands; they usually aren't sturdy enough.

❀ Ideally, mount the hardware at each window before taking measurements for your window treatment. More accurate measurements can be taken if the hardware is in place.

❀ Enlist a partner to help you install drapery hardware. Two sets of eyes are better than one when deciding on placement, and two sets of hands make the installation easier.

❀ If you'll be placing hardware over an existing treatment that will remain in place, allow for necessary clearance between the layers (depth, as well as height and length).

This same guideline applies when installing a soft treatment over existing vertical or horizontal blinds. Remember to allow room to manipulate the blinds. The recommended distance is a 2-inch clearance between the layers.

☼ The curtain rod must be level for the window treatment to hang straight. The only way to determine if the rod is truly straight is to use a carpenter's level.

☼ The most secure place to mount your hardware is into a stud. The structure of houses usually dictates that wooden 2-by-4s surround each window opening. The easiest way to find these studs is to knock firmly on the wall with the heel of your clenched fist. A solid sound means you have located a stud; a hollow sound tells you to keep knocking. Once you've found the studs around the window, mark them at the level you plan to hang the brackets.

☼ If you cannot locate a stud, use wall anchors for additional support for the rod. Window treatments can be awfully heavy, and you do not want the rod to come out of the wall after the curtains are hung.

Installing Rods, Brackets, and Holdbacks

Proper installation of hardware will literally keep your window treatment attached to the wall and enable it to withstand daily use.

1. Hold the brackets where desired on the wall above the window; mark the screw locations by poking a pencil through the screw holes in each bracket.

2. If you cannot secure the screws into studs, use wall anchors for additional support. A spreading anchor consists of a bolt and metal sleeve. Toggle bolts have spring-loaded winglike toggles that expand after they have been pushed through the wall. Plastic wall anchors expand when the screw is inserted.

3. Using the screw-hole marks as a guide, drill holes slightly smaller in diameter than the screws or the wall anchors.

4. If you're using a spreading anchor bolt, tap it into the drilled hole with a hammer. Align the bracket and screw

over the anchor bolt and tighten the screw. The anchor bolt will expand and flatten against the back of the wall (fig. 1).

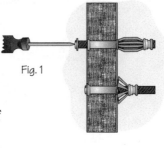

Fig. 1

5. If you're using a toggle bolt, insert it into the drilled hole by squeezing the "wings" so the toggle bolt is flat. Push the toggle bolt into the hole; tap it with a hammer so it is flush with the wall. The wings will spread out against the back of the wall when the screw is in place.

6. If you're using plastic wall anchors, tap the anchor into the hole with a hammer (fig. 2). Place the screw through the hole in the bracket and align it with the wall anchor. Tighten the screw slowly so the wall anchor expands (fig. 3).

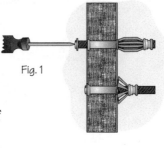

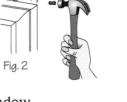

2"- 4"

2"- 4"

Fig. 2

Fig. 3

7. If you're installing a rod over an extra-wide window, additional supports may be needed to help hold the weight of the window treatment; otherwise, it may sag in the center. Additional brackets are usually added at 30-inch intervals across the width of the windows. These can usually be purchased where you purchase the rods.

8. Use these same types of wall anchors to install holdbacks.

Preparing a Mounting Board

A mounting board is not meant to show. To camouflage the board, we recommend covering the board with fabric or painting it to match the wall color.

1. If you choose to cover the board, wrap it as if you are wrapping a package, and staple the fabric to the underside of the board to hold it in place (figs. 4a and 4b).

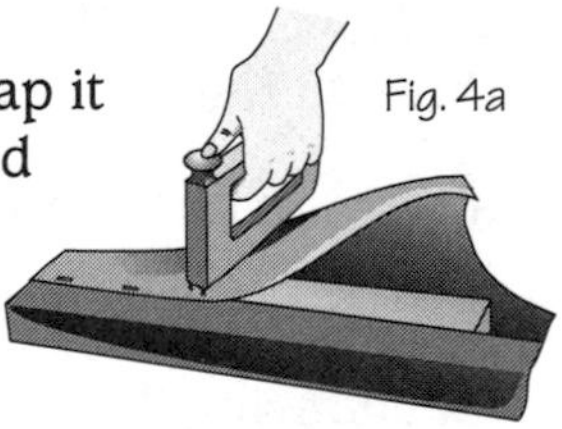

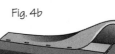

Fig. 4a

Fig. 4b

2. Miter the fabric at the corners. The fabric should be as flat as possible against the board. If necessary, trim away excess fabric.

Installing a Mounting Board

A board-mounted window treatment is very easy to make and install. A 1-by-2, 1-by-3, 1-by-4, 1-by-6, or 1-by-8 piece of wood (available at home centers) is placed above the window like a shelf to which the window treatment is attached with staples. It is mounted to the wall with angle brackets. Wider boards are often used to mount valances over rod-hung treatments. Terminology for board measurements is misleading. The actual measurements of the wood used for a mounting board will differ from its named size. For example, boards referred to as 1-by-2s actually measure about $3/4$ inch by $1\,5/8$ inches. Carpenters call the former measurements "nominal dimensions," or dimensions that are not really what they say they are. Actual measurements will also vary slightly depending on the type of wood and the mill. The following measurements are closer to what you will find when you purchase wood for your mounting board.

NOMINAL MEASUREMENTS	ACTUAL MEASUREMENTS
1-by-2	$3/4$ inch by $1\,5/8$ inches
1-by-3	$3/4$ inch by $2\,1/2$ inches
1-by-4	$3/4$ inch by $3\,1/2$ inches
1-by-6	$3/4$ inch by $5\,1/2$ inches
1-by-8	$3/4$ inch by $7\,1/4$ inches

Follow these tips when installing a mounting board.

Fig. 5

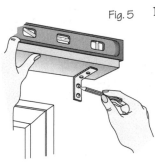

1. Mark the screw placements for the angle brackets on the underside of the board. Drill screw holes into the board; the size of the holes should be slightly smaller than the size of the screws you are using. Screw the brackets to the board. If the mounting board is covered with fabric, make a pilot hole through the fabric and into the board with an awl to prevent the threads of the fabric from twisting around the screw.

2. The most secure place to install a mounting board is into a stud. Usually, wooden 2-by-4s surround a window opening.

Fig. 6

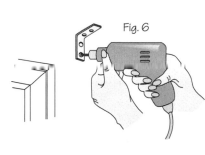

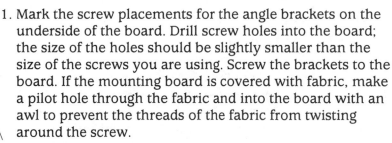

3. Position the board over the window and make sure the board is level. Mark the exact position of the screw holes on the wall (fig. 5).

4. Remove the angle brackets from the board and secure the brackets to the wall (fig. 6). Use the

appropriate wall anchors as described above in Installing Rods, Brackets, and Holdbacks.

5. After attaching the window treatment to the board, place the mounting board over the angle brackets (fig. 7). Hold the board in place and screw the angle brackets to the board.

Inserting Cup Hooks into a Wall

When purchasing cup hooks, select a style that has the longest screw. Use a drill bit that is slightly smaller than the cup hook screw to drill a pilot hole where each cup hook is to be inserted.

Fig. 7

For plaster walls, or for a different look, cut a 1-by-4-inch board 2 to 4 inches longer than the width of the window. Paint the board the desired color. Insert the cup hooks into the wide, flat side of the board instead of directly into the wall. Mount the board to the wall with large screws. To conceal the heads of the screws, recess the screw heads and cover them with wooden plugs (available in craft and hardware stores).

4 – Fabric

Usable Fabric Widths

Fabrics that are manufactured specifically for home décor are usually printed on wider fabrics than used for crafts or apparel. The selvages are included in the fabric width measurement (usually 54 inches, but it can vary). Decorator fabrics are printed so that the design motifs are easily matched at the sides when fabric widths are stitched together. The entire printed area between selvages is considered to be the usable width. On 45-inch-wide fabrics, the design is also printed from selvage to selvage. However, the design motifs do not repeat predictably along the selvage edges. Many times, the same roller that is used to print decorator fabrics is used to print narrower fabrics, and portions of the print are simply left off the sides. Therefore, the designs cannot be matched as easily. If you study the fabric, you may be able to find a motif that matches, but it will often be toward the center of the fabric. This may cause wasted fabric when matching patterns. So when matching printed designs, the usable width of 45-inch-wide fabrics is actually much narrower than the measured width.

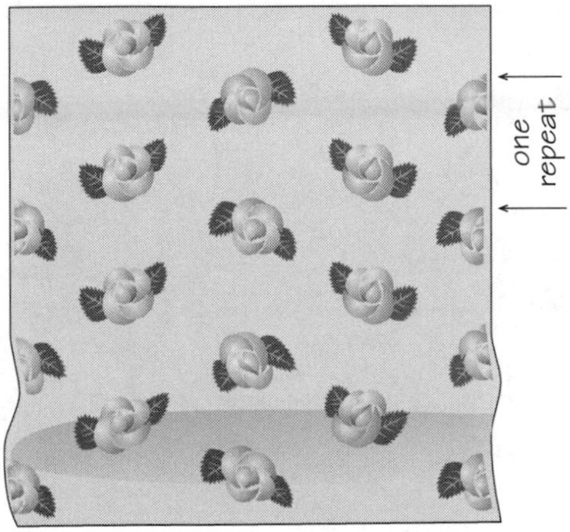

Fabric Repeats

one repeat

Fig. 8

Patterned fabrics have motifs or designs that repeat uniformly both vertically and horizontally. A "repeat" is the length of one full motif. It is the distance from an element on one motif to the same element on the next motif. When looking for the repeat, examine the selvage. Find a distinguishing feature of the printed motif and scan along the selvage until you see the same feature (fig 8). The distance can vary from 1 to 36 inches or more. If your fabric has a prominent repeat design, you must determine where the design will fall on the finished panel. Regardless of how many window treatments are in the same room, they must be cut so the design is in the same position on every treatment. Use these guidelines to determine where the design should fall.

❉ For floor-length panels, place one full repeat design just below the top edge of the window treatment; this is where the eye travels first.

❉ For sill-length panels, the placement is just the reverse— one full repeat design should end at the hem. If you have floor- and sill-length window treatments in the same room, follow the floor-length guideline.

Cutting Fabric

In theory, fabric needs to be "on grain," or straight, for a treatment to hang correctly. The grain of fabric refers to the direction of the threads. Being on grain means that the crosswise threads are perpendicular to the lengthwise threads and that the fabric is straight. Ideally, the printed pattern should align with the grain line. In reality, few fabrics are printed precisely on grain. In fact, it is more common to find the design to be printed off grain as much as 1 1/2 to 2 inches. Fabric mills consider this amount to fall within their acceptable range of print deviation. Pulling the fabric (described below) may partially or completely correct this situation. However, many decorator fabrics have finishes applied to the surface. Consequently, the threads are more secure and cannot be as easily manipulated. After attempting to straighten the fabric, you will have to decide if you can work with the fabric as is. In general, we recommend that if your fabric has a predominant design, it is more important to cut along the design line rather than the grain line if the difference is no more than 3/4 inch.

Follow these instructions to straighten the design on your fabric.

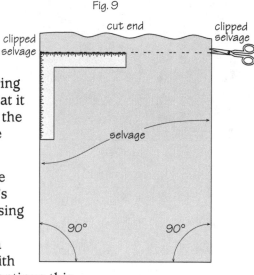

Fig. 9

1. Work on a large, flat surface.

2. Unroll several yards of fabric, right side up. Bring the selvages together, and fold the fabric so that it lies flat without ripples. If the motifs match at the selvage, make a small snip with scissors in the selvage area through both layers.

3. Open the fabric to a single thickness, right side up. At the snip, align one blade of a carpenter's square with one selvage of the fabric (fig.9). Using the other blade as a straightedge, draw a line across the fabric beginning at the snip. Align a yardstick (we like to use a see-through one) with the carpenter's square to lengthen this line. Continue this line across the width of the fabric.

4. Ideally, the line will connect to the snip at the opposite edge, forming a perfect right angle with the selvage. If the line is just slightly off at the selvage (3/4 inch or less) (fig. 10a), you may be able to straighten the design by pulling on the fabric. Trim the selvage from the side that appears short. Then pull the fabric from that corner to the opposite diagonal corner. For fabric longer than 2 yards, work by pulling shorter diagonal sections (fig. 10b). If a slight difference remains after pulling, it is better to follow a prominent design line for the cut edge rather than the grain line. However, if all attempts to match the designs are unsuccessful

Fig. 10a

edge to be pulled

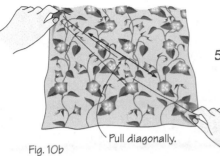

Pull diagonally.
Fig. 10b

and the difference is more than 1 inch, consider using another fabric.

5. When stripes and plaids are printed off grain, the error is obvious. If you find this problem, choose a fabric design that is woven, not printed. (A woven design looks the same on both sides, whereas a printed fabric has obvious right and wrong sides.)

Addressing Take-Up

For many window treatments, multiple fabric widths need to be cut and joined together to obtain the necessary size. Be aware that any time a vertical seam is stitched (including the side hems) the potential for the seam to "draw up" increases. Since seams are necessary when joining widths, we recommend that you cut the fabric four inches longer than the determined cut length, stitch the widths together, and then cut the stitched width lengths to the correct cut length. Avoid unnecessary vertical seams.

Cutting Multiple Fabric Widths

Treatments requiring multiple widths can appear almost seamless if the cutting has been done properly.

1. Before cutting into your fabric, determine its printed direction by studying the design. The direction of a design with flowers, stems, and leaves is easy to discern, but other fabric designs may not be so obvious. Many fabrics have a directional arrow printed on the selvage to help you determine the direction of the print.

Fig. 11

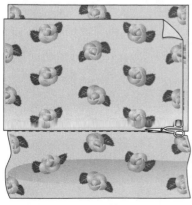

2. From the straightened end of the fabric, measure the cut length along the selvage, and place a mark.

3. Use a carpenter's square and a straightedge to draw a line across the width of the fabric at the mark. Cut along this line. This is the first squared-off length.

4. To cut additional widths, use the first length as a guide. Place it directly on top of the remaining fabric, matching motifs (fig. 11). If you have had to pull the fabric to straighten the first length, then you must do the same to each successive length of fabric.

5. Use a straightedge to mark the cutting line.

6. After each panel is cut, snip a small corner off the top of each panel so you can quickly distinguish between the top and bottom of the panels.

7. If the right and wrong sides are hard to differentiate or if the printed direction is not obvious, place a piece of masking tape on the right side or top edge of your fabric to avoid confusion.

Stitching Fabric Widths Together

When joining multiple widths of fabric, you need to determine seam placement.

☀ If 1 1/2 widths are required to create one curtain panel, cut 1 width in half lengthwise and stitch the half width to the outside edge of each full width (fig. 12).

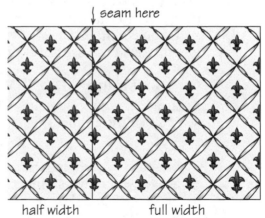

Fig. 12

seam here

half width · · · · · · · · · · full width

☀ If 2 full widths of fabric are required to create one curtain panel, stitch the widths together side by side unless you are making a valance. In that case, cut one width in half lengthwise and stitch one half width to each side of the full width.

☀ If 3 full widths of fabric are required for a panel, stitch the widths together side by side. This arrangement does not result in a center seam.

Matching Repeat Designs

On professionally made window treatments, the repeat designs match at all seams. Extra fabric is needed to accomplish this. Each set of project instructions in this book includes information on how to calculate the extra yardage, but the rule of thumb is to allow one repeat for each cut length of fabric.

To ensure matching repeat designs, you may fuse-baste the seams by using a paper-backed fusible tape. It's essential to use a tape that can be stitched through; some no-sew adhesives can gum up your needle. However, fuse-basting will prevent you from pressing seams open as directed in individual instructions, and the resulting seam may be bulkier.

Follow these instructions to fuse-baste a seam.

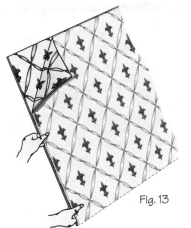

Fig. 13

1. Lay the full width of the fabric on a large work surface, right side up.

2. Lay the second piece of fabric right side down directly on top of the first width; motifs should align along the selvage edge (fig. 13).

3. Turn the edge of the top fabric toward the wrong side until the motifs match exactly (fig. 14) and press.

4. Place a strip of paper-backed fusible tape, adhesive side down, on the pressed-under edge of the top panel close to the fold. Follow the package instructions for iron temperature and steam setting. Iron on the paper side of the tape; allow it to cool and then remove the paper.

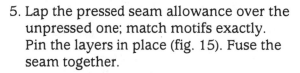

Fig. 14

5. Lap the pressed seam allowance over the unpressed one; match motifs exactly. Pin the layers in place (fig. 15). Fuse the seam together.

fusible tape   Fig. 15

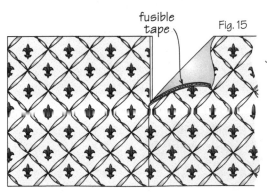

6. Arrange the panels right sides together. Stitch directly in the creased line. The motifs will be perfectly matched! Press the fused seam to one side.

7 If you have not trimmed away the selvages, do so now.

8. Usually, the fabric is cut to the cut width measurement after the widths of fabric are joined. To do this, trim

equal amounts of fabric from both side edges to obtain the cut width (fig. 16). (If you cut the excess fabric from one edge only, the design will appear lopsided.)

Advantages of Lining Your Window Treatments

Lined window treatments have many advantages.

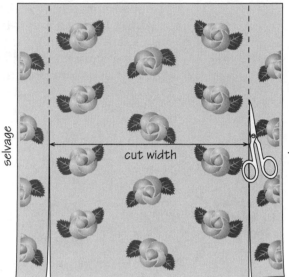

Fig. 16

* While you'll incur some additional cost, lining extends the life of a window treatment, enhances its appearance, increases insulation, and makes light-weight to medium-weight fabrics hang better. In the long run, it will save you money.

* Lining provides a little more privacy and reduces the amount of light, noise, and dust that filter through a window.

* Lining hides construction details and, if all window treatments in the house are lined with the same color, gives windows a unified appearance on the outside.

Here are some tips for selecting and using lining.

* White and off-white are the two most popular lining colors and are less noticeable than other colors when viewed from the outside. However, another color or coordinating decorator fabric can be used for lining if it aesthetically enhances the window treatment from both inside and outside the window. (In the text of the projects, we refer to the fabric used to line as "lining," regardless of what type of fabric is used.)

* Select fabrics designed specifically for lining. Quality lining fabrics are made from durable fibers or a blend of fibers that are resistant to sunlight deterioration and water stains. Usually these fabrics are cotton or cotton-

polyester blends, and many have protective finishes that will contribute to the durability of the window treatment.

☼ Choose blackout lining when you want to block out any light that might disrupt a good night's sleep. Blackout lining is not really black but is usually white or cream. It is also available in a variety of colors. It has a soft, rubbery feel on one side and a smooth outer surface. Blackout lining is also nice to use when you have a window that faces the sun during the day. The blackout lining actually blocks the sunlight so that the curtain doesn't look transparent.

☼ If you choose a fabric other than standard lining fabric, it must be compatible with the decorator fabric. It must be the same width and the same or lighter weight and must have the same care requirements.

☼ Preshrink the lining if you preshrink the decorator fabric before beginning your project.

☼ Try to use linings made from 100 percent cotton if at all possible. Linings that contain polyester may be distorted when pressed.

5 – Sewing and Handling Decorator Fabrics

Stitching Successfully

"A stitch in time saves nine." It may be an old saying, but it is still true. Time taken to create a good stitch the first time it is sewn will save ripping and repairing stitches made in haste. A good quality machine stitch is smooth to the touch on both sides of the fabric. It should not be loose enough to have loops or tight enough to cause puckering. Ideally, neither the top nor the bottom thread should show on the opposite side. If you are having problems achieving a good quality machine stitch, refer to Troubleshooting Tips on page 203.

Part III – Window Treatments 101

Here are some general sewing tips for a successful project.

☀ For all of the projects in this book, use a 1/2-inch seam allowance unless otherwise instructed.

☀ To help yourself sew a straight line, measure the appropriate distance (1/2 inch in most cases) from the needle and place a piece of masking tape on the sewing machine bed. Use this as your seam guide.

☀ Stitch a few test seams to determine the correct stitch length for your fabric. If the seam puckers, try adjusting the stitch length. A seam that puckers even slightly will prevent a curtain from hanging straight. See Troubleshooting Tips on page 203 for more sewing help.

☀ Always place pins perpendicular to the edge of the fabric with the pin heads toward the cut edge. Do not sew over the pins.

☀ Try not to lose pins inside a curtain—use extra-long pins with large heads (normally used for quilting) so they are easy to see. Forgotten pins can become enclosed inside hems or other areas that have been stitched closed.

☀ Backstitch at the beginning and end of each seam to secure the stitches in place. To backstitch, first take a few stitches in reverse, then continue forward for the remainder of the seam.

☀ Do not overcast seam allowances unless specifically instructed or unless overcasting is absolutely necessary because of easily frayed fabric edges. Each stitching line causes the fabric to draw up somewhat. Puckered seam allowances can result if the fabric has too much stitching. Also, overcasting can produce a ridge that may show through to the front of the fabric after pressing.

☀ Always stitch from the top to the bottom of a curtain. This way, if the fabric shifts slightly as you sew, the mismatched area will fall into the hem area, where it won't be as noticeable.

☀ Do not consider the selvage as part of the seam allowance. The selvage is woven more tightly than the body of the fabric and a seam that includes the selvage may pucker. Therefore, remove all selvages before constructing a project.

Troubleshooting Tips

Problems such as skipped stitches, puckering, or pulled-up seams are easily corrected. If the following tips don't solve the problem you are experiencing, consult your local sewing machine dealer. It might be time for a tune-up!

☀ Change the needle (even if you started with a new needle as we recommend). A burr at the point of the needle can snag, pucker, or cause skipped stitches.

☀ Use a smaller size needle to correct puckering.

☀ If you're using heavy thread and it hangs up in the needle, use a larger needle.

☀ Change the thread. Uneven slubs in your thread can catch in the needle and cause skipping.

☀ Change the presser foot. Choose a foot that is flat on the bottom—not grooved for special techniques. The groove can draw up the fabric, causing it to pucker.

☀ Lower the tension on your sewing machine. Because all machines are different, refer to your operation manual. The gauge that controls the upper thread has numbers: the lower the number, the lower the tension and the looser the stitch. (Don't drop the tension too close to zero, which is no tension at all!) The bottom thread tension usually is set with a tiny screw (usually on the bobbin case). Turning the screw very slightly to the left drops the tension. Always check your sewing machine manual before adjusting the machine tension. If you don't have the manual, consider taking the machine to your local sewing machine dealer for this quick adjustment. Adjusting the lower tension should be done only if all other suggestions do not solve the problem.

☀ Hold the fabric taut as you sew but don't pull it as it goes through the machine.

☀ If the seam still puckers, place a piece of paper (such as adding machine tape) or tearaway stabilizer between the fabric and the feed dog. Tear away the paper or stabilizer when finished stitching the seam.

Creating Even Seams

If the fabric was cut correctly, an uneven seam means that one layer has crawled or slipped, and the fabric edges at the end of the seam are not even. To avoid this, try the following.

❁ Pin the fabric well before stitching. Place a pin at the beginning and end of the seam. Add a pin at the exact center then fill the area in between with additional pins to ease in any extra length. Remove each pin just before stitching over it.

❁ Use a roller foot or a walking foot to keep fabrics moving at the same speed under the needle.

❁ Place the layer that appears longer on the bottom when sewing. The feed dog will help control any slipping.

❁ If one layer has crawled considerably, don't simply cut off the excess at the end of the seam. Instead, remove enough stitches to even out the seam. Repin the fabric and stitch the seam again.

Creating Flat Seams

To prevent a ridge on the front of the fabric that is created by multiple fabric edges in the seam allowance, grade the seam. Grading refers to a method of trimming seam allowances to avoid a ridge at the edge of the seam allowance. To grade, trim each layer of the seam allowance to a different width. Grade seam allowances when they will be turned in the same direction, as opposed to pressed open or flat. Generally, trim more from the seam allowance of the lining or contrasting fabric than from the decorator fabric so that the seam allowance of the decorator fabric is wider than the seam allowance of the lining fabric (fig. 17).

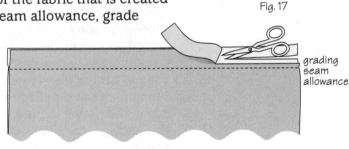

Fig. 17

grading seam allowance

Making Smooth Curves

Curved edges or shapes make window treatments interesting. When sewing a curved edge, use a short stitch length and stitch slowly and accurately; the seam allowance must be consistent in width. For curved edges to lie flat, the seam allowances must be graded and then clipped and/or notched at regular intervals.

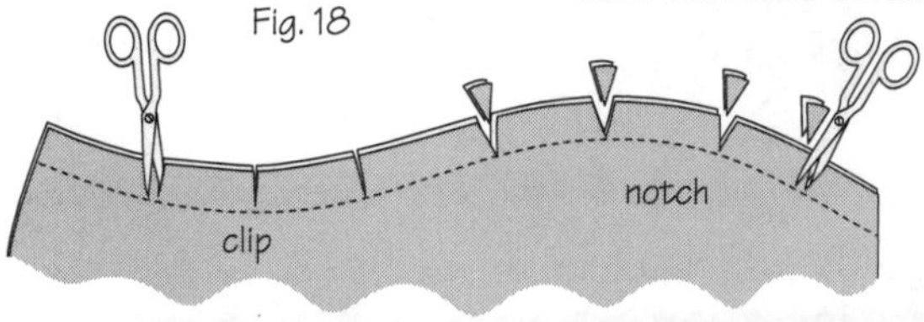

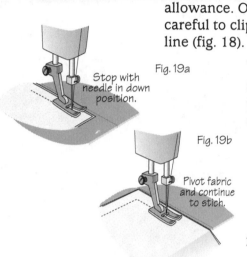

Fig. 18

clip

notch

Clipping refers to making a snip into the seam allowance; notching means cutting small wedges from the seam allowance. On an outward curve, notch the seam allowance. On an inward curve, clip the seam allowance. Be careful to clip and notch to, but not through, the stitching line (fig. 18).

Fig. 19a

Stop with needle in down position.

Turning and Cutting Corners and Points

Several steps are required to turn a corner precisely and create a sharply defined point or edge.

Fig. 19b

Pivot fabric and continue to stich.

1. When you come to a corner or point while sewing a seam, stop with the needle down, raise the presser foot, rotate the fabric, lower the presser foot, and continue stitching (figs. 19a and 19b).

2. Due to the nature of some fabrics, corners and points may become distorted. This is often the case with loosely woven, stretchy, or very heavy fabrics. To keep the corners square, "blunt" the corners. Blunting the corners gives the trimmed seam allowances more room, so there's no distortion when the corners are turned right side out. For lightweight fabrics, make one stitch diagonally across the corner (fig. 20a). Make two on medium-weight fabrics (fig. 20b) and three on heavy fabrics (fig. 20c).

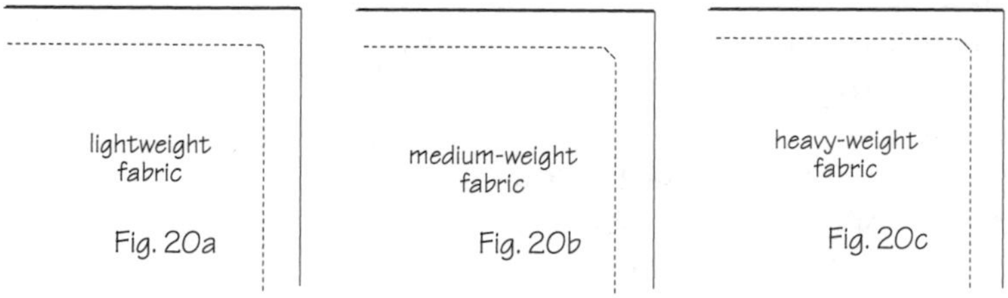

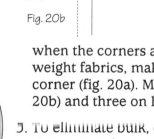

lightweight fabric

Fig. 20a

medium-weight fabric

Fig. 20b

heavy-weight fabric

Fig. 20c

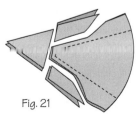

Fig. 21

3. To eliminate bulk, clip the corners diagonally (fig. 21). Next, taper the seam allowances away from the corner; the sharper the point, the farther away from the corner the seam allowance must be trimmed.

4. Turn the fabric right side out. At each corner, use a point turner to gently push the fabric out from the inside to create a sharp point. Press the seam so that neither fabric is visible from the opposite side.

Hems

❀ Custom-made curtains, draperies, and valances have double hems at the bottom and side edges. Side edges are double-hemmed (1 1/2 inches) unless they are incorporated into a "pillowcased" lining, as is done when making many of the valances in this book. Double hems are double the thickness of a single hem.

❀ In this book, the bottom hem for floor-length curtains is a double 4-inch hem. However, if your fabric is sheer, increase this to a double 6-inch hem. The bottom hem of a valance can be a double 2- or 3-inch hem. When possible, hem the bottom first and then the sides. This will ensure a clean finish along the side edges because the folds of the bottom hem will not show. The lining hem is usually 1 inch shorter than the hem of the decorator fabric. Always hem the lining and decorator fabric separately for the bottom hem.

❀ To create a double 4-inch hem at the bottom of a decorator fabric panel, fold over and press 8 inches toward the wrong side. Next, tuck in the top of the hem 4 inches to meet the fold. Blindstitch or handstitch the hem (fig. 22). To hem the lining fabric, create a double 3-inch hem. Fold over and press 6 inches of fabric toward the wrong side. Next, tuck in the top of the hem 3 inches to meet the fold. Blindstitch or handstitch the hem.

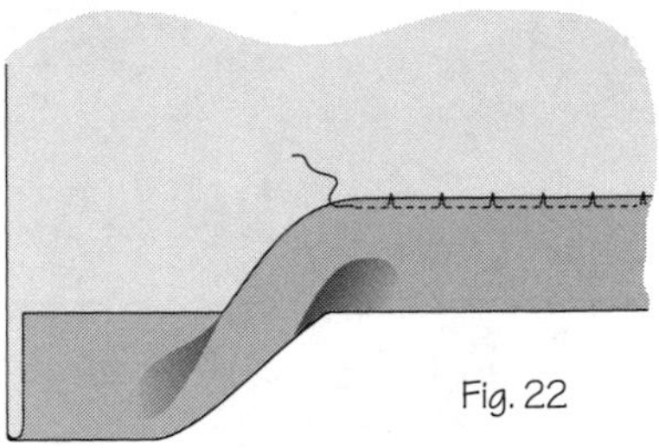

Fig. 22

❀ To create a double 1 1/2-inch hem at the sides of a decorator fabric panel, fold over and press 3 inches toward the wrong side. Next, tuck in the top of the hem 1 1/2 inches to meet the fold. Blindstitch or handstitch the hem (fig. 23).

❀ For a professional look for any style of window treatment, make the hems as invisible as possible. Professional workrooms have special blind stitch hemming machines that do just that. Most home sewing machines also have a blind stitch feature as well as a special blind-stitch presser

Fig. 23

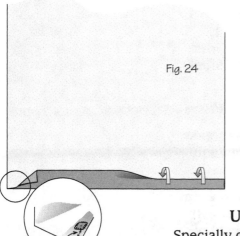

Fig. 24

foot to help guide the stitching. However, the stitch is completely different and often leaves a visible dent or too large of a stitch on the front of the treatment. Test the stitch on a scrap of your decorator fabric and if either problem happens, try setting the needle to take smaller "bites" into the fabric or loosen the top tension slightly. If the dent is unsightly, you may need to handstitch your hems for the most invisible hemlines. If the fabric shifts when you're stitching a blind hem, hand-baste the hem in place first.

Using Drapery Weights

Specially designed precovered drapery weights will help ensure that your window treatments hang well. Insert a weight into the bottom hem area at each corner (fig. 24) and/or at the bottom of each vertical seam. If the weight is not precovered, you must first cover the weight with muslin to prevent the weight from discoloring the decorator fabric.

☼ – Sheer Fabrics

Working with Sheer Fabrics

Decorative sheers are delightfully wispy, floating fabrics that are wonderful for window treatments. But working with them can be a different matter. Sheers wiggle and slip. It sometimes seems that they are alive as they slither around while you try in vain to control them. But do not despair. A little preparation, practice, and patience will yield very satisfying results. The following tips will help you work through potential problems before they happen.

☼ Buy an extra half yard or yard of fabric to use for testing.

☼ Work on a large surface—both for cutting and sewing to prevent voluminous amounts of fabric from sliding to the floor.

☼ Choose window treatment designs that allow the fabric to hang softly. We have grouped several designs together that we feel look great in sheers in a section called "Sheer Illusions" (page 33). Other designs in the book are also appropriate. Consider using sheer fabrics for Crisscross Valance (page 3), Cancan Valance (page 150), Leaf Motif (page 49), and Waiting for Inspiration (page 9).

Straightening Sheer Fabrics

Sheer fabrics often seem to have a mind of their own. Make sure they hang as you intend by checking and straightening the fabric before cutting and sewing.

✺ For best results when working with sheer fabrics, sew on the grain line of the fabric. To find the grain line, snip the cut edge parallel to the selvage edge and pull a lengthwise thread. Cut along the thread line to remove the selvage (a must) and to cut the straightest edge. If the crosswise grain is perpendicular to the lengthwise grain, you can do the same thing when cutting a crosswise edge. If not, mark and cut the edge as instructed in Cutting Fabric, page 195.

✺ Loosely woven cotton or gauze-like fabrics, such as scrim, have grain lines that are very visible and easily manipulated. To cut an edge along the crosswise or lengthwise grain, always cut along a thread line. First cut off the selvage; then cut along a thread line on the crosswise grain. If the thread line is difficult to see, pull a crosswise thread and cut along the pulled thread. With the restricting selvage removed, the entire piece of fabric should be easy to arrange so that the grain lines are perpendicular. If you find this to be true, continue to cut all pieces on the thread line. The fabric will automatically revert to the straightest grain when the curtain is hung. If you don't find this to be true, mark and cut the crosswise grain as instructed in Cutting Fabric, page 195.

Cutting Sheer Fabrics

You must control the fabric when cutting, not the other way around. Make sure the cut line is as you intend by following these tips.

✺ For the straightest line, always rest the bottom blade of the shears on the cutting surface when cutting.

Raising it off the table when cutting can leave you with a zigzag edge.

❀ Cut one layer at a time. More than one layer can slip, and the result will be pieces of different sizes.

❀ Do not allow the fabric to hang off the edge of the work surface. It may all flow off the surface like running water! Have a chair in place to catch the spillover.

❀ Crinkled sheers (often called "crash") have permanently pressed-in wrinkles. Allow the fabric to remain relaxed when cutting it. Pulling may distort the fabric and prevent accurate cutting. It is normal for the cutting line to have tiny notches as the wrinkles are cut through. Otherwise, cut and handle the crinkled sheers as you would other synthetic sheers.

Sewing Sheer Fabrics

The ultrathin quality of sheer fabrics means less margin for error than with heavier-weight decorator fabrics. Extra precautions will ensure well-stitched seams.

❀ Set your sewing machine stitch slightly shorter than normal (2 to 2.5 or 12 to 14 stitches per inch).

❀ Use the proper thread tension to achieve a smooth seam. *Always* consult your sewing machine manual before changing the tension. The lower the number, the looser the tension; the higher the number, the tighter the tension. Sheer fabrics will be easier to sew and have a better stitch quality if you lower the thread tension slightly.

❀ Use a throat plate with a smaller needle hole to eliminate puckering or skipped stitches.

❀ It's best to use a new, fine, sharp machine needle— universal size 70/10 is best for sheers. If using an old needle, check the tip for rough edges that can cause puckering or snags.

❀ If skipped stitches or puckering still occurs, check the thread. Poor quality thread (usually found in bargain bins) can have slubs, which can catch in the needle, causing puckering.

❋ Sew with a flat-bottomed presser foot. Any groove on the underside of the foot can cause the fabric to pull up and pucker or skip stitches.

❋ If the feed dog snags or puckers your sheer fabric, purchase a roll of paper adding-machine tape. Place the paper between the fabric and the feed dog. Carefully tear away the paper when the seam is complete. (Test this process on a scrap of fabric first.)

❋ Keep the fabric taut while sewing, but do not pull it as it goes through the machine.

❋ For best results, use hand stitches to hem rather than a machine stitch.

❋ Test all machine adjustments on a scrap of fabric before sewing on your project.

Sewing French Seams

A French seam is used as a seam finish for fabrics when the seam will show through to the right side (as in sheer fabrics), when both sides of the fabric are visible, or when there is no lining to cover the wrong side of the fabric. Here's how to sew a French seam.

Fig. 25

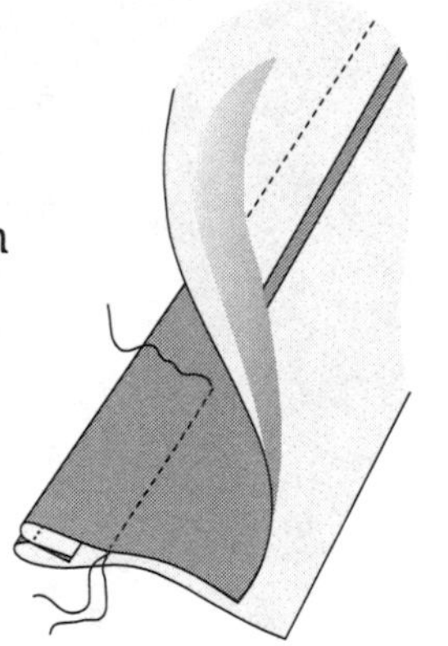

1. Stitch a seam using a $1/4$-inch seam allowance with the fabrics placed wrong sides together.

2. Trim the seam allowance to $1/8$ inch and press the seam to one side.

3. Fold the fabric so the right sides are together and the seam is along the edge. Stitch another $1/4$-inch seam, encasing the $1/8$-inch edges in the seam (fig. 25).

Pressing Sheer Fabrics

Depending on the fiber content, some sheer fabrics will not take a crease. Polyester and nylon are synthetic fibers and may not be easy to press, whereas cotton is a natural fiber and holds a crease better. Knowing this before you start will aid you in making a sheer curtain.

❋ Test for the correct ironing temperature. Most synthetic sheers require a cool setting, but cotton sheers can benefit from higher heat. Test-press measured sections for shrinkage with and without steam. (Steam can shrink the fabric.)

☼ Use folded strips of fabric to check for the ability to press in a crease or to iron out a pressed-in crease. If your fabric will not hold a crease, you may need to alter the hemming procedure for your project: mark the fold with a disappearing-ink pen (available in fabric stores), then pin, sew, and press.

☼ If steam heat shrinks your fabric, use a protective iron shoe over the soleplate of your iron to help diffuse the heat. This attachment is sold in the notions department of fabric stores. Test this on a scrap of fabric before using it on your project.

☼ For quick reference later on, keep a written record of the iron settings that work best.

Combining a Flat Sheer Fabric with a Crinkled Sheer Fabric

Crinkled sheer fabrics offer tantalizing texture in a window treatment while maintaining the translucent quality so desirable in sheer fabrics. The pressed-in crinkles require some extra care, however, especially when you join the crinkled fabric with a flat sheer fabric. Test the following techniques on fabric scraps first.

☼ Measure and cut each piece separately. Because of the flexible nature of the crinkled texture, pieces with identical measurements may appear to be different sizes. The tiny pleats and folds often create an accordion-type effect when they are cut through.

☼ Pin the crinkled sheer to the flat sheer. If the crinkled fabric balloons out over the edge of the flat fabric, ease it in to fit the edge of the flat fabric. To ease the crinkled sheer, pin both pieces together at each end and in the middle. Then fill in with more pins every 3 to 4 inches.

☼ Machine-stitch with the crinkled layer on top. Use a walking foot if possible.

❋ Pressed-in wrinkles may "crawl," causing the crinkled layer to appear longer. This fullness must be eased in to avoid real puckering. To ease in wrinkled fullness, pin as above, and pull the grain line of the crinkled piece sideways slightly as you sew. To do this, place your index finger on one side of the foot and your middle finger on the opposite side of the foot. Spread your fingers slightly as you sew, while pressing down on the fabric. This method is for minor easing only. If the fabric slips more than 1/16 inch within a pinned section, remove it from the machine and examine it for possible repinning.

7 – Decorative Trims

Working with Decorative Trims

Decorative trims offer style and dimension to your window treatments, transforming even an ordinary fabric into a decorator's dream. Rich-textured trims are much like jewelry; they accent shapes and colors to make the entire ensemble more appealing.

Trims are designed to be attached to fabric in one of two ways—into the seam as you construct your project or directly to the surface to embellish an already completed project. All trims are constructed with one or both of two components—an insertion edge and a decorative edge (fig. 26). When attached, only the decorative edge (the fringe or cording) is visible. The insertion edge has several different names, such as "header edge," "gimp edge," and "lip edge," depending on the trim. But no matter what it is called, the insertion edge is still just a plain old seam allowance.

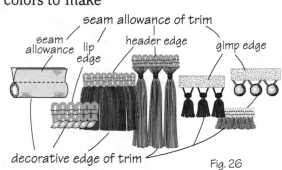

seam allowance of trim

seam allowance

lip edge

header edge

gimp edge

decorative edge of trim

Fig. 26

Fabric stores have an array of trim styles to coordinate with your fabric. Although trims may differ widely in style, they actually have quite a bit in common. Likewise, the techniques used to sew them are similar. A few sewing tips will make using trims seem downright easy! And while some trims may seem expensive, a small amount of trim can create a million-dollar look that appears custom-made by a professional decorator. This "perceived value" is inherent in decorative trims. So if you have never attempted to sew these exotic beauties, now is the time to start! By following these easy tips, you'll be competing for compliments with the pros in no time.

Choosing Trims

Choosing the best trim for your fabric is similar to picking a mat and frame for a photograph. The proper color, shape, and size will highlight the best features of the fabric and create a masterpiece.

❀ Trims have a right side and a wrong side. Sometimes a trim is more decorative on one side than the other, so it is easy to see which is the right side. Or the wrong side may have visible chain stitching in the seam allowance. If you can't find the right side, there may be no difference, and then it probably doesn't matter.

❀ Choose a trim that is of a similar weight to your fabric. For example, use a lightweight fringe on a sheer fabric rather than heavy bullion fringe. A trim that is too heavy can stretch and distort your window treatment.

❀ Decorative trims are manufactured in many fibers. The most common are cotton, acrylic, rayon, and acetate. Of these, rayon is the best choice for its vibrant colors and durability. It can be glossy for dressy décor or have a softer sheen for casual decorating. Rayon is often confused with acetate. While they are very similar, rayon is a more stable fiber; it will wear better and will not fade as fast. Note that blended fibers may fade at different rates, causing a multihued trim over time.

❀ Choose a trim that requires the same care as your fabric. Because of noncolorfast dyes and delicate construction, trims are usually not washable and must be dry cleaned. We do not recommend washing window treatments. However, if you choose to launder your window treatment, choose a trim that can also be washed. If you are unsure about the care required, test first by sewing a sample as you would the finished project. Measure the sample before and after laundering and inspect for shrinkage and color fastness.

Trim Tips to Make Handling Easier

The many cut ends and added thickness of trims can present a brand-new challenge when incorporating them into a project. Here we offer some solutions.

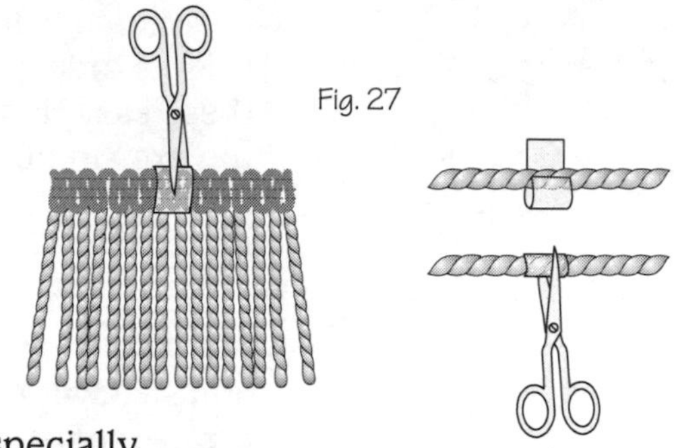

Fig. 27

❋ Wrap the cut end of a trim with tape to prevent raveling. To cut a trim, wrap the section to be cut with tape; then cut through the taped section (fig. 27). This is especially important for twisted cord. Carefully remove the tape just before stitching.

❋ The lip edge of cord-edge often gets distorted when wrapped around the narrow reels used in retail stores. When purchased, the trim may have kinks or folds that may cause the lip edge to draw up and create puckering when stitched (it may actually curl). To prevent puckering, clip the edge to, but not through, the inner row of trim stitching until the trim relaxes and flattens out. Do this before stitching it into a seam.

❋ Use long quilting pins with large glass or plastic heads so the pins don't bend or get lost in thick trims.

❋ Pin trims as you sew them, not in advance, for easier handling. Make sure you have allowed enough trim for ease before starting (about 3/8 inch for every 12 inches of seam). Then pin only the amount you can handle at one time. Pin 3 to 4 inches, adding 1/8 inch for ease and stitch; then pin the next 3 to 4 inches with ease and stitch. Repeat this process as needed, pinning as you go.

❋ Leave the unused trim in a pile in your lap as you sew to keep the weight of the trim from pulling against the stitching.

❋ Multiple rows of stitching connect the loops or threads that form a fringe or the insertion edge connected to the cord. These rows of stitching need to be hidden within the seam allowance of a project. When inserting trim into

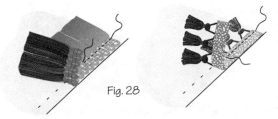
Fig. 28

a seam, position the trim so the inner-most row of trim stitching lines up with the seam line; this is where to stitch (fig. 28). Keep in mind that the seam allowance of the trim may be different from the 1/2-inch seam allowance of the window treatment.

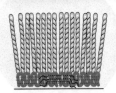
Fig. 29

❀ These multiple rows of stitches are usually chainstitched. When these threads are cut, they will unravel with normal handling (especially on bullion fringe). To prevent this from happening, secure the cut ends of the trim by stitching over the chain stitching when attaching the trim in a seam. This may require additional stitching in the header area (fig. 29).

Trim Tips for Best Sewing Results

Tried-and-true techniques make sewing trims hassle-free. Here are some helpful hints.

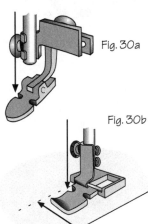
Fig. 30a

Fig. 30b

❀ Using a zipper foot to attach most trims will enable you to stitch as close as possible to the decorative edge of fringes or cord. Older sewing machine models have zipper feet that slide from side to side so that you can move the foot to one side of the needle for close trim stitching (fig. 30a). Newer zipper feet are often too wide for close stitching. To remedy this, adjust the needle position to the left or right to move the needle closer to the edge of the foot (fig. 30b).

❀ Use a size 90/16 sewing machine needle to sew most trims. Smaller needle sizes can be used when required for fine fabrics, such as sheers, but they are more likely to break when thick trims are sewn in a seam. Stitch more slowly on thick trims to prevent needles from breaking.

❀ Lengthen the stitch on your sewing machine to 3 or 3.5 (about 8-10 stitches per inch). Decorative trims often drag in the machine, causing the stitches to shorten. These are very difficult to remove if you make a mistake!

❀ Always ease trim to fit the fabric. The easiest way to do this is to lay the trim on the fabric so that the trim buckles slightly (about 1/8 inch) with every 3 to 4 inches of fabric. Pin trim in place just before sewing. Flatten the buckled trim as you sew (fig. 31). Repeat with the remaining trim, 3 to 4 inches at a time.

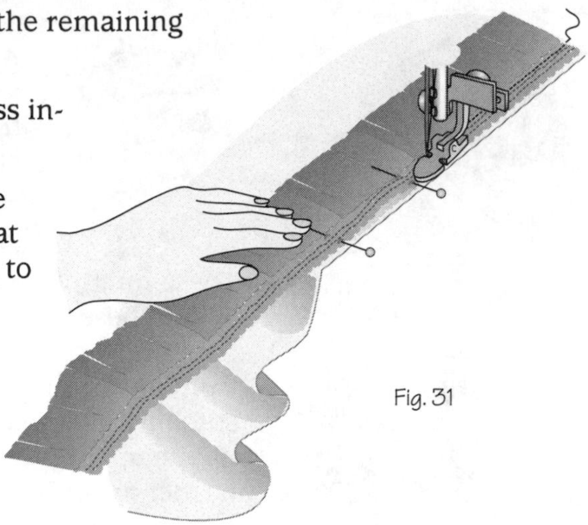

☀ Never pull the trim while sewing unless instructed to do so.

☀ Where all four sides of a treatment are trimmed, begin and end your sewing at the center of a side, never at a corner, to avoid bulk. Try to choose a side that will be inconspicuous on the finished project.

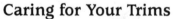

Fig. 31

☀ If the project calls for trim along one side only, you must start at a corner. In this case, place the cut edge of the trim flush with the side seam allowance or run the end of the cord into the seam allowance of the edge being trimmed. This avoids both the corner and the adjacent side seam. (See figs. 35 and 52 for cord-edge and welting.)

Caring for Your Trims

Trims that are handled constantly, such as a fringe on the leading edge of a curtain, can become tangled. These tips will help you make trims more manageable.

☀ Use a hand steamer or steam iron to steam fringe ends to remove kinks. Use a kitchen mitt on your hand as a portable "ironing board" when pressing already-hung curtains.

☀ Unruly tassels or fringes can be brushed softly with a hairbrush to untangle and fluff them. Select a brush with plastic bristles that are spaced 1/4 inch apart and have little balls on the tips. Uneven fringe ends can be trimmed with scissors. (However, don't cut looped or twisted bullion fringes. They will just unwind!)

Trim Specifics

While all trims have many things in common, the design details of certain trims may require special handling. Follow these specific recommendations for problem-free sewing.

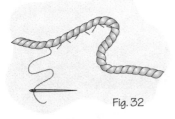

Fig. 32

Cord

Cord comes in many diameters and textures. You can use it to tie back a curtain, create loops for tab-top curtains, or embellish a surface where there is no seam.

✸ To cut cord, wrap tape around the section to be cut. Then cut through the tape to prevent raveling.

✸ Handstitch cords inconspicuously with a slip stitch if there is no attached edge (fig. 32).

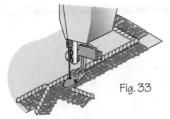

Fig. 33

CORD-EDGE (CORD WITH AN ATTACHED LIP EDGE)

Cord-edge is cord with an attached seam allowance or lip edge for machine-stitched seam insertion. Always use a zipper foot to attach cord-edge. To sew narrow cord-edge (³/16 to ¹/4 inch wide), place the cut end of the cord over the edge of the fabric; stitch over the cord on the seam line, and continue stitching flush to the cord. To finish, overlap the beginning of the trim and run the cut end into the seam allowance (fig. 33).

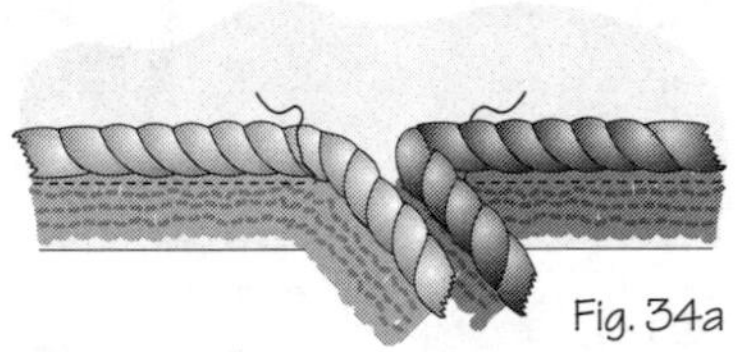

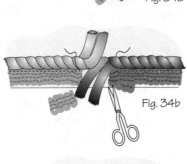

Fig. 34a

Fig. 34b

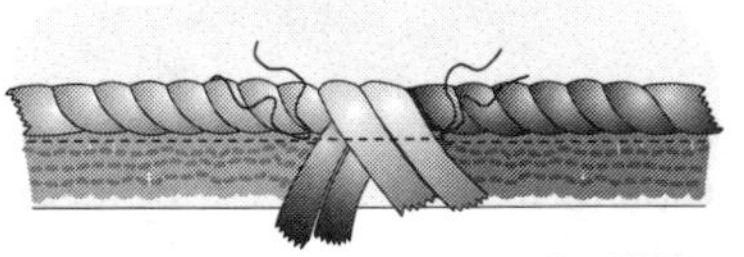

Fig. 34c

While wide cord-edge (³/8 to ¹/2 inch wide) is very similar to the smaller kind, it is often stiffer. Test the cord-edge before stitching to see if one side lies on the fabric more evenly than the other. If so, stitch it in this position. Stitching is the same as for the narrow cord-edge. However, the stiff nature of the wide cord-edge makes overlapping ends difficult. An easier (and less visible) method is to retwist the ends where they join. To do this, leave a 3-inch unstitched tail of cord-edge at each end of the trim. Leave about 1¹/2 inches between the beginning and ending stitches (fig. 34a). Remove the lip edge on both tails by clipping the thread that attaches the lip. Untwist the cord in the tail sections only (fig. 34b). Overlap the cord at the seam line so the twists are parallel and the cord ends hang off the edge of the fabric (fig. 34c). The joined cord will appear to be continuous and the untwisted cord ends will have become flat enough to stitch over. Stitch flush to the retwisted section to finish.

The following tips apply to both narrow and wide cord-edge.

☀ Cord-edge that runs along one seam only (such as at the bottom of a valance) must be finished at each end of the seam. Leave 1 1/2 inches of extra cord at each end; remove the lip, as above, from each end section. Begin and end the seam by bending the cord end so it is flush to the end seam allowance; untwist the cord in the seam allowance to flatten the twists. Stitch over the flattened cord section; then continue stitching as close as possible to the cord to attach it (fig. 35). The cord should not be stitched into the end seam allowances.

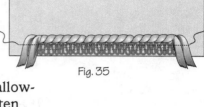

Fig. 35

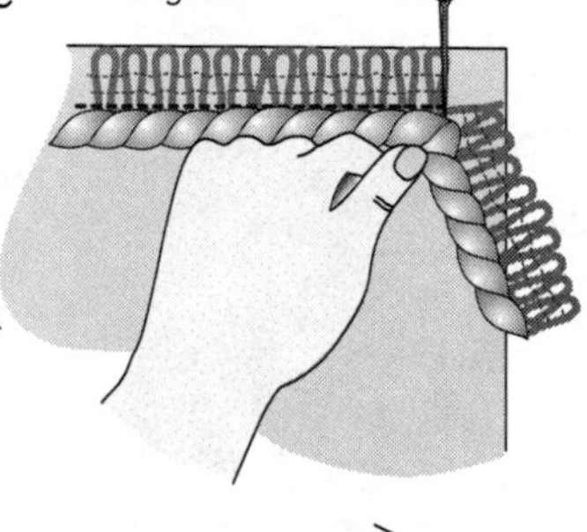

☀ To create sharp corners, stitch to within 1 inch of the corner and stop. At the corner clip the lip edge of the cord-edge to, but not through, the innermost row of stitching. Stitch to the corner and stop with the needle in the down position. Raise the foot, pivot the fabric, and with the foot still raised, use your thumb to gently push the cord away from you (fig. 36). Lower the foot and continue to sew, easing the trim as you go.

Fig. 36

☀ To create smooth curves, clip the lip edge to, but not through, the innermost row of trim stitching before sewing. Ease the cord-edge to fit the curved fabric edge (fig. 37). It is not necessary to buckle the cord as you do in straight applications.

Fig. 37

☀ Please note that when you're stitching cord-edge with a zipper foot, the needle is quite exposed and stitching takes place very close to your fingers. Your fingers can slip off stiff cord and get caught by the needle. Remember to stitch slowly and carefully. Stitched fingers are not conducive to a fun sewing experience!

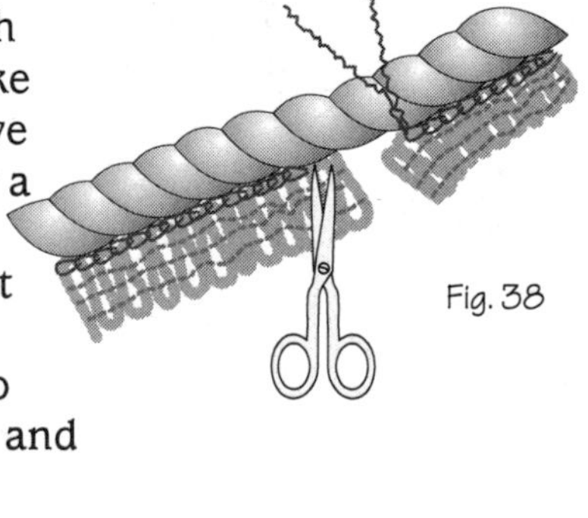

☀ Occasionally a project will call for two cords—one with and one without a lip edge. Not all manufacturers make matching styles, however. To create plain cord, remove the attached lip edge by clipping the stitching (usually a chain stitch) that attaches it to the cord. It is usually embedded in the side of the cord (fig. 38). (The hardest part is finding the correct end of the stitch to pull!) A chain stitch will continue to unravel where attached to the cord, however, so make sure to reinforce the cord and

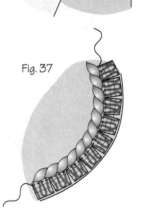

Fig. 38

lip edge at the point where the stitches were removed with machine or hand stitching.

Fringes

Fringes come in many styles. The thinner varieties are usually used for window treatments because they hang so gracefully. Here are some tips for working with fringes.

☀ The seam allowance, or header edge, of fringe is permanently stitched. A row of protective chain stitching is often used along the decorative edge of the fringe to keep the cut ends flat and away from the needle while you are stitching. (This is why fringe often doesn't look like fringe on the store shelf.) Leave the chain stitching attached until you have completed your project. Then remove it by pulling on one of the threads (fig. 39).

Fig. 39

☀ When determining the finished length of your window treatment, consider the length of any fringe you plan to use. A design calling for a finished length equal to $1/5$ or $1/6$ of the window height may need to be shortened slightly to accommodate a 5-inch-long fringe. Test the length first by pinning the fringe to a paper pattern. Tape the pattern to the mounted hardware to check the effect of the added length before cutting out your project.

☀ Fringe is easy to join. Usually you can just butt the cut ends together and reinforce the joint with extra stitching (fig. 40). If the header edge of the fringe is thin, overlap it 1 inch and turn the top end under $1/2$ inch.

Fig. 40

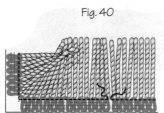

☀ To create sharp corners, stitch to within 1 inch of a corner and stop. At the corner, clip the fringe to, but not through, the innermost row of stitching (fig. 40). Stitch to the corner; with the needle in the down position, raise the foot and pivot the fabric. Give the fringe a little extra ease at the corner by pushing it away from you slightly. Lower the presser foot and continue to stitch.

☀ Bullion fringe can be long or short, heavy or lightweight. It is constructed as one continuous set of threads that are twisted and looped into fringes. Tape the cut end securely to handle the fringe. Remove the tape just before you sew this trim, and add extra stitching to prevent raveling.

❈ Tassel fringe has small tassels attached to a flat decorative edge (gimp edge), which also serves as its seam allowance. Insert this edge into the seam so only the tassels show (fig. 41), or place it on the surface of your window treatment. If you use it as a surface detail, place one row of stitching along each edge of the gimp to secure it.

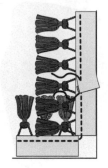

Fig. 41

Novelty Fringes

Novelty fringes can be any shape or size, including ball fringe, ostrich and confetti fringes, and a variety of beaded, dimensional styles. These trendy trims are all quite different from each other and often can be either inserted into a seam or used for surface embellishment. Since their construction varies greatly, inspect the trim before sewing. Decide which style of trim your novelty fringe most closely resembles, and use the methods outlined for that trim. Beaded fringe may not appear to resemble any of your listed trim styles. However, its flat twill tape edge must be inserted into a seam as you would tassel or ball fringe. Take care to control the beaded fringe while stitching to prevent it from flipping into your stitching path. Sewing over the beads can break the needle.

Fig. 42

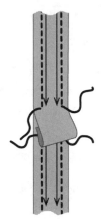

Braid

Braid, also known as gimp, is a simple flat trim finished on both edges. Stitch it as a surface detail to add interesting texture. Or glue it to cover the raw edge or staples on a structured window treatment.

 Before stitching braid, pin it well, easing it to fit the fabric. (Braid can sometimes wiggle around.) Machine-stitch along each edge with a cording or embroidery foot. Stitch each row in the same direction. Use a walking foot, if available, to prevent crawling. Overlap and turn under the top cut end to finish (fig. 42).

❈ To glue braid, place a bead of fabric glue on the surface to be covered. Then press the braid into the glue.

Filler Cord

This strange-looking web-covered cotton cord is used as the filler or center of fabric-covered welting and cording. With its loose construction, it is not durable unless it is covered with a fabric casing, but it is strong and smooth when covered. (Twisted cable cord, its alternative, will leave visible bumps when covered.)

Welting

The terms welting and piping are often used interchangeably, but they are different. Both trims are constructed by wrapping a bias fabric casing around a filler cord. Piping usually has a thin filler (about 1/8 inch in diameter) and is often used in apparel. Welting, most commonly used in home decorating, has a thicker filler cord, available in widths from 1/8 inch to 2 inches. Welting can be purchased ready-made in limited colors and sizes, or you can make your own.

MAKING YOUR OWN WELTING

Making your own welting gives you endless options and is much easier than you think. Specific directions follow.

1. Select a filler cord diameter that suits the project.

Fig. 43

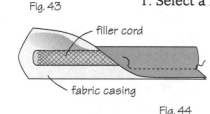

filler cord

fabric casing

Fig. 44

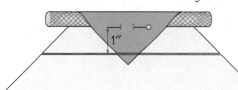

1"

2. Bias strips of fabric are used to cover the cord. The cut width of the strip depends on the diameter of the cord and the weight of the fabric. The strip should be wide enough to wrap around the cord plus form a 1/2-inch seam allowance (fig. 43).

3. Make a template for the bias strip pieces. Fold a corner of fabric or tissue paper around the cord and encase the cord snugly. Pin to secure. Measure 1 inch out from the pin and cut (fig. 44). Use this template to cut bias strips.

4. Cut and piece the bias strips (directions follow).

5. Press the entire length of the strip. Stretch the fabric slightly as you press it to ensure the covering will be smooth.

6. Lay the cord in the center of the wrong side of the fabric. Fold the fabric strip around the cord so the raw edges are even.

7. Attach a zipper foot or piping foot to your sewing machine, following the manufacturer's instructions. Stitch close to the cord but not tightly against it (fig. 45). Trim the seam allowances to 1/2 inch.

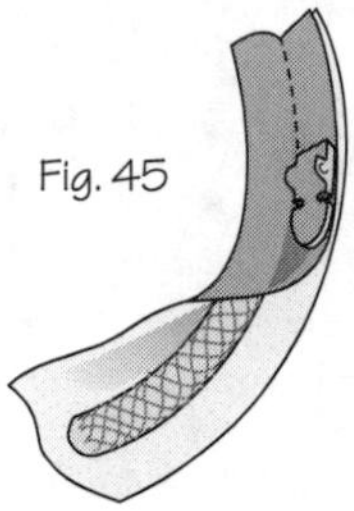

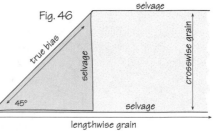

Fig. 45

CUTTING BIAS STRIPS

Approximately 26 yards of 1³/₄-inch-wide bias strips or 20 yards of 2¹/₄-inch-wide strips can be cut from 1 yard of 54-inch-wide fabric.

1. Use a carpenter's square to mark and cut a straight edge along one end of the fabric.

2. Fold the cut edge toward the selvage at a 45-degree angle. Finger-press each folded corner to mark the bias edge (fig. 46).

Fig. 46

selvage
true bias
selvage
crosswise grain
45°
selvage
lengthwise grain

3. Use a fabric pen or pencil and a straightedge to draw a line connecting the two finger-pressed marks; then draw lines parallel to the first line using the template (fig. 47). On the shorter pieces that do not extend all the way from selvage to selvage, draw a short line parallel to the selvage at each end of the strip. Cut along all the lines.

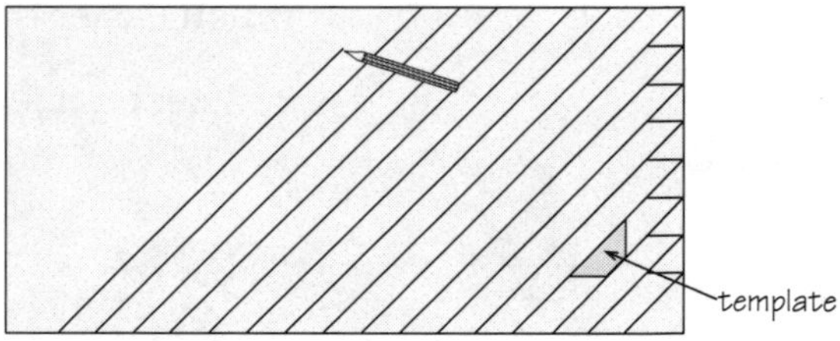

template

Fig. 47

4. Place the short ends of the strips right sides together, forming a right angle; offset the tips slightly so the cut edges match at the seam lines. Stitch the strips together with a 1/4-inch seam allowance (fig. 48). Continue sewing strips together in this way until you have one long strip. Press all seams open.

SEWING WELTING INTO A SEAM

These tips will help you sew welting into a seam easily.

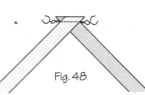

Fig. 48

❀ Use a zipper foot to stitch welting as close as possible to the fabric-covered cord. Newer sewing machines have zipper feet that are often too wide for close stitching. To stitch as close as possible to the cord, move the needle position to the side until the needle comes down close to the outer edge of the foot. Be sure to adjust the seam allowance measurement as the needle position changes. Trim seam allowance to 1/2 inch.

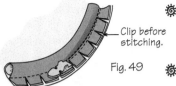

Clip before stitching.

Fig. 49

☀ Avoid puckering by easing the welting to fit the seam. For the smoothest curves, clip the welting seam allowance before stitching (fig. 49).

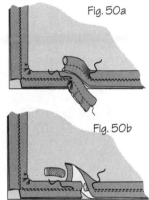

Fig. 50a

Fig. 50b

☀ If the welting is stitched around an entire project, start at the center of one side. To eliminate bulk, avoid starting at a corner. The welting itself should be placed just beyond the 1/2-inch seam line so the welting seam allowance is on top of the seam allowance of the project. Stitch directly on the seam line so your stitching is right against the cord. Begin and end each seam with an unstitched section of welting 1 to 1 1/2 inches long (fig. 50a). At the point of overlap, cut the excess welting so the ends overlap by 1 1/2 inches. Open the casing on the longer end. Clip the excess filler cord so the cord ends butt together inside the opened casing. Fold under the end of the top casing 1/2 inch so it covers the welting and rewrap the cord, enclosing the joined ends (fig. 50b). Stitch across the overlapped fabric on the seam line to finish (fig. 50c).

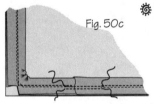

Fig. 50c

☀ To create sharp corners, stitch to within 1 inch of a corner and stop. At the corner, clip to, but not through, the casing stitch line. Stitch to the corner; with the needle in the down position, raise the presser foot and pivot the fabric. To create the sharpest corner, before lowering the foot use your thumb to push the corner welting away from you (fig. 51). Then lower the foot and continue stitching.

Fig. 51

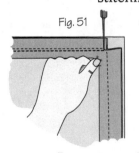

☀ Welting that runs along one seam only, such as the bottom edge of a valance, must be finished at each end of the seam. Allow 1 1/2 inches of extra welting at each end of the seam. Open up each end of the welting casing and cut off the filler cord so it stops just short of each end seam allowance. (Don't forget to allow a little ease!) Refold the casing and manipulate the empty flat section so it curves off of the fabric edge, flush with the end seam allowance (fig. 52). Do this at both ends. Stitch the welting to the fabric, stitching over the flattened sections to finish.

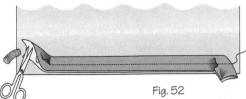

Fig. 52

Fabric-Covered Cording

Fabric-covered cording is similar to welting, except that the seam allowance is tucked inside the casing, creating a round, finished cording for surface embellishment.

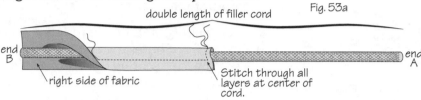

Fig. 53a

double length of filler cord

end B

right side of fabric

Stitch through all layers at center of cord.

end A

This type of cording is often placed where there is no construction seam, so it must be glued or handstitched to your project. Follow the instructions given above for cutting and sewing bias strips, except cut each strip 1/4 inch wider. Then follow these steps to cover the cord.

Fig. 53b

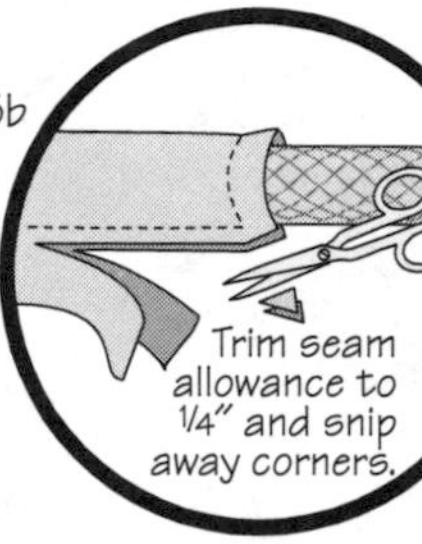

Trim seam allowance to 1/4" and snip away corners.

1. To create this cording you will need filler cord measuring 2 times the required finished length. Mark the exact middle point of the filler cord. This is your starting point. Center the filler cord on the right side of the fabric strip so the marked point lines up with one short cut end of the fabric. Fold the fabric right sides together so it encases the cord. Starting at the fabric fold, at the marked center point of the cord, use a zipper foot to stitch

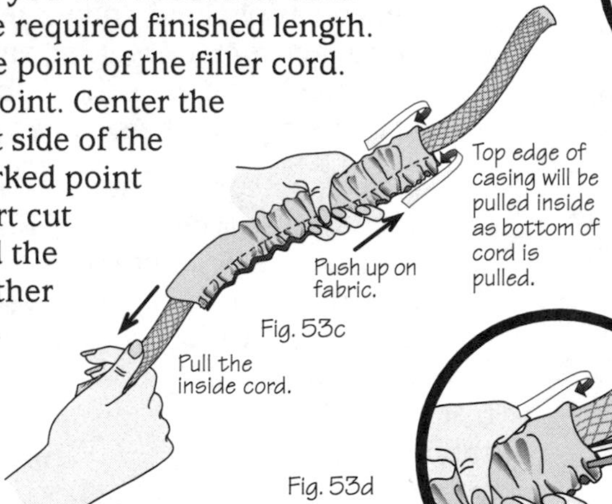

Top edge of casing will be pulled inside as bottom of cord is pulled.

Push up on fabric.

Fig. 53c

Pull the inside cord.

Fig. 53d

Help the casing roll inside with a pair of tweezers.

Push the fabric up to start.

across the cord through all layers to secure. Stitch slowly to avoid breaking a needle. At the side of the cord, stop with the needle in the down position, raise the foot, and pivot the cord. Lower the foot and continue stitching down the long edge of the casing next to the cord (fig. 53a). Do not stitch so close as to catch the cord itself in your stitching. The casing must remain loose enough so you can turn it right side out.

2. Trim the seam allowance to about 1/4 inch (fig. 53b).

3. To turn the casing right side out, pull the end of the cord that has been covered

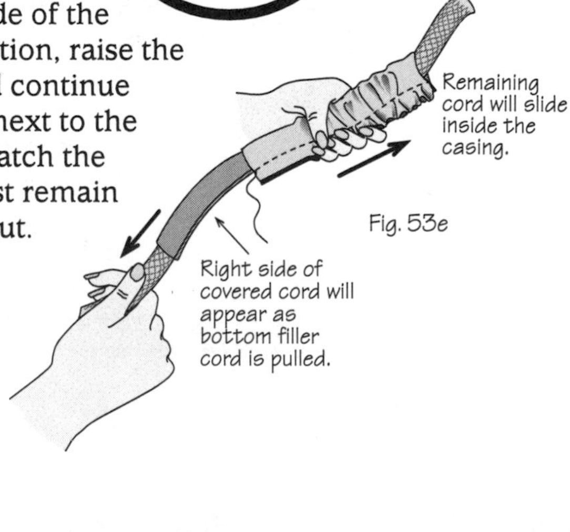

Remaining cord will slide inside the casing.

Fig. 53e

Right side of covered cord will appear as bottom filler cord is pulled.

until the fabric gathers slightly along the stitched length (fig. 53c). At the stitched end of the cord, push the now gathered fabric toward the uncovered portion of the cord. Use tweezers (sewing tweezers work best) to grab the fabric and manipulate the gathered folds so they roll over the stitching. At the same time, use the tweezers to gently push the cord and fabric inside at the stitched end until the seam allowance disappears inside the casing (fig. 53d).

4. Continue to gently pull the covered cord with one hand while you push the gathered fabric up over the stitched end with the other. As the fabric casing starts to slide, keep one hand pushing upward at the top end while the other pulls the filler cord downward at the covered end. The uncovered cord at the top end will slip inside the fabric casing as you pull from the covered end. The fabric-covered cord, right side out, will appear as you pull (fig. 53e).

Tassels

Tassels are available in many shapes and sizes, including large elaborate creations with ceramic heads and beads. The most common tassels are 3 inches long. These come in two styles—tassels with a 1/2-inch top loop and those with a 3-inch top loop. The length of the loop suggests the method of attachment.

Fig. 54

❁ Tassels constructed with a 3-inch loop at the top can be easily machine-stitched. Place a tassel on the right side of the fabric with its cut ends pointing toward the center of the fabric and its head just outside of the seam allowance. The tassel loop will hang off the edge of the fabric (often at a corner or point). There must be enough space beside the head of the tassel to allow a zipper foot to stitch on the seam line without catching the threads of the tassel. Stitch across the loop on the seam line (fig. 54). When the lining has been attached, use scissors to cut the loop. Knot the two loop ends flush to the stitched seam to prevent them from pulling loose.

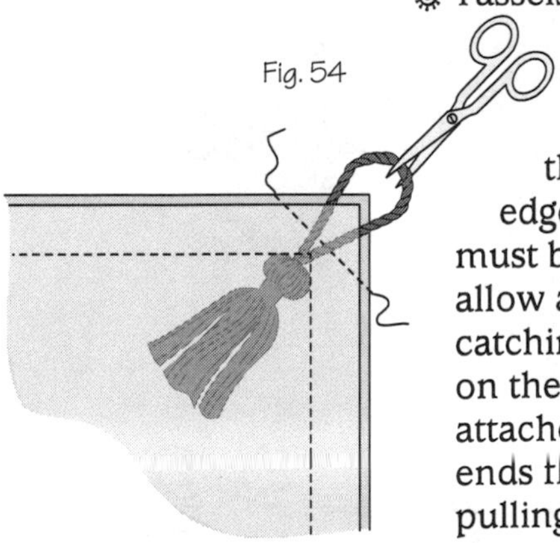

❁ Tassels with a 1/2-inch loop are usually handstitched to a project. This loop may be adjustable.

8 – Buttons and Buttonholes

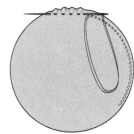

Covering Buttons

Buttons covered with fabric are a wonderful finishing touch for many of the window treatments in this book. Commercial kits are available that make this process easy. The two most available types of buttons to cover are the type with the shank attached to the back piece of the button and the type with the shank attached to the button itself. Cover buttons with the shank attached to the back of the button often come in a kit containing a rubber-like mold to hold the button and a pusher to make it easier to pop on the back. Since this kind of button has no teeth to secure the fabric around the button form, we suggest the following tips to help pull fabric smoothly.

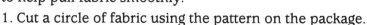

Fig. 55

1. Cut a circle of fabric using the pattern on the package.

2. Handsew a row of running stitches around the outside edge of the circle. Leave the needle and thread attached to the fabric (fig. 55).

Fig. 56

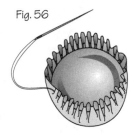

3. Place the button in the center of the wrong side of the fabric circle. Gather the fabric around the button by gently pulling on the needle and thread (fig. 56). Push the covered button into the mold. Tighten the gathers and secure them by taking a few hand stitches (fig. 57).

4. Use the pusher to pop the back into position; then pop the button out of the mold.

Fig. 57

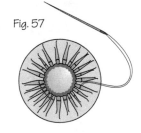

Cover buttons with the shank attached to the button itself are much stronger for home decorating. They have teeth inside the button form to hold the fabric in place. However, they have no mold to help with the fabric positioning. Here are some tips.

1. Cut a circle of fabric following the pattern on the package.

Fig. 58

2. For heavier fabrics, use small scissors to clip the pleats that form inside the button as you tuck in the fabric (fig. 58).

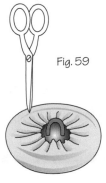

Fig. 59

3. Use the eraser on a pencil or the tip of your scissors to secure the fabric under the teeth (fig. 59).

4. Occasionally, the silver shine of the button shows through the fabric. To prevent this, cut a second, smaller circle of fabric. Place this between the button and the larger circle of fabric.

Some kits combine the best of both types—the cover button with the teeth and the mold with a pusher. If this combination is not available in your area, we recommend that you purchase two packages—one with a mold and a pusher, and one containing buttons of the same size with teeth (fig. 60).

Fig. 60

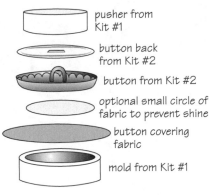

pusher from Kit #1

button back from Kit #2

button from Kit #2

optional small circle of fabric to prevent shine

button covering fabric

mold from Kit #1

Sewing on Buttons

We recommend a slightly different (and actually easier) technique to sew a button to a window treatment or other home decorating project.

1. Use heavy thread such as carpet thread or waxed button thread to attach buttons. Waxed thread bonds to itself when handstitched to keep the button from slipping. With waxed thread, two stitches and a knot are sufficient to hold the button. If waxed button thread is not available in your area, pass the heavy thread through beeswax (available at fabric stores) to obtain the same no-slip effect.

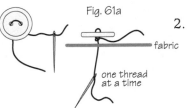

Fig. 61a

fabric

one thread at a time

2. Cut a piece of waxed thread 18 inches long for each button. Insert both ends of the thread through the holes of a flat button, from front to back, and knot the thread on the underside of the button (fig. 61a). Or tie the thread to the shank of the button (fig. 61b). With either style of button, both thread ends should be even in length.

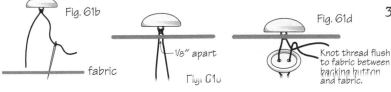

Fig. 61b

fabric

1/8" apart

Fig. 61c

Fig. 61d

Knot thread flush to fabric between backing button and fabric.

3. Use a sharp needle with an extra-large eye, such as a doll needle, to handle the heavy thread. Insert one thread end only through the needle.

Take one stitch with one thread end from the front to the back of the project. Unthread the needle. Rethread it with the second thread end. Stitch so this end comes out

1/8-inch from the first stitch (fig. 61c). Unthread the needle to attach the backing button.

4. A backing button is a clear button that is placed on the back of the fabric directly behind a decorative button to reinforce the stitches and prevent puckering. Pass one thread end through the backing button from the bottom to the top and then back through the second hole from the top to the bottom. Knot the thread ends together tightly between the backing button and the fabric (fig. 61d). Clip the thread ends.

Better Buttonholes

Easy sewing adjustments can be made for strong, beautiful buttonholes.

☀ Lower the top tension one number to create a more satiny stitch.

☀ To prevent stretched buttonholes, place a piece of interfacing between the layers of fabric. This is especially helpful if making buttonholes in sheer or flimsy fabric.

☀ Trim any seam allowance between fabric layers that might come close to the buttonhole. An uneven surface can create an uneven buttonhole.

Fig. 62

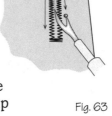

☀ Test all buttonholes on a scrap of fabric folded to the same thickness as your project first! Practice makes perfect.

☀ A seam ripper is the most common method of cutting open a buttonhole. To use a ripper, first use the tip of the ripper to score the length of the buttonhole. This will help to separate the stitches and prevent cut threads. To score, pass the tip of the ripper between the rows of stitching from bar tack to bar tack (fig. 62). Start at the end farthest away from you and drag the point of the ripper toward you. Place a straight pin across one end of the buttonhole just inside the bar tack. Insert the point of the ripper between the rows of stitching just inside the bar tack closest to you (fig. 63). Hold the fabric taut at each end of the buttonhole. Slowly push the ripper blade between the rows of stitching, away from you, toward the straight pin. The pin will stop the ripper from going too far.

Fig. 63

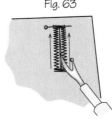

Glossary

A

Acetate–A manufactured cellulose fiber used in fabric and decorative trims.

Angle bracket–An L-shaped piece of metal on which shelving is supported on a wall.

Appliqué–A surface decoration in which a material is cut out and stitched, embroidered, or pasted on another material.

Apron–The bottom portion of a window frame that is flush against the wall.

Awl–A woodworking tool with a sharp point that creates holes in wood when tapped with a hammer. Also a sewing implement used to create holes in fabric (no hammer required).

B

Backing button–A clear button that is placed on the back of the fabric directly behind a decorative button to reinforce the stitches and prevent puckering.

Backstitch–A stitch used to secure the beginning and end of a row of machine stitching. This is accomplished by stitching back and forth over the same stitches two or three times.

Ball fringe–A decorative trim constructed of fluffy dangling balls.

Banding–A strip of fabric that is folded around the edge of fabric and topstitched.

Bar tack–Overlapping stitches that are made to close each end of a buttonhole to prevent the buttonhole from ripping. These stitches are twice as wide as the stitching that forms the sides of the buttonhole.

Baste–To sew a row of temporary stitches; can be done by machine or hand or with fusible tape.

Batiste–A lightweight, somewhat sheer fabric; available in solid colors or prints.

Batting–A fluffy substance used for padding; available prepackaged or by the yard.

Bay window–A style of window that has three or more side-by-side windows that are angled outward.

Bead–A thin, narrow line of glue that is applied to a surface.

Bell wire–Thin wire traditionally used for doorbells that easily bends and holds its shape. It can be used in window treatments to help an edge retain its shape, such as at the corner of a return.

Bias–The 45-degree diagonal direction between the lengthwise and crosswise grains of fabric. Also called true bias.

Blackout lining–A heavy, opaque fabric that is room darkening.

Blind stitch–A stitch specifically used for hemming window treatments. It consists of several straight stitches, then a stitch that moves to the side and "bites" the fabric to hold the hem in place.

Bobbin–A spool-like thread holder that supplies the bottom thread for a machine stitch. It is placed in a compartment directly below the needle.

Bow window–A style of window with the glass portion curved into a semicircle.

Box pleat–A flat pleat that has a fold of fabric laid behind each side of the pleat.

Brackets–Devices that are attached to the wall where a rod is placed.

Braid–A narrow decorative trim finished on two edges. Also known as gimp.

Broadcloth–A cotton fabric with a very fine crosswise thread. Similar to muslin in a solid color.

Brocade–A rich jacquard-style fabric with an allover pattern that appears to be embroidered, often emphasized by contrasting colors on the surface.

Bullion fringe–A decorative trim consisting of a continuous series of threads looped and twisted into a long fringe.

Buttonhole scissors–Small scissors that are used to cut open buttonholes. They are designed with a notched blade and a setscrew that limits the cutting action to the size of the buttonhole.

 C

Calico–A closely woven, inexpensive cloth made from cotton; often associated with quilting.

Carpenter's square–An L-shaped measuring device that enables one to measure length and width simultaneously or to mark a 90-degree angle.

Carpet thread–Coarse, strong thread traditionally used for mending carpets.

Casement window–A window that swings outward on side hinges.

Chain stitch–A stitch consisting of one or more continuous threads that form continuous hooked loops; easy to remove by pulling one end of the stitch. This stitch is often used in the construction of decorative trims.

Chambray–A plain woven fabric with lengthwise colored threads and crosswise white threads. Most commonly blue and white.

Chiffon–A thin, gauze-like fabric usually used for apparel.

Chintz–A cotton fabric with a glazed, shiny finish.

Clip–To make small scissor cuts into a seam allowance to allow movement of fabric, especially around a curved edge.

Confetti fringe–A style of fringe that has small tufts of fiber sandwiched within the ply of a yarn. The many contrasting-colored tufts make the fringe resemble confetti.

Cord-edge–A twisted cord with a seam allowance or lip edge attached for seam insertion.

Cording–A twisted cord used as decorative trim.

Cording foot–A special presser foot with a groove on the underside to accommodate the thickness of cording.

Cornice–A window treatment that covers the top portion of a window; usually made from wood and covered with batting and fabric.

Cover button–A form that is covered with fabric and has a special backing that once snapped in place will form a button.

Crash–See crinkled voile.

Crawl–An unplanned, uneven movement of one fabric over another.

Crinkled voile–A sheer fabric with many pressed-in wrinkles. Also known as crash.

Crosswise grain–The threads that run perpendicular to the lengthwise grain and the selvage edges. Also known as woof, weft, or filling.

Cup hook–A small hook that can be screwed into a wall and has an open cuplike hook from which to hang something.

Cut length–The fabric measurement that equals the vertical length of a window treatment plus any allowances for construction details such as hems or seams.

Cut width–The fabric measurement from side edge to side edge after widths of fabric are stitched together but before any construction begins. The measurement allows for needed fullness, seam allowances, and hems.

D

Damask–A firm jacquard-style fabric, similar to brocade but reversible.

Decorator fabric–The main fabric in a window treatment. Also known as the face fabric in the professional window treatment industry.

Decorator rods–Decorative hardware from which valances or curtains hang. These rods are meant to be visible.

Denim–A strong cotton twill fabric, most often made with blue lengthwise threads and gray or white crosswise threads. What blue jeans are made of.

Desired finished length–This is the lowest point on the window where you want a valance or curtain to end.

Doll needle–An extra-long needle used for doll making. Also useful for attaching buttons through thick fabrics.

Dormer window–A style of window that projects through the roof line.

Double-faced satin–A ribbon with a satiny finish on both sides.

Drapery rings–Wooden or metal rings that slide onto rods; secured to a window treatment with either stitches or an attached clip.

Dress goods–A term that refers to 45-inch-wide fabrics that are usually used for garments but can also be used in home decorating projects.

Dressing–The styling and positioning of the fabric in a window treatment.

Drill bit–A device that is inserted into a drill to make a hole in a wall or wooden surface.

Duck–A very durable, closely woven fabric of varying weights. Printed or solid.

Douppioni–An unevenly woven silk fabric.

Dye lot–A color run of fabric or decorative trim that may vary slightly in color from one batch to the next.

E

Ease–The extra amount of fabric or trim included in a measurement to ensure that it will not bind or be too small.

Edge-stitch–To sew an even row of stitching along a pressed or seamed edge of fabric.

Embossing–A finish created with heat and moisture by raising or recessing the surface in a chosen design. The process is often accomplished with velvet, a rubber stamp, and a hot, dry iron.

Embroidery foot–A presser foot that is used for machine embroidery. It has a wide opening between the toes with a wide channel on the underside to accommodate raised stitching.

Embroidery scissors–A small, sharply pointed scissors that is used for needlework, ripping, clipping, and opening buttonholes.

Epoxy glue–A nonwater-soluble type glue that will bond a variety of surfaces together.

Eyebrow–A term that refers to a window with a wide, oval top section that resembles the shape of an eyebrow.

Eyelet–A semisheer fabric with a decorative surface that features holes and shapes surrounded by surface embroidery. Also a small circular metal reinforcement for holes that are made in window treatments and garments.

F

Fabric finishes–Processes that a fabric goes through to make it more durable, decorative, or serviceable. Finishes are usually applied with chemicals or by mechanical pressure.

Face–The front or decorative side of fabric used for home accessories.

Face board–A term used for the front part of a cornice.

Facing–A piece of fabric that is attached to an edge to conceal the raw edges and the wrong side of the fabric.

Feed dog–A toothed mechanism in a sewing machine that is under the needle and presser foot and moves the fabric when sewing.

Filler cord–A web-covered cotton cord used inside welting or fabric-covered cord.

Finger-press–A technique of pressing a small section of fabric without an iron; fabrics are flattened and creased between the thumb and forefinger.

Finial–An ornamental accent used at the end of a curtain rod.

Finished length–The measurement equal to the vertical length of a treatment after the top and bottom edges are finished.

Finished width–The measurement of a window treatment that equals the sum of the following: the horizontal length of the rod between brackets plus returns, if any, plus yardage for the desired fullness needed to create the treatment. It is the width of the treatment after all seams and side hems are sewn.

Finishing nails–Nails with small, unobtrusive heads.

Fishing line–A strong, clear, thread used for extra support to secure window treatments.

Fray–The process by which threads in a woven fabric come loose or unravel from the body of the fabric.

French door–A style of door that has two hinged doors with rectangular panes of glass divided by wood grids.

French seam–A seam finish used when both sides of the fabric can be seen or there is no lining to cover the wrong side; especially effective on sheer fabrics. One-half inch of fabric is allowed for this process.

Fullness–The amount of fabric shirred, gathered, or pleated onto a rod to create a window treatment. Fullness is calculated by multiplying the length of the rod (sometimes including the returns) by a number, usually 1 1/2, 2, 2 1/2, or 3 but sometimes higher. The number depends on the style of the window treatment.

Fuse–To adhere two layers together with a bonding agent and heat (usually from an iron).

Fusible tape–See paper-backed fusible tape.

Fusible webbing–A wide, paper-backed adhesive that is activated when heated with an iron. Used to hold two pieces of fabric together. Available by the yard.

G

Gather–A term referring to a method of stitching that evenly pulls up fabric, creating a ruffle-like effect.

Georgette–A sheer, rather wiry fabric, printed or solid.

Gimp–A simple flat trim finished on both edges that is often used on upholstery. Also attached to trims as an insertion edge. Also known as braid.

Gimp edge–The edge attached to decorative trims to enable them to be inserted into a seam.

Gingham–A fabric with dyed yarns woven in specific intervals to create a check design.

Grade–A seam trimming process where two or more seam allowances are trimmed to different widths so the seam lies smoothly.

Grain–See lengthwise grain and crosswise grain.

Grain line–Refers to thread direction— lengthwise or crosswise. Any diagonal that intersects these two grain lines is known as bias.

Grid-marked–Describes fabric or paper that is printed with evenly spaced marks for accurate measurement. Also refers to marked spacing on see-through rulers.

Grommets–Large eyelets or metal rings pressed through fabrics.

Grosgrain (ribbon)–Woven ribbon that has a cross-rib design.

H

Handkerchief linen–A lightweight linen usually associated with hankies or apparel.

Handwheel–The round mechanism on the right hand side of a sewing machine that can be turned manually to raise and lower the needle.

Header edge–The top, looped, and permanently stitched edge of fringe—usually inserted into a seam allowance.

Hem–The side or bottom area of a window treatment that is turned under twice and stitched into place.

Holdback–A short metal rod with a decorative medallion or finial designed to hold draperies at the side of a window.

Hook-and-loop tape–A type of fastener that has threadlike hooks on one side and threadlike loops on the other; the two sides adhere to each other when pressed together.

I

Inside mount–Brackets or a mounting board installed inside the window frame rather than on the surrounding wall.

Installation–The process of securing window hardware or mounting boards to the wall with nails and screws.

Glossary

Interfacing–A nonwoven or woven fabric that is stiffened to add body to soft fabrics. May have an adhesive layer that will secure it to the fabric when heat is applied.

J

Jacquard–The name of a loom that produces an intricately woven fabric with a raised design. The fabric produced is also referred to by this name.

L

Lawn–A light, thin, gauzy cotton that is crisper than voile but not as crisp as organdy.

Leading edge–The inside vertical edge of a curtain—the edge that leads or moves forward when the curtain is pulled closed.

Lengthwise grain–The fabric threads that are parallel to the selvage edge. Also known as the warp.

Level–A carpenter's tool that is used to determine if something is evenly positioned on a horizontal or vertical plane.

Lining–A solid (usually white or off-white) fabric that is sewn onto the back of a window treatment to protect the decorator fabric from sun damage, add a layer of insulation, make a window treatment hang more attractively, and give a uniform appearance to all treatments when they're viewed from the outside.

Lip edge–The edge attached to cord so that it can be inserted into a seam.

Liquid seam sealant–A liquid that, when applied to the cut edge of fabric, will eliminate fraying.

Loop turner–A long, extra–thin sewing tool with a hook at the tip that is traditionally used for turning loops or pulling threads through to the opposite side.

M

Matelassé (double cloth)–A soft fabric with a puckered, quilted appearance, created by two sets of lengthwise and two sets of crosswise threads simultaneously woven into separate fabrics, then woven together into a pattern.

Miter–The junction formed by joining or folding fabric to make an angle. Also the process of forming such an angle.

Molly bolt–A wall anchor with elbows that flare out inside the wall when the anchor is screwed in; used to strengthen hollow walls where wood-framing studs are absent.

Monofilament thread–A fine, clear or smoky-colored nylon thread that appears invisible when stitched to fabrics of many colors. Most often used when a colored thread might show. Heavier monofilament threads are used to invisibly attach returns or other unsecured edges in place. Heavy monofilament thread is often called fishing line.

Motif–A single design or decorative pattern within a larger design.

Mounting board–A 1-by-2-, 1-by-3-, 1-by-4-, 1-by-6-, or 1-by-8-inch piece of wood to which a valance is attached. It is mounted to the wall with angle brackets. Deeper boards are often used to mount valances over rod treatments.

Muslin–An inexpensive plain-weave cotton fabric that is classified as either "bleached" or "unbleached."

N

Nap–The directional raised fibers on a fabric surface.

Nondirectional–A term used to refer to fabrics that have no discernable direction in their printed design. The print is neither up nor down.

Notch–A small wedge that is cut from the seam allowance to allow movement of fabric, especially around an outwardly curved edge.

Novelty trims–Unusual, trendy trims created for special effects.

⊙

Organdy–A lightweight sheer cotton fabric with a permanently crisp finish.

Organza–A very plain, stiff, sheer woven fabric made from nylon, polyester, silk, or acrylic.

Ostrich fringe–A shaggy novelty fringe resembling ostrich feathers.

Outside mount–Brackets installed outside the window frame or on the ceiling.

Overcast–A machine stitch that encases the raw edges to prevent the fabric from raveling.

Overlock–A stitch that is the result of a serger or overlock machine. The stitch encases the raw edge within a loopy stitch.

℘

Palladian–A style of window that is arched on the top edge.

Paper-backed fusible tape–A tape of varying widths that has a coating of glue or adhesive on one side that is activated when heated with an iron. Used to hold two pieces of fabric together.

Parallelogram–A four-sided geometric shape whose opposite sides are parallel.

Percale–A high-quality, woven cotton fabric.

Perle cotton–A lustrous heavy thread usually used for embroidery. Its larger diameter makes it desirable for use as reinforcement of buttonholes or for raised decorative stitching.

Pillowcased lining–A method of lining a window treatment where the sides of the lining and the sides of the window treatment are stitched right sides together and then turned right sides out.

Pilot hole–A tiny hole that is drilled into a wall or wood prior to inserting a screw.

Pinmark–A method to temporarily mark a position with a straight pin.

Piping–See welting.

Piping foot–See cording foot.

Pleat–Fabric that has been folded on itself and stitched at one end with the other end open.

Ply–A set of threads twisted together to form a cord.

Point turner–A flat pointed tool used to push out a point from the wrong side to the right side without damaging the fabric.

Preshrink–The process of removing residual shrinkage in fabric before any construction process begins.

Press cloth–Fabric that is placed between an iron and decorator fabric for protection against scorching and iron shine.

Presser foot–A sewing machine attachment that mounts behind the needle and is raised or lowered to hold fabric in place while sewing.

Projection–The distance a bracket and rod or mounting extends from the wall.

Puddling–Occurs when the bottom edge of a floor-length window treatment is allowed to pool on the floor.

ℛ

Railroad–The process of cutting fabric so the lengthwise grain runs horizontally on the finished project.

Ranch windows–A strip of windows installed high on a wall for ventilation and light but not for a view.

Glossary

Rayon–A manufactured cellulose fiber that is used in the construction of decorative trims and fabrics.

Repeat–The distance from an element on one motif to the same element on the next motif; usually measured along the selvage edge.

Return–The length of the end projection of a mounting board or the distance a rod bracket extends from the wall.

Rod–What a window treatment is placed on. It is placed in brackets that are installed above the window.

Roller foot–A presser foot that has one or more metal rollers between the toes to allow the foot to roll smoothly over thick layers of fabric.

Roman shade–A style of window treatment that is easily raised and lowered by means of a series of cords.

Rosette–A circular decorative embellishment made of fabric or decorative trim used to draw attention to a specific point, such as the corner of a window treatment.

Running stitch–A small, but not tiny, stitch of equal length—part of a continuous series of similar stitches.

S
___

Sateen–A fabric with a smooth, lustrous, satiny finish constructed when long, smooth crosswise (weft) yarns float over four or eight lengthwise (warp) yarns.

Scrim–An open-mesh, plain-weave cotton fabric.

Seam allowance–The area that extends from the stitching line to the cut outer edge of a sewn seam.

Seam gauge–A tool with a movable dial or slide to assist in measuring accurately.

Seam ripper–A small tool with a pointed hook at one end. The point is used to pick (or rip out) stitches from fabric, and the inside curve of the hook is designed for cutting seams. A seam ripper is often used to cut through the center of buttonholes.

Self-lining–Refers to using the same fabric to line a treatment as you use to make a treatment.

Selvage–The finished lengthwise edges of fabric that run down each side.

Serge–A utility machine stitch that is done on an overlock machine or serger. It cuts a clean edge and wraps it with stitching at the same time to prevent raveling.

Shade cord–A firm, smooth nylon cord primarily used to rig Roman shades and other drawn-up window treatments.

Shank–The small protruding loop on the underside of a button, used to attach the button to a project.

Sheer–A term used for a translucent, lightweight fabric.

Sheeting–A plain woven cloth that comes in light, medium, or heavy weights. Usually refers to the weight of fabric used for bedsheets.

Shirr–The process of making soft gathers.

Sill length–The finished length of a window treatment where the bottom edge touches the sill of a window.

Sliding glass doors–Glass doors that slide open.

Slip stitch–A hidden handstitch that connects two layers of fabric or trim to a fabric. A looser temporary version is used to aid in the precise matching of stripes, plaids, and prints at seam lines.

Slub–A yarn that is uneven or irregular or an uneven section of sewing thread.

Soleplate–The flat surface of an iron from which heat and steam emerge.

Spreading anchor–A wall anchor that spreads on the back of drywall to offer support.

Stabilizer–A nonwoven material that is

layered onto the back of a fabric to provide additional weight and body while the fabric is being heavily stitched as in making buttonholes or machine embroidery.

Stationary treatment–A window treatment that does not open or close for privacy.

Stitch in the ditch–The process of inconspicuously connecting more than one layer of fabric by stitching in the crevice of a previously stitched seam.

Straightedge–The edge of a ruler or measuring device that can be easily traced.

Studs–The wooden supports that are behind walls; the "bones" of a house.

Swag–A draped fabric window treatment shaped in a semicircle.

T

Tabs–Extensions of fabric that are formed into loops or ties used to hang a curtain from a curtain rod.

Tack–A handstitch that is used during construction to hold two or more layers in place. Also used for marking.

Taffeta–A plain, reversible, woven fabric with a sheen, often woven so that the color seems to change when viewed from different angles.

Tails–The extended areas of a window treatment that hang down the sides of the window.

Take-up–The inadvertent shortening of fabric (in width or length) caused by multiple seams, hems, and folds.

Tapestry–A heavy textured fabric that is woven on a jacquard loom.

Tassel–A group of threads or yarns that are bound together at the top to form a decorative accent. Hangs freely by means of a top loop or attachment.

Tension–The tightness of the top and bottom threads in a machine-stitched seam. Controlled by a dial on the sewing machine that increases or decreases the pressure on the threads as they are fed through the machine. Machines have a separate tension control for the top thread and for the bottom (bobbin) thread.

Tension rod–A curtain rod or shower rod that is mounted between two walls without brackets. The rod contracts to fit inside an area and has springs that when released will apply pressure against the walls to stay secure.

Throat plate–The metal plate directly under the needle of a sewing machine.

Ticking–A striped cloth made of tightly woven twill, traditionally used for mattresses.

Tieback–A decorative fastener made from fabric or other materials that is attached to the side of the window to hold back curtains or draperies.

Toggle bolt–A wall anchor that forms a brace inside the wall; used to strengthen hollow walls where wood-framing studs are absent.

Toile–A French term referring to a fabric with scenic designs.

Topstitch–Machine stitching on the right (top) side of an item for decorative or functional purposes, often along the edge.

Trapezoid–A four-sided geometric shape where only two opposite sides are parallel.

Tulle–A transparent netting that is often used for bridal veils.

Twill–A fabric identified by woven diagonal lines.

Twisted cable cord–A ropelike cording that is constructed of separately twisted groups of thread, usually used for craft projects or drawstrings. Cotton or polyester.

Glossary

U

Usable fabric width–The area of a fabric that is not marred by printed brand names or the binding selvage edge.

V

Valance–A fabric top treatment for windows.

Velvet–A soft, pile fabric.

Voile–A fine, sheer fabric that is crisp to the touch.

W

Walking foot–A special feature or attachment that feeds both layers of fabric under the sewing machine needle at the same speed so that neither layer crawls.

Wall anchors–Weight-support devices that are inserted into walls where wood-framing studs are absent.

Waxed button thread–A thread that has had beeswax applied to the surface to strengthen it for handsewing. The addition of beeswax reduces the tendency for the thread to tangle and knot during the sewing process.

Welting–A cord wrapped with bias fabric to be used as a decorative edging when inserted in a seam. Also known as piping.

Window wall–A wall that consists of nothing but windows from one end to another.

Wing Needle–A style of needle that has a flat projection or wing at each side. It creates a large hole when it is used to stitch. Primarily used for hemstitching where the large hole accents the stitched design.

Wood glue–A glue that is specially formulated to hold two pieces of wood together.

Y

Yardstick–A measuring device that is usually made from wood that is exactly 1 yard in length.

Z

Zigzag–A type of machine stitch where the needle swings left to right as it stitches, creating a evenly notched stitch.

Zipper foot–A narrow sewing machine presser foot designed to sit at one side of the needle so that stitching can be guided very close to a zipper, welting, or other decorative trims.

Index

Index

Meet The Authors

Donna Babylon

Donna's passion for fabrics, colors, and textures combined with her gift of teaching has been the driving force in her diverse career in sewing and decorating. Donna has watched her career unfold in front of her with fascinating twists and turns, leading to establishing her own publishing company, Windsor Oak Publishing, in 1991.

Her enthusiasm is contagious when it comes to helping individuals decorate their homes. She believes everyone is creative and can have wonderful and professional results in do-it-yourself projects. To help unlock people's creativity, she has written 12 books on home decorating, speaks frequently at consumer conferences around the country, designs a line of patterns for The McCall Pattern Company, and has appeared on over 200 national television programs. She is always looking for clever ways to save money when decorating—but only if they result in an expensive look.

Donna lives in Maryland with her two cats, Ashley and Teakah, where she enjoys quiet country living and the wildlife that surrounds her home. She considers her home her laboratory and is always experimenting with various projects that eventually appear in her books, as patterns, and in numerous television segments on Home and Garden Television, PBS, and the Discovery Channel. In her free time, she enjoys attending rock concerts and is an avid bicyclist and downhill skier.

Victoria Waller

Designing is more of a lifestyle than a vocation for Vicki. Working from her home office in San Mateo, California, she lives and breathes her work. Vicki has worked in the sewing and craft industries for over 27 years, honing her skills as a seamstress, artist, designer, and writer. Floor-to-ceiling displays of trims, lace, antique buttons, and all forms of embellishment surround her and offer constant inspiration.

Her background covers diverse areas such as sewing machine sales, clothing design and patternmaking, graphic design and fine art, display and photo styling, and writing. These creative endeavors have culminated in her current position as the designer for the Hollywood Trims line of decorative trims and the Dritz Corporation.

Vicki has written numerous booklets and how-to pamphlets featuring the use of decorative trims on pillows, window treatments, and home accessories. Her books *Trims and Tassels*, *Bed Coverings* (Friedman/Fairfax), and *Pin Beading* (Design Originals) are examples of her belief that "design is design is design." Each abounds with beautiful photography and stimulating ideas.

Vicki feels that inspiration is at the heart of all design. And antiquing and gardening provide some of her best inspiration.